The Afterlife Book

HEAVEN, HELL, AND LIFE AFTER DEATH

MARIE D. JONES AND LARRY FLAXMAN

VISIBLE INK PRESS

DETROIT

ALSO FROM VISIBLE INK PRESS

Secret Societies: The Complete
Guide to Histories, Rites, and
Rituals
By Nick Redfern
ISBN: 978-1-57859-483-2

The Spirit Book: The Encyclopedia of Clairvoyance, Channeling,
and Spirit Communication
By Raymond Buckland
ISBN: 978-1-57859-172-5
(ebook)

Supernatural Gods: Spiritual
Mysteries, Psychic Experiences,
and Scientific Truths
By Jim Willis
ISBN: 978-1-57859-660-7

Time Travel: The Science and
Science Fiction
By Nick Redfern
ISBN: 978-1-57859-723-9

Unexplained! Strange Sightings,
Incredible Occurrences, and Puz-
zling Physical Phenomena, 3rd
edition
By Jerome Clark
ISBN: 978-1-57859-344-6

The Vampire Book: The Encyclopedia of the Undead, 3rd
edition
By J. Gordon Melton
ISBN: 978-1-57859-281-4

The Werewolf Book: The Encyclopedia of Shape-Shifting Beings,
2nd edition
By Brad Steiger
ISBN: 978-1-57859-367-5

The Zombie Book: The Ency-
clopedia of the Living Dead
By Brad Steiger and Nick
Redfern
ISBN: 978-1-57859-504-4

"REAL NIGHTMARES"
E-BOOKS BY BRAD STEIGER

Book 1: *True and Truly Scary Unexplained Phenomenon*

Book 2: *The Unexplained Phenomena and Tales of the Unknown*

Book 3: *Things That Go Bump in the Night*

Book 4: *Things That Prowl and Growl in the Night*

Book 5: *Fiends That Want Your Blood*

Book 6: *Unexpected Visitors and Unwanted Guests*

Book 7: *Dark and Deadly Demons*

Book 8: *Phantoms, Apparitions, and Ghosts*

Book 9: *Alien Strangers and Foreign Worlds*

Book 10: *Ghastly and Grisly Spooks*

Book 11: *Secret Schemes and Conspiring Cabals*

Book 12: *Freaks, Fiends, and Evil Spirits*

PLEASE VISIT US AT VISIBLEINKPRESS.COM.

ABOUT THE AUTHORS

Marie D. Jones is a fully trained disaster response/preparedness member of Community Emergency Response Teams (CERT) through FEMA and the Department of Homeland Security, and she is a licensed ham radio operator (KI6YES). She is the author of over fifteen nonfiction books on cutting-edge science, the paranormal,  conspiracies, ancient knowledge, and unknown mysteries, including Visible Ink Press' *Demons, the Devil, and Fallen Angels* plus *PSIence: How New Discoveries in Quantum Physics and New Science May Explain the Existence of Paranormal Phenomena, 2013: End of Days or a New Beginning, Supervolcano: The Catastrophic Event That Changed the Course of Human History*, and *The Grid: Exploring the Hidden Infrastructure of Reality*. She is a regular contributor to *New Dawn Magazine, FATE, Paranoia Magazine*, and other periodicals. Jones has been interviewed on over a thousand radio shows worldwide, including *Coast-to-Coast AM*. She makes her home in San Marcos, California, and is the mom to one very brilliant son, Max.

For nearly two decades, **Larry Flaxman** has been actively involved in paranormal research and hands-on field investigation, emphasizing the scientific method to unexplained phenomena. His books with Marie D.  Jones include *11:11 The Time Prompt Phenomenon, Mind Wars*, and *This Book Is from the Future*. He has appeared on the Discovery Channel's *Ghost Lab* and the History Channel's *Ancient Aliens*. His numerous radio credits include *Coast-to-Coast AM, The Shirley MacLaine Show, The Jeff Rense Show, Rob McConnell's X-Zone, TAPS Family Radio*, and *Paranormal Podcast*.

TABLE OF CONTENTS

THE
AFTERLIFE BOOK

Visible Ink Press®
43311 Joy Rd., #414
Canton, MI 48187-2075

Visible Ink Press is a registered trademark of Visible Ink Press LLC.

Most Visible Ink Press books are available at special quantity discounts when purchased in bulk by corporations, organizations, or groups. Customized printings, special imprints, messages, and excerpts can be produced to meet your needs. For more information, contact Special Markets Director, Visible Ink Press, www.visibleinkpress.com, or 734-667-3211.

Managing Editor: Kevin S. Hile
Cover Design: Graphikitchen, LLC
Page Design: Alessandro Cinelli, Cinelli Design
Typesetting: Marco Divita, The Graphix Group
Proofreaders: Christa Gainer and Shoshana Hurwitz
Indexer: Larry Baker
Cover and chapter page images: Shutterstock.

ISBNs
Paperback: 978-1-57859-761-1
Ebook: 978-1-57859-822-9
Hardbound: 978-1-57859-821-2

Cataloging-in-Publication data is on file at the Library of Congress.

Printed in the United States of America.

10 9 8 7 6 5 4 3 2 1

PHOTO SOURCES

Allposters.com: p. 163.
American Philosophical Society: p. 197.
Osama Shukir Muhammed Amin FRCP (Glasg): p. 219.
Boston Sunday Post: p. 61.
Cirone–Musi, Festival della Scienza: p. 114.
Cmichel67 (Wikicommons): p. 168.
Dandebat.dk: p. 72.
Derby Museum and Art Gallery: p. 236.
Dura–Europos synagogue: p. 24.
Egyptian Museum, Cairo, Egypt: p. 34.
Fibonacci (Wikicommons): p. 162.
Gutenberg.kk.dk: p. 91.
John Hill: p. 42.
Himalayanart.org: p. 80.
Robert Lanza: p. 59.
Library of Congress: p. 186.
Louvre Museum: p. 50.
MM (Wikicommons): p. 57.
National Geographic: 220.
National Institutes of Health: p. 212.
Paramount Pictures: p. 221.
Pixar Animation Studios: p. 120.
Press2014 (Wikicommons): p. 64.
Carole Raddato: p. 94.
Sgerbik (Wikicommons): p. 112.
Shutterstock: pp. 3. 6, 8, 9, 14, 16, 19, 20, 21, 22, 31, 32, 37, 40, 48, 65, 71, 75, 79, 89, 100, 103, 107, 110, 111, 124, 126, 128, 133, 136, 139, 150, 157, 160, 172, 175, 177, 178, 184, 188, 190, 193, 198, 204, 206, 208, 211, 215, 223, 226, 234, 241, 243.
John Singer: p. 231.
StagiaireMGIMO (Wikicommons): p. 146.
Theosophical Society: p. 147.
TriStar Pictures/Roth Films: p. 153.
W. David and GayEtta Hemingway Foundation: p. 142.
Walters Art Museum: p. 53.
Warner Bros. Pictures: p. 86.
Wellcome Images: p. 45.
Kenneth C. Zirkel: p. 119.
Public domain: pp. 84, 131, 201, 227.

DEDICATION

To Max and Mary Essa.

ACKNOWLEDGMENTS

I, Marie, would love to thank Lisa Hagan, my longtime agent and friend, who is a wonderful person and a fabulous agent. I am a lucky girl to have her as both. I would love to thank Roger Jänecke and the staff at Visible Ink Press, the best publisher on Earth. I mean that! Thank you, Roger, for allowing me the privilege to write such great books and work with you and your awesome team!

Thank you to every reader, fan, follower, listener, and friend I have made over the years from my work. You guys mean the world to me, and I do it for you. Your support is what holds me up during the long, hard hours of writing!

Larry, thanks for the many years and intense conversations about the paranormal and the books, articles, and radio shows we have done together. It has been one heck of a ride; you've inspired me to think in new ways and expand my perception of reality, and I am grateful for it all. May this book extend that lucky streak and be another big hit for us!

Thank you so much to my family. My mom, Milly, who is my number one cheerleader, and my siblings, Angella and John, who love and support me. Thanks to my dad, John, who inspired my love of all things science. Also, to my wonderful extended family and my gal pals and good friends! But most of all, thanks to the reason for my being, my sun and moon and stars: my son, Max. You are my life and I know that death will never end the love I have for you.

* * *

I, Larry, am truly blessed to have so many wonderful people in my life, and to thank them all would take an entire book itself!

In the interest of time, I would like to first thank my mom and dad, who, while in spirit, have both motivated and pushed me harder than I could ever have imagined. I'd also like to thank Mary Essa, my daughter, who not only motivates me to be the best father I can be but also reminds me that while every writer's work is their art she is truly my masterpiece.

Next (but certainly not least!), I'd like to express my gratitude to Sherry, my best friend, soulmate, and better half. She was just as vital to the completion of this book as I was, from late-night brainstorming meetings to reading early manuscripts and providing valuable input.

It is as difficult as it sounds to take an idea and turn it into a book for publication. The experience is mentally and emotionally challenging, but super gratifying in the end. I'd like to express my gratitude to the individuals that contributed to making this possible.

Of course, my sincerest thank you goes to my writing partner, Marie D. Jones. It seems like only yesterday that I read a copy of *PSIence* and rolled the dice to email her. Even after 10 books, hundreds of magazine pieces, and numerous radio appearances, we're still a formidable force!

Finally, I'd want to express my gratitude to Roger Jänecke, the publisher of Visible Ink Press, as well as my literary agent, Lisa Hagan.

INTRODUCTION: THE BIG QUESTION

There are three big existential questions human beings ask at some point in their lives.

1. Why am I here?

2. Are we alone in the universe?

3. Is there life after death?

All three questions are, in a bizarre way, linked. We want to know if our lives have meaning and if we matter, and this frequently requires us to consider the limitations of human life. We really want to believe that we were placed here for a reason and that our lives will not be snuffed away in the blink of an eye. We want to know whether we possess an immortal component—our consciousness or our soul.

Most people believe existence, in some form, goes on. We might even say everyone would like to believe in an immortal soul or spirit, including those diehards who say they are not afraid. Oh, they are afraid. Even the most religious and spiritual folks quiver when faced with death. It's easy to shrug off the fear of something when it's not staring you in the face.

According to recent Pew Research Center polls on afterlife beliefs, the majority of people in the United States believe in the afterlife. They also believe in the existence of Heaven and Hell. Depending on the poll year, approximately 65 to 70 percent say they do. Almost three-quarters of adults believe in God. Unaffiliated religious people made up 37 percent of the population, agnostics 26 percent, and atheists 3 percent. The figure for belief in Hell was a little lower at 62 percent of all Americans, implying that more people believe they will never see the fiery bowels of punishing fury and will instead receive the golden ticket to the pearly gates.

According to a CBS News poll conducted in April 2014, three out of every four people believed in the existence of Heaven and Hell. Eighty-two percent thought they were on their way to Heaven. The same poll asked how often people consider their own deaths: 14 percent said a lot, 31 percent said a little, and 54 percent said not at all. This appears to be the polar opposite of normal human behavior, which drives our actions based on an innate desire to survive and thrive. We believe that people are constantly thinking about death but are not consciously aware of it because to them, eating, sleeping, taking medications, and other actions have as their foundation the desire to live to see another day.

These are just polls, of course, with a very limited numbers of respondents and sometimes skewed demographics. Go on social media and do an informal poll and no doubt more people than not will say they believe there is something beyond death, even if they are not sure what. Ask people if they want to live longer and most will say yes. Who wouldn't want more time with loved ones, or to travel, or to pursue dreams and goals, or to just be alive? Not everyone, but most.

This book will not give you a definitive answer as to whether life after death is real or merely wishful thinking. It will take you, instead, on a journey through the science behind energy and consciousness and the brain's response to death, the pharmaceutical and spiritual quests for immortality, the myth and religious beliefs and traditions, including reincarnation, the personal experiences of those who have stepped beyond the veil for a glimpse, what observing nature has to say about death and rebirth, and even a touch or two from the paranormal world of ghosts and spirit communications and what clues they might hold for us.

Death may not be an end at all but rather a transformation or significant change. It could be a symbolic, archetypal representation of an ending and a new beginning. In the Tarot card deck, the death card represents not a permanent death, but the death of something like a relationship, a cycle, or a current situation that needs closure and requires a new beginning. The esoteric concept of death is one of change because all changes require something to die or end before the next phase can begin.

To be sure, it will be a journey, but the final destination will continue to elude us all until it happens to each of us. The goal is to shed some light on a deep, deep mystery, possibly the deepest of all, while also providing some hope and comfort along the way.

What Happens When We Die?

The first step to eternal life is you have to die.
—Chuck Palahniuk

Death, the last sleep? No, it is the final awakening.
—Walter Scott

My view of the afterlife is that it's made of different levels, depending on how spiritual a life we live.
—John Edward

It has been claimed that space is the final frontier, but this is not the case. Death is a fact. We might one day travel across galaxies and live to tell the tale. Death, on the other hand, may not provide the same level of comfort. We are left in the dark about where we "go" when we die, if we even go anywhere at all.

Before even contemplating life after death, we need to understand death itself—at least, physical death—and what happens to our bodies from the moment we take our last breath on. It is a process with specific steps that effect the body, brain, cells, and all our "parts." It is the tangible part of dying that leads to the expression "ashes to ashes, dust to dust," with a whole lot of steps in between.

According to the 31st edition of *Dorland's Illustrated Medical Dictionary*, death is "the cessation of life; permanent ces-

1

sation of all vital bodily functions. For legal and medical purposes, the following definition of death has been proposed–the irreversible cessation of all of the following: (1) total cerebral function, usually assessed by EEG as flat line, (2) spontaneous function of the respiratory system, and (3) spontaneous function of the circulatory system...."

Death is an absolute certainty. From the moment of birth, we all begin the slow process of dying. It's not a matter of "if," it is a matter of "when."

Death a thousand years ago was not the same as death today. We now have the technology to keep people alive longer and to cure many of the diseases that once took people's lives. People today can live much longer lives if they take good care of themselves, avoid accidents and natural disasters, and postpone the inevitable moment when they will leave this world.

And what happens after that? First, we need to look at what leads up to it.

We grow old. We get sick. We are victims of unfortunate circumstances that shorten our lives. Often death comes quickly and without warning, but sometimes it's a longer, slower process that allows us too much time to think about what will happen next, if anything at all.

THE HOSPICE MOVEMENT

Before physical death occurs, we might be in the hospital with a major illness or at home recovering from a devastating heart attack, the progression of cancer, or another terminal illness. We might feel totally healthy, only to not wake up one morning, to die calmly and peacefully in our sleep. Death comes in a variety of ways and forms, and neither we nor our loved ones are always prepared.

The word "hospice" comes from the Latin *hospes*, which has two meanings–"guest" and "host." The concept is ancient, even primitive, as indigenous cultures would take care of the dying since they did not have hospitals or rest homes for their elderly. In the 11th century c.e., the Roman Catholic Church adopted the practice of offering a place of hospitality and care for the sick and dying. The first of this type of hospice may have dated back to the Crusades, then it became more widespread in the Middle Ages, before other religious orders took on different traditions.

Jeanne Garnier, a young widower and bereaved mother, founded the Dames de Calaire in Lyon, France, in the mid–1800s to care for dying patients. Dying was considered a failure of the medical system at the time, and those who were terminally ill were not welcome in hospitals, which were primarily focused on curing patients. Six more hospice facilities were established in New York and Paris between 1874 and 1899.

The concept of hospice—a place to spend one's last days comfortably—goes back many centuries.

The hospice concept spread to Ireland where the Irish Sisters of Charity opened Our Lady's Hospice in Dublin. England opened St. Joseph's Hospice in London soon after.

The modern hospice movement was the work of British physician Dame Cicely Saunders, who worked in London around 1948 as a nurse. She worked specifically with terminally ill patients and even earned a medical degree in 1957. While she was a medical social worker, she encountered a dying patient named David Tasma in 1948, which led to her founding St Christopher's House in London in 1967. Dr. Mary Baines worked with Dame Cicely and was instrumental in the advancement of palliative care. In the United Kingdom alone, there are now over 220 hospices in operation.

Other noted hospice centers included the Marie Curie Cancer Care and the Sue Ryder Foundation, both of which contributed to the development of care for terminally ill patients and their families. The main focus was on the needs of not only the patients but also the families dealing with a terminally ill loved one.

In 1969, Dr. Elisabeth Kübler-Ross published *On Death and Dying*, which included hundreds of interviews with dying patients and emphasized the benefits of home care over institutional treatment for the terminally ill. The author promoted the concept that the dying deserved the right to determine their own end–of–life care and whether they wished to die in a hospice center or at home.

In 1974, the first hospice in the United States was founded. Connecticut Hospice in Branford, Connecticut, was founded by Florence Wald, along with two pediatricians and a chaplain. That same year, two U.S. senators—Frank Church of Idaho and Frank Moss of Utah—introduced legislation for federal funding for hospice programs, but it wasn't until 1986 when the Medicare Hospice Benefit was enacted, giving states the option to include hospices in their Medicaid programs. Hospice care was also made an option for terminally ill nursing home residents.

It would be another 30 years before more legislation passed and funding was increased. By 2004, over one million Americans had received hospice care services, and by 2005, there were over 4,000 hospice providers.

Today, hospice care is widely available, and many people prefer to die in their own homes or the homes of loved ones, with hospice care provided by trained staff who come into the home and teach family members how to care for the terminally ill. In the September 2018 issue of Marie Claire, Adrian Tookman, medical director at Marie Curie Hospital in Hampstead, England, stated, "Good hospice care helps people living with a terminal illness achieve the best possible quality of life. The philosophy behind the hospice movement is about making the most of the time you have left, no matter what prognosis you have."

Tookman said that it is about providing not only physical comfort but also emotional support for the dying and their family and friends. A hospice should be a comfortable, homey, and relaxed place, unlike a noisy, bustling hospital. "Hospices can help prepare people for death," Tookman said, because death is such a taboo subject in our culture and one that is difficult to discuss. Many hospices and hospice home services also provide spiritual counseling as well as practical financial planning for funerals and dealing with finances after the death of the loved one.

Dying is not easy no matter where it occurs, but hospice is there, whether at a licensed facility or at home with loved ones, to make the experience and transition a little bit easier and provide a dignity and level of concern that might not be found elsewhere.

THE BODILY DEATH PROCESS

We are biological organisms, and when we die, our bodies decompose and disintegrate. Oxygen, hydrogen, carbon, calcium, nitrogen, and phosphorus make up the human body. These constitute 99 percent of our physical forms, with the remaining 1 percent made up of potassium, sulfur, sodium, chlorine, and magnesium. It's difficult to look in the mirror and imagine ourselves as a jumble of elements and minerals, because these don't carry much weight in and of themselves. Add approximately 60 percent water, because water makes up the majority of our body weight, and you have the composition we call our bodily form.

A number of systems–such as circulatory, respiratory, and digestive–work in tandem to get what our bodies need when they need it so we can function. Death is a slow cutting–off of those systems, as each one shuts down at a different point in time. Several series of events occur within our biological and cellular levels that go through stages from a few seconds to a few hours after death, including the ceasing of functioning of the heart, brain, and lungs, and eventually the beginning of decomposition, which can be sped up or slowed down based on environmental conditions such as cold, heat, or humidity levels. Decomposition speeds up in hot and humid environments and slows down in cold and arid ones. Mortuaries are usually colder and drier for this reason, to slow decomposition until the person's body can be properly embalmed or cremated.

We forget that our "flesh vehicle" deteriorates over time just like a car would, whether temporarily due to disease or permanently due to death, since we link so much of our humanity with our personalities. This causes us to forget that our bodies age just like any other vehicle. It is difficult to picture our life coming to an end on a simply physical basis, but that is exactly what death is, at least according to the facts that we know about it.

"I regard the brain as a computer which will stop working when its components fail. There is no Heaven or afterlife for broken down computers; that is a fairy story for people afraid of the dark." –Stephen Hawking

THE POST-MORTEM TIMELINE

Death can occur when the heart stops beating, the brain stops working, or we stop breathing, or so we think. Clinical death in a hospital is described as the absence of a pulse, absence of breathing, absence of reflexes, and the absence of pupil contraction to bright light. Death occurs when either the circulatory or respiratory functions stop and cannot be reversed, or when the entire brain, including the stem, ceases to function. Trained emergency responders look for specific signs of irreversible death to determine whether resuscitation should be attempted and when it is no longer an option. Death does not happen in an instant. It's not "fade to black, end of story, and that's all she wrote." For up to ten minutes after we die, our brains continue to work and may be aware that we are dead. At some point, the entire brain shuts down, but does awareness?

Sam Parnia, M.D., Ph.D., writes in "What Can Science Tell Us About Death?" for the New York Academy of Sciences that death occurs when the heart stops beating. "We call this death by cardiopulmonary criteria and it is how death is defined for more than 95 percent of people. A person stops breathing and their brain shuts down, causing all life processes to cease." Recent medical discoveries have allowed us to artificially keep a patient's heart beating even if their brain has died. Legally, they will still be declared dead based upon irreversible brain death.

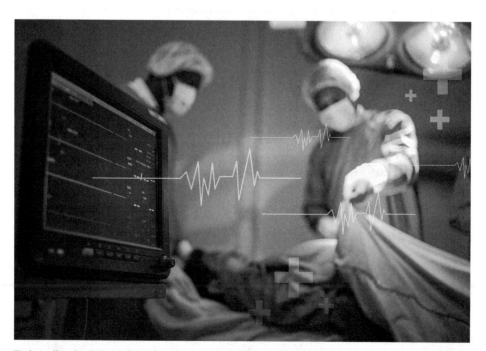

Technically, death is defined by physicians as when there is no more breathing, no pulse, no reflexes, and no respiration, and there is a failure to revive these bodily functions.

Parnia goes on to say that when a person dies, their cells, as well as their brain, begin their own death process. After death, it may be hours or days before the brain and other organs are irreversibly damaged.

THE FIRST HOUR

At the moment of death, our bodies go into a state called primary flaccidity. The muscles relax, eyelids lose tension, the jaw may drop open, pupils dilate, and joints and limbs become very flexible. The skin will begin to sag, and larger bony areas or joints may be more pronounced without plump skin to cover them up. Along with our muscles, our sphincters relax and release urine and feces.

Brain cells begin to die within moments of death.

Pallor mortis occurs within moments of the end of heart activity, as blood drains out of smaller veins into the skin, causing our skin to look pale or grey.

This process, known as algor mortis or the "death chill," causes the body temperature to drop from its usual level of 98.6 degrees Fahrenheit to the temperature of the surrounding air. The temperature of a person's body can drop consistently at a rate of approximately 1.5 degrees Fahrenheit every hour.

HOURS TWO TO SIX

Livor mortis kicks in, which is the process by which gravity pulls the blood down to ground level and can often cause a red-purple discoloration in feet and legs from the accumulation of blood.

Then, around the third hour, there are chemical changes in the body, which releases a gel-like substance that stiffens the muscles, a process known as rigor mortis, starting with the eyelids, jaw, and neck muscles. It takes a few hours as rigor mortis travels over the rest of the body, with the fingers and toes the last to stiffen.

HOURS SEVEN TO TWELVE AND BEYOND

The body turns blue between eight and twelve hours after death.

At about twelve hours into death, the body's muscles achieve maximum stiffness, give or take a little time due to age, weather, gender, or physical condition. It becomes difficult to move the dead person's limbs at this point, and the fingers and toes may be crooked and hard to straighten, if possible. The process of rigor mortis is complete at around the twelve–hour mark.

As a result of the chemical changes, the cells and internal tissue begin to decay. Secondary flaccidity occurs when muscles loosen and continue to loosen for up to three days. Skin shrinks, and it gives the illusion of hair and nails growing. Rigor mortis begins to dissipate, but in the opposite direction now, with the fingers and toes first, and the face last.

This process takes about 48 hours, and when it is finished, the body's muscles are relaxed and moveable.

Twenty–four hours after death, skin cells begin to die off.

After three to four months, the skin's color changes from yellowish–green to brownish–black as blood vessels

If a body is not embalmed, it takes about two or three months for the flesh to completely disintegrate, leaving only the skeleton. The body still decomposes with embalming, but it takes longer for the process to be complete.

What Is the Death Rattle?

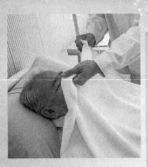

When someone is critically ill and on the verge of death, they may experience terminal respiratory secretions, also known as the death rattle. This is a distinct sound made by a person just before death. It sounds horrifying, but it is not painful and occurs frequently when the sick person is extremely weak or goes in and out of consciousness.

The last sound many make as they pass away is a respiratory sound sometimes called the "death rattle."

In their weakened state, they are unable to clear secretions, such as from the back of the throat, which is made up of saliva and mucus, through coughing or swallowing. As the dying person's breathing becomes irregular, even labored, it becomes even more difficult for them to expel the secretions. When they inhale deeply, the forceful air moves against the secretions at the back of their throat, producing the strange, wet crackling or gargling sound.

The sound might be soft or harsh, and it can startle loved ones who hear it because they think the person is drowning or choking on their spittle. To minimize the death rattle, the person can be turned on their side with their head elevated to help the secretions out of the back of the throat. Alleviating the death rattle does not stop death but can be more comforting for those who are sitting with the dying person.

deteriorate and the iron inside leaks out and oxidizes. The molecular structure that holds cells together disintegrates, and the body's tissues collapse into a watery mush.

A year later, if buried, the clothes the body is buried in disintegrate from the body's acidic fluids and toxins. Nylon seams and waistbands survive a lot longer.

After ten years, chemical reactions in the body convert fat in the legs and buttocks into a soapy substance known as "grave wax." The body would begin to mummify in drier conditions. After 50 years, tissues have liquefied and vanished, leaving only tendons, which will disintegrate after about 80 years. What is left is a delicate and brittle mineral frame that collapses after a century, as the bones become dust.

Ultimately, all that will be left are teeth, the grave wax, and any nylon fibers or threads from the clothing.

This is the typical scenario for an embalmed body, but it also depends on the embalming quality, the length of time between death and embalming, the moisture and acidity of the earth in which the body is buried, the size and weight of the body, the availability of oxygen, and the type of coffin. Softer woods, such as pine, degrade faster than harder woods.

A dead body buried about six feet in the ground without a coffin and without embalming would take about two to three months to turn into a skeleton.

How People Die Today

Do Not Stand at My Grave and Weep
Mary Elizabeth Frye

Do not stand at my grave and weep.
I am not there; I do not sleep.
I am a thousand winds that blow,
I am the diamond glints on snow,
I am the sun on ripened grain,
I am the gentle autumn rain.
When you awaken in the morning's hush,
I am the swift uplifting rush
Of quiet birds in circled flight.
I am the soft stars that shine at night.
Do not stand at my grave and cry.
I am not there; I did not die.

The darkness of death is like the evening twilight; it makes all objects
appear more lovely to the dying.
—Jean Paul

Decisions must be made after death. What should be done with the body? How should survivors pay tribute to the deceased? What were their last wishes? What are the religious and spiritual traditions? The body must first be preserved while the remaining loved ones decide how best to lay the body to rest in a way that both honors the deceased and fits within the budget available. While no one likes to

11

think of money as a factor in end–of–life decisions, it is a harsh reality and one of the main reasons many people choose life insurance or death benefits to pay for their own funerals and services.

EMBALMING

Because a dead body won't last for long without decomposing, we embalm it. The primary goal of embalming is to preserve the body for as long as possible, though one could argue that once it's in the ground, who cares how long it looks like a human body? But preferences are strong in many countries for preservation to last a long time for those left to carry on once someone has died. It might be purely symbolic, for when loved ones visit a grave and wish to imagine the deceased still in their full human form.

Embalming became the common method of preserving bodies for transport, but after the war, demand decreased.

When a body is to be publicly viewed as part of a funeral, there will be an embalming, which has been used for thousands of years to preserve a dead body and stop decomposition. The ancient Egyptians had a similar process to slow down decomposition through mummification, and other ancient cultures had their own methods of preserving the bodies of the deceased.

Modern arterial embalming began in the United States during the Civil War, when Abraham Lincoln's friend Ephraim Ellsworth, an Army officer and law clerk, was killed. Dr. Thomas Holmes of New York had been experimenting with embalming methods used in France. He cared for Ellsworth's body so that he could be returned to his hometown of New York and buried ten days after his death.

This practice grew in popularity as more soldiers died far from home and their families desired to bury them nearby. Embalming became the common method of preserving bodies for transport, but after the war, demand decreased. By the end of the nineteenth century, however, the practice had increased as the undertaker's role became an important part of society, and more trained undertakers opened funeral parlors well into the new century.

Family and friends could travel long distances to attend a funeral and view the well-preserved body in an open casket.

The first step in arterial embalming is to give the body a bath and replace the blood and other body fluids with a formaldehyde-based preservative. This includes chemicals like methanol, ethanol, phenol, and maybe even dyes that make pale skin look darker. Natural oils could be used instead of chemical fluids, but they don't preserve the body as long as chemical fluids. They are worth looking into if you want a more natural approach and the viewing will be held soon after the death.

The eyes are secured in a closed position with glue, and the lower jaw is secured with wiring or sewing so that the face can be molded into a desired position. Body cavities are filled, and internal organs are drained of fluids and gas.

Following embalming, the body is dressed in a favorite family outfit and prepared for viewing using restorative art and cosmetology. Hair is washed and styled as well. If the body has been subjected to trauma or tissue donation, the embalmer can perform restorative work to restore it to its original state. There are embalmers trained in post-mortem reconstructive surgery who can do an extraordinary job restoring a body to its former condition in severe situations such as major accidents, burns, or other extreme death conditions.

Funerals are generally held within a week or less from the time of death but can be held up to two weeks later. Many families use funeral homes to handle the preparations and arrangements. A service may be held at a funeral home or a specified location, such as a beach or park, or a place listed in the last will of the deceased.

Families can wait much longer if a body is cremated, but it is usually done within a month of death. If there are reasons why the funeral must be delayed or it is difficult to find next of kin to sign off on a funeral or even cremation, bodies can be "put on ice" or refrigerated for a specific amount of time per each funeral home (some states in the United States do not allow refrigeration of bodies). If the body is the subject of an ongoing police investigation, the coroner must first authorize burial or cremation.

OBITUARIES, MEMORIALS, AND TRIBUTES

After death, we pay tribute in many other ways. We mourn, we memorialize, and we tell the world who we have lost in the form of obituaries.

Obituaries, or "obits" for short, are public pronouncements, usually in newspapers, of a recent death. Obits can be printed for known figures or everyday citizens, and are intended to serve as a short biography of the positive aspects of one's life. Usually life–affirming and a way to tell others where and when the funeral service will be, they can also be funny or opinionated, depending on the person submitting them.

There are two kinds of obits: death notices, which are brief and factual notices of the time, place, and cause of death and who the next of kin are; and memorials, which are more detailed notices by a family member or friend.

There are prewritten obits on file at news outlets for notable people who are still alive. This allows the news outlet

A memorial is a traditional way to pay tribute to someone who has passed away. Typically, a memorial includes photos of the deceased, flowers, and sometimes other objects that are reminders of the person who has passed.

to immediately publish a highly detailed obit of the person when they die. These are often updated with new information as the person lives on, and the *New York Times* alone is said to have a collection of over 1,700 advance obits, constantly adding new ones to its files. The problem with these lies in human error. In 2003, CNN reported the deaths of seven major public figures who were still alive, and in 2020, Radio France Internationale published up to 100 premature obituaries. It happens, along with premature obits that are the result of faked deaths, clerical errors, close calls with death, hoaxes, imposters, military personnel missing in action, kidnap victims, and misidentified corpses.

People of note are frequently honored with a full-page obituary in magazines or publications related to their life's work or career. Sports heroes, military heroes, and medical heroes may also be featured in publications.

A necrology is a register or list of the death records of those who were members of a specific organization or group, and it can be much shorter than a personal obituary. Local historical necrologies, which provide interesting tidbits of information that may not be found elsewhere, can often teach us a lot.

On social media outlets, it's common to see an In Memoriam page for accounts of those who have died, which allows friends and followers to continue to post messages of love and even birthday greetings. This applies to pets, too, as many pages exist honoring a lost pet with photos and memories. Since the days of the Roman Empire, the words "In Memoriam," followed by the name, have appeared on gravestones, monuments, and statues, as well as book or poem dedications. One such example is the poem "In Memoriam" by Alfred Tennyson, written over the course of 17 years to honor and mourn the death of his good friend Arthur Hallam.

To commemorate their life, public figures may be given a memorial park, statue, holiday, street name, or other grand gesture. Memorials are also built to remember those who died in wars and terrorist attacks.

On a more personal level, people frequently memorialize the locations of a loved one who died in a car accident with mini shrines containing personal objects, flowers, and photographs, as well as a religious symbol such as a cross or Star of David. It is common to see a memorial or shrine to a loved one, even a beloved pet, in private backyards, as we seek to keep some part of them alive through our own love and memories of them.

MODERN FUNERAL TRADITIONS

The typical Western funeral might begin with a viewing or visitation where either close family members or the public can come and view the body in the casket the night before the burial. The body is laid out in a nice outfit and the face and hair are done. People might offer flowers or bend to kiss the deceased's forehead. It's up to the desires of the family or the religious customs.

Visitations are usually followed with food at a family member's home. The Irish hold a wake that can last up to three days before the burial and include food, drink, and song. Prefuneral gatherings serve to allow people to come together and remember with joy, and grieve together, before the final service. It is a chance to bond over the loved one who is no longer there and celebrate life and honor death.

Funeral processions can range from the modest to huge, elaborate, televised events such as this one when Queen Elizabeth II passed away in 2022.

If the body is not cremated, the funeral then follows. A clergy member or someone from the funeral home officiates the service, which can be held at a funeral home or elsewhere. People listen to readings from holy texts or poems, possibly accompanied by music or singing of hymns or personal songs. Before attendees gather to head to the burial site, someone close to the deceased may give the eulogy, and depending on the religious tradition of the family, there may be readings from the Bible or other text.

A procession of cars will follow the lead hearse with the coffin inside to the burial site, usually with lights or blinkers flashing to alert others. It is common to see lines of dozens of cars for police officer or firefighter funerals. Pallbearers are often male family members or close friends of the person who died. They carry the body from the chapel, funeral home, or church to the hearse and then from the hearse to the burial service. Pallbearers usually sit in a designated area during the service.

Once everyone arrives at the burial grounds, they stand around the open grave, and there may be more readings and another eulogy. Then the coffin is lowered into the grave and people may be asked to throw a flower or handful of dirt on top of it. This is often reserved only for close family, but the rules can be flexible. Once the service ends, the attendees leave and go to a family home for lunch or disperse to their own homes. The coffin is then covered with dirt.

There are variations, but that is the most common funeral service. Military rites are performed at the burial service if the deceased served in the armed forces. Coffins are kept closed during the burial ceremony according to most religions. In Eastern Orthodox funerals, coffins are reopened right before the body is laid to rest to give loved ones a chance to say farewells. There are also services that involve the placement of an urn containing the deceased's cremated ashes into a family crypt or mausoleum.

MODERN DEATH TRADITIONS

Several years ago, author Marie had the pleasure of attending a very special funeral for her ex-husband's cousin, a popular surfer who had died while diving for sea bass. His friends and family crowded into a seaside church to laugh and tell stories and celebrate. So many people showed up to honor this young man's life that the crowds spilled out onto the street. Later we all headed to the beach, where his fellow surfers rode out and made a circle at sea, tossing his ashes into the waters. The sea bass he had caught while diving was cooked and passed around for all to taste, an unusual but powerful way to honor the cycle of nature and the circle of life. This is called a "Paddle Out" and has become a very popular method of celebrating the life of a deceased diver, surfer, swimmer, or beach lover in Southern California.

Other modern methods of celebrating death include humorous parties where attendees tell funny stories about the deceased as a way to focus on the joy that person brought them. The normal, somber funerals still occur, but for some, there is a need to see their beloved off to the "other side" with lightness and laughs. People throw "Come as the Deceased" parties where attendees dress up and act like the dead person, but all in good fun and respect. Other celebrations may involve watching old movies or videos filled with photos of the deceased with family, friends, colleagues, or just having fun enjoying their lives.

Residents of New Orleans, Louisiana, in the United States will be familiar with the Jazz Funeral, a procession that combines West African, French, and African American traditions in which funeral mourners march behind an elaborate marching band or a brass jazz band. The march is led by the family and loved ones of the deceased and moves from the family home to the funeral parlor or church, then on to the cemetery where the body is laid to rest.

As the march progresses, music can shift from solemn tones like hymns to more joyful and celebratory music to accompany the point of burial where the last goodbyes are said and mourners "cut the body loose." It's common for the mourners to break out in dance and do everything from twirl parasols and handkerchiefs to strut and wave their arms in the air. These dancers are called the "second line" behind the band, and the whole point is to first grieve death, then celebrate life.

The spreading of ashes can be itself a ceremony, with those in attendance taking turns spreading some ash and saying something about the deceased, renting a speedboat to deposit ashes in the ocean, or even hiking to the tops of mountains to cast the ashes off into the valleys below. If the deceased specified a certain desire in their last will, it is honored. If not, those who knew the person well might plan something special that the deceased would have loved if alive, such as taking the ashes to a particular park where they often played baseball or a lake in the woods where they loved to fish.

Commemorating dead pets is just as unique to the person or persons who loved the pet. There are pet funerals and places that cremate pets and return their bones and ashes in beautiful urns or boxes, along with a cement paw print and commemorative poem. Some people buy elaborate pet coffins and pay good money for a plot in a local pet cemetery, while others choose to bury their pets at home. It is no longer considered unusual to spend thousands of dollars honoring

Dogs, cats, and other pets have become like family members for many people, so it is not surprising that pets, too, are being buried and memorialized just like humans these days.

a dead pet just as we would a person, as they are considered important and beloved family members.

The truth is, there are as many ways to commemorate a death as there are people, including virtual ceremonies posted to social media to include those who could not attend in person, allowing them to post their memories and prayers of comfort for the family. Unless the family is adhering to a specific religious or cultural tradition, anything goes when sending off a loved one to the Great Beyond.

Deathversaries have become a "thing," with people gathering at grave sites or homes to celebrate the day of the death of a loved one with food and drink, as they would a wedding anniversary.

BURIAL VS. CREMATION

What to do with the body is the most important decision to make after death. This could be stated in the deceased's last will and testament. Burial and cremation are the two most common methods, and each has advantages and disadvantages. Some religious traditions require burial. Funerals, caskets, and plots to bury the body can cost thousands, if not tens of thousands of dollars, depending on the quality of the casket and the location of the plot. There are also fees for transporting the body to the plot and for the actual burial.

Cremation is becoming more popular as a way of holding down costs (a burial plot is not needed) but also because some people prefer not to think about their bodies slowly decaying underground.

Cremation is a much cheaper alternative for many who cannot afford a funeral, or for those who are not religious and wish to spread the ashes in a specific location to honor the dead. According to the Cremation Association of North America (CANA), the rate of cremation has risen from 48.6 percent in 2015 to 54.3 percent in 2021. A Harris poll conducted by the Funeral and Memorial Information Council (FAMIC) found that 65 percent of Americans would prefer to be cremated. People love the idea of either keeping the ashes of their loved one on a shelf or fireplace mantle in a fancy urn, or spreading them in a special place, but many states now have laws against spreading ashes in ponds, lakes, waterways, and the ocean.

Backyard burials and environmental burials are new alternatives. People may opt to bury a loved one in the backyard of a family home in a homemade casket with a specially made marker. To preserve the environment, we now can choose to have our ashes intermingled with tree seeds in tree pods that allow our bodies to nourish the soil and grow new life. The family can bury the tree pod on their own property or at a tree pod facility, as not every city may allow human remains buried on private property (imagine selling the home later and having to dig up Grandpa when the home inspector finds out).

Biodegradable caskets are now available for those who are concerned about burying another casket that will take over a century to decompose. You can also bury a body without a casket in a green cemetery, a wonderful way to return the body to nature—ashes to ashes, dust to dust, organic matter back into organic matter—all while reducing the carbon footprint.

RELIGIOUS BELIEFS ABOUT BURIAL AND CREMATION

Cremation is becoming a common and widely accepted choice, and most religious groups accept the practice. The ancient Greeks did it all the time, but the ancient Hebrews only used burial. Both ways were used by the ancient Romans. Some religious people believe that cremation is a sin and could stop the body from being resurrected because the body is no longer considered whole. On the other hand, a body buried quickly decomposes, so these traditions are being pushed to change with the times.

The Catholic Church once prohibited cremation but later changed its policies to allow Catholics to be cremated after funeral rites are performed on the body. Many Catholic families now choose cremation as a more cost-effective option, and the church has changed its rules to allow funeral rites to be performed with the ashes present after cremation.

> The Church earnestly recommends that the pious custom of burial be retained; but it does not forbid cremation, unless this is chosen for reasons which are contrary to Christian teaching.
>
> –The Code of Canon Law, 1985, #1176.3

Cremation is permitted by Lutherans, and you can have a traditional Lutheran funeral and cremation. Methodists do not oppose cremation, and it is possible to be cremated as part of a traditional Methodist funeral. Cremation is not pro-

Islam prohibits people from being cremated. Even further, Muslims are not allowed to even witness a cremation. This is because cremation is considered a disrespectful way to treat the deceased's body.

The Environmental Effects of Cremation and Burial

Crematoriums are not just an American problem. This one in Thailand also emits considerable pollutants.

Traditional burial impacts the environment in many negative ways, leaving behind approximately 800,000 gallons of formaldehyde in embalming fluid each year. A 10-acre cemetery leaves behind approximately 1,000 tons of casket steel and enough wood to build over 40 houses. In addition, overcrowded cemeteries leave little room for plants, trees, or animal life. Then there is the negative impact of cut flowers left at grave sites on the environment. Most of the cut flowers are grown in South America where intensive amounts of pesticide are used, many currently banned in North America. Those pesticides leech into the soil if the plants are left behind to rot at the gravesite.

Biodegradable caskets made of wood, cardboard, or wicker are not only less expensive than traditional caskets, but they also break down into the earth much more quickly. Another option is to simply put a shroud over the body. Some cemeteries will only take shrouds or caskets that break down over time. You may decline embalming because it is not required by law unless the body is being transported or the deceased had a communicable disease.

In California, there is a service called Better Place Forests that allows you to choose a tree in one of the company's many forests to turn into a memorial tree. Once cremated, your ashes are mixed in with the local soil and returned to the base of your chosen tree and become a part of the living forest. You get special access to the forest to hike and visit to watch your tree grow once you purchase it, and once you are buried there, your children and grandchildren can come visit your tree in the beauty of a natural setting. The company claims it is a way to protect the forestland and honor the dead at the same time.

Effects of Cremation

The crematoria emissions of vaporized mercury are dispersed into the air and eventually fall back to earth in the form of acid rain de-

cont'd on next page

cont'd from previous page

posited on water and land. These toxins get into our food sources and then our bodies, and ashes get into the groundwater from those who choose to ignore local or state laws and illegally spread ashes. Contrary to popular belief, you cannot spread a loved one's ashes anywhere you want as you might see in the movies.

What You Can Do to Help

Ask the crematorium about its use of pollutant filters and mercury emissions. In addition, request that it remove and recycle prosthetic limbs, pacemakers, and other medical implants. If you intend to bury the cremated ashes, use a biodegradable urn. A newer method called promession involves the use of freeze drying and prepares the body in a way that mimics natural decomposition. This process, developed by Swedish biologist Susanne Wiigh-Mäsak, comes from the Italian word for "promise" and enables the body to be fully decomposed into the earth in one year. It can be used in both burials and cremations.

hibited by the Anglican Church before or after a funeral, and cremation is not opposed by Baptists.

For Jews, the rules regarding cremation vary. Conservative and Orthodox Jews don't allow cremation, but a Rabbi is permitted to perform funeral rites of a cremated person. Cremation is becoming more popular amongst Reform Jews, and several Reform rabbis will perform funeral rites at the interment of a person who has been cremated. Jewish law does insist that the dead be buried and that the responsibility for interment details is left to the family.

Even if the deceased left instructions for cremation, the family should arrange for burial in a Jewish cemetery because of the belief that our bodies belong not to us but rather to God. This does not apply if the person was cremated against their will. It is still appropriate to do mitzvot and recite the mourner's prayer in remembrance of their soul.

Jehovah's Witnesses don't believe in the physical resurrection; they believe that the spirit will be resurrected and

A Personal Jewish Perspective on Death and Dying

This c. 247 C.E. fresco from the Temple of Bel in present-day Syria depicts the resurrection of the dead.

When it comes to death, a traditional Jewish joke states that there is no such thing as Heaven or Hell: we all go to the same place, where Moses and Rabbi Akiva continue to teach everlasting courses from the Bible and the Talmud. Those who are righteous will experience eternal enjoyment, while those who are evil-minded will suffer indefinitely.

But what exactly does Judaism believe? In this regard, Jewish tradition is notoriously unclear. The immortality of the soul, the presence of a future world, and the resurrection of the dead are all key issues in Jewish tradition, but what these concepts are and how they connect to one another have remained a mystery for most of the millennia.

Let's dive deeper into what Jews believe about death and the hereafter.

Traditional Judaism believes death is not the end of human existence. However, because Judaism is more focused on the present than with eternity, there is limited official doctrine about the hereafter, allowing room for personal interpretation. For example, an Orthodox Jew may believe that the souls of the dead of those who were good in life will move to a world similar to Christian paradise, that they are reincarnated many times, or that they just await the return of the messiah, at which point they will be awakened. Similarly, Orthodox Jews may believe that the souls of the wicked are tormented by the demons they created or that evil souls are obliterated and cease to exist upon death.

According to some experts, belief in the afterlife is a late-evolutionary Jewish concept. The Torah, while emphasizing immediate, tangible, physical rewards and punishments over abstract future repercussions, also provides unambiguous evidence for the belief in life after death. The Torah states that the devout will be reunited with their loved ones after death, whereas the wicked will be barred from this reunion.

cont'd on next page

cont'd from previous page

When a person commits certain offenses, such as murder or rape, they are "cut off from their people," according to Jewish belief. This punishment is known as kareit (kah-REHYT) (literally, "cutting off," but more commonly interpreted as "spiritual excision") and refers to the soul's loss of a portion of the World to Come.

The dead, according to traditional Judaism, will be resurrected one day. This idea differentiated the Pharisees from the Sadducees (the intellectual forefathers of Rabbinical Judaism). The Sadducees rejected this idea because it was not addressed directly in the Torah. The idea was hinted at in various passages but required "creative" interpretation, according to the Pharisees.

One of Rabbi Moses ben Maimon's 13 Principles of Faith is belief in the resurrection of the dead. The second blessing of the three-times-a-day Shemoneh Esrei prayer contains several references to resurrection.

During the messianic age, the dead will be resurrected. When the messiah arrives to inaugurate the perfect world of peace and prosperity, the righteous dead will be resurrected and given the opportunity to experience the perfected world that their righteousness helped to build. The wicked dead will not be raised from the dead.

Resurrection, according to certain mystical schools of thought, is a continuous process rather than a one-time event. The spirits of the pious are reborn to complete the ongoing work of tikkun olam, or world repair. Some authors claim that reincarnation is common, while others claim that it only happens in rare cases, such as when the soul has unfinished business. Reincarnation can also explain the old Jewish belief that every Jewish soul in history was present at Sinai when the covenant with G-d was made.

Another interpretation holds that the soul existed prior to the body and that these unborn souls were present in some way at Sinai.

Reincarnation is a belief held by many Hasidic Jewish communities, as well as more mystically inclined Jews.

In Hebrew, the spiritual afterlife is known as Olam Ha-Ba (oh-LAHM hah-BAH), or the World to Come, which used to refer to the messianic age. The Olam Ha-Ba is a higher plane of existence.

cont'd on next page

cont'd from previous page

One Mishnah rabbi claims that "this world is similar to the lobby before the Olam Ha-Ba. Preparing for the dining hall begins in the foyer." Similarly, according to the Talmud, "This world corresponds to Shabbat eve, and the Olam Ha-Ba corresponds to Shabbat itself. Those who prepare meals on Shabbat evening will have food to eat on Shabbat." We prepare for the Olam Ha-Ba by studying the Torah and doing good.

According to the Talmud, everyone in Israel has a stake in the Olam Ha-Ba. But not all "shares" are created equal. A virtuous person receives a larger portion of the Olam Ha-Ba than the average person. A person's share may be reduced as a result of poor behavior. There are several statements in the Talmud that a specific mitzvah will guarantee a person's place in the Olam Ha-Ba, or that a specific transgression will cause a person's share in the Olam Ha-Ba to be taken away, but these are frequently regarded as exaggeration or overly enthusiastic approval or condemnation.

Some interpret these teachings to mean that Jews want to "earn their way into Heaven" by performing mitzvot. This is a blatant misinterpretation of the Jewish religion. It's important to remember that, unlike other religions, Judaism isn't concerned with how to enter Heaven. Judaism is concerned with present life and how to live it.

Nonetheless, Jews believe that their place in the Olam Ha-Ba is determined by a meritocracy based on their actions rather than who they are or what religion they practice.

Gan Eden (GAHN ehy-DEHN) is the place of spiritual reward for Judaism's faithful (the Garden of Eden). This is not the same garden as Adam and Eve's, but it is a spiritually beautiful garden. The specifics vary greatly from report to report. According to one tradition, the peace felt when keeping Shabbat perfectly amounts to one-sixth of the afterlife's delights. Some traditions suggest the bliss of the afterlife is comparable to the pleasures of sex or a warm, sunny day. The living, on the other hand, are simply unable to grasp the essence of this location, just as the blind are unable to perceive color.

Gan Eden, according to Jewish belief, only accepts the most moral people. For punishment and/or purification, the average person is sent to Gehinnom (guh-hee-NOHM) (in Yiddish, Ge-

cont'd on next page

---

cont'd from previous page

henna), but also known as She'ol and other names. According to one mystical interpretation, every sin we commit creates a corresponding angel of destruction, or a demon, and when we die, the demons we created punish us. Gehinnom, according to some interpretations, is a realm of cruel punishment, similar to the Christian Hell of fire and brimstone. Other authors simply see it as a time to reflect objectively on our lives, acknowledge the harm we've done and the opportunities we've missed, and mourn. Each person only has 12 months in Gehinnom before ascending to Olam Ha-Ba to take his or her position.

Only the most heinous offenders will not ascend at the end of this 12-month period; their souls suffer for an entire year. Sources differ on what happens at the end of the year: some say the bad spirit is completely extinguished and no longer exists, while others believe the soul remains in a constant state of awareness of their regrets.

This 12-month period is mentioned several times in the Talmud, and it is linked to grief cycles and Kaddish recitation.

To summarize, Jewish belief in a hereafter is both straightforward and complex. Though we have no way of knowing if there is another life or if there is a reward for what we achieve, it appears that our reward will be determined by the type of life we have led up to this point. As a result, let us make every effort to carry out God's plan for us as precisely and joyfully as possible, because we will undoubtedly reap a variety of benefits, the most important of which will be the satisfaction of seeing a better world as a result of our efforts.

---

their physical body is not needed. There are no rules against cremation. Members follow local customs and norms for burying the dead if they choose to.

Buddhism encourages cremation. The spiritual founder of Buddhism, Siddhartha Gautama, known as the Buddha, was cremated on a funeral pyre, and many choose to follow his example. The family may choose to enshrine the cremated remains or scatter them. Cremation is considered the traditional option, but a family can choose burial if they please. Hinduism also encourages cremation. Hindus believe cremation helps with the disposal of physical remains and ushers the soul of the deceased. When someone dies, the Hindus believe the soul leaves the body and enters another until it achieves Mukti, when it has reached perfection. Cremation helps the soul get closer to Mukti.

There are religions that do not allow cremation. Muslims are prohibited from cremating loved ones. Islam is very strict about its opposition to cremation, and a Muslim cannot even be the witness to a cremation. The dead body is treated with the same respect in Islam as when alive. Bodies are buried in graveyards after funeral rites are performed.

Mormons don't forbid cremation, but they also don't encourage it. Because they believe that the soul is connected to the physical body, the Church of Jesus Christ of Latter-day Saints (LDS) prefers burial. However, if you choose cremation, the LDS memorial services can still be done.

The Eastern Orthodox Church generally prohibits cremation, believing the body is sacred and should be buried intact.

As the cost of burials and burial plots rises, it will be interesting to see if even the strictest religious traditions allow adherents to choose a less expensive way of remembering their deceased loved ones.

Death and Dying around the World

*Seeing death as the end of life is like seeing the horizon
as the end of the ocean.*
—David Searls

*If we can prove an afterlife, then we have less pressure
to make our physical life last forever.*
—Chuck Palahniuk

There is an afterlife. I am convinced of this.
—Paulo Coelho

People all over the world mourn, grieve, and honor the dead. Funeral or burial traditions vary by culture, with some emphasizing mourning and others emphasizing the celebration of the transition from death to another, better place.

HALLOWEEN AND DÍA DE LOS MUERTOS

Every October 31st, kids and adults alike hit the streets or attend parties donned in costumes to trick or treat for candy or just hang out with friends. It's one night each year people can become someone else, but that was not the original intent of Halloween. People don't realize that they are re-enacting remnants of ancient folk customs paying respects to the dead and to the souls of the departed. Halloween is based on ancient pagan beliefs about life, death, and the veil between the living and the dead. Pagans celebrated changes

29

from the warm, sunny days of summer to the coming of the harvest and the cold winter months to follow, and Halloween traditions symbolized the dying of the year. It was a time to remember the dead and to honor them as the veil thinned, allowing them to come visit the living for a short time.

Halloween has its roots in the ancient Celtic festival Samhain (pronounced SOW–in), which was one of the most important festival quarter days of the year. Samhain begins on the eve of October 31st and ends with the beginning of the Celtic New Year on November 1st. During this time, Celts believed the otherwise solid boundaries that separated the living and dead became thin and mutable, with the veil at its thinnest on the eve of Samhain.

This time of year also marks the harvest and readying for the cold winter months when the sun sets earlier and the nights become longer. Trees shed their leaves, animals prepare for hibernation, and humans prepare for the coming winter when hopefully they've stored up some of fall's harvest to get them through to the time of rebirth, or spring.

After the Roman conquest, the Christian Church merged traditions of Samhain into their own celebration of martyrs and saints–November 1st–and it became All Saints Day (with the following day, November 2nd, as All Soul's Day). This festival was called All–Hallows, and the previous evening was called All Hallows' Eve–later becoming what we know and love as the present–day Halloween.

The way we celebrate Halloween still consists of many ancient traditions such as dressing up in costumes, having parades, playing scary tricks on people, decorating homes, making treats, and lighting bonfires. Dressing in costumes comes from the Celtic belief that the ghosts of the dead and the fairy folk liked to roam the fields and roads on Halloween, and the best way to avoid them would be to wear a mask or costume so the spirits and fairies would think you were one of them. Thus early costumes were a bit more frightening and did not yet include the sexy nurse or kitten costumes of today!

Europeans leave offerings of food or "treats" on their doorsteps for the dead spirits and fairies, which evolved into modern–day trick or treating. Offering treats for the dead is an integral part of many such festivals, including the colorful

Day of the Dead, or Día de los Muertos, celebrated in Mexico, Latin America, and parts of North America.

Día de los Muertos includes traditions such as decorating with skulls and making treats like pan de muertos, or bread of the dead, and the famous colorful sugar skulls called calaveras. This holiday blends customs and traditions of the invading Spanish conquistadores with those of indigenous Mesoamerica.

The Aztec Festival of the Dead was originally a two-month festival presided over by Mictecacíhuatl, Goddess of the Dead and the Underworld, known to the Aztecs as Mictlán. In pre-Columbian beliefs, Mictlán was a peaceful realm where souls rested until Día de los Muertos arrived and they could visit the living. Celebrants placed offerings to the dead, such as food, photographs, flowers, and candles, on homemade altars.

ANCIENT AND PAGAN DEATH RITUALS

Death rituals obviously go back as far as humankind, and we have the remains of once-sacred sites to prove it, sites

In Mexico, Día de los Muertos (Day of the Dead) is a festive, happy occasion honoring ancestors and remembering them with love.

Celebrating Departed Souls

Lights placed in a cemetery in Pécs, Hungary, on All Soul's Day.

With the arrival of the Spanish and Christianity, the new rulers of Mexico attempted to hijack the pagan celebrations dedicated to the dead under the auspices of All Saints Day (November 1st) and All Souls Day (November 2nd). The dates of these two Catholic holidays are now celebrated in Mexico as Día de los Muertos.

November 1st is a somber day to remember children who have died. In many Mexican towns, church bells ring in the morning to call on the deceased children, or Angelitos, to come and visit their loved ones. On November 2nd, deceased adult spirits are then welcomed to return to their family home for a visit. Celebrations may include reading poems written to the dead and offerings of food, drinks, and special cempasúchil flowers (marigolds), as well as plenty of bread of the dead and brightly colored calaveras with names of people (living or dead) painted on them.

Families may gather in cemeteries on the eve of November 2nd, Día de los Muertos, and hold a commemorative feast at the grave-

cont'd on next page

cont'd from previous page

sites of the deceased. It is a time of visiting with the dead and living family members and leaving food, sweets, and brightly colored tissue paper decorations on the gravesite, as well as grooming supplies needed for the spirits to clean up after their long journey from their world into the world of the living.

There may also be music, cooking, and dancing, characteristic of the lighter and more festive celebrations of ancient pre-Columbian times.

Adapted in part from the
National Endowment for the Humanities, neh.gov

such as the pre–Stonehenge megaliths recently found in Dartmoor, England. These nine megaliths predate Stonehenge and have been carbon dated to approximately 3500 B.C.E. The standing stones mark the rising midsummer sun and setting midwinter sun. Mass quantities of pig bones found near the site suggest that some type of death ritual occurred here, a kind of feast that marked the passage into the darkness of the underworld, according to archaeologist Mike Pitts, one of the key figures in this amazing discovery. Another stone mound called Cut Hill appears to have been a burial place and the site of accompanying rituals and ceremonies.

Maya

To the ancient Maya, death was also considered a transition. The good souls would be taken directly to Heaven, while the evil would be transported to Xilbalba, the underworld, where they would suffer for all eternity (much like the Judeo–Christian Heaven/Hell). To the Maya, some individuals upon death became deities. Maize was used to symbolize rebirth and was often placed in the mouths of the dead, who might also be buried with whistles, stones, and engravings designed to help them navigate the spirit world.

Lavish tombs were built for the revered, usually at the bottom of funerary pyramids consisting of nine steps, to symbolize the nine platforms of the underworld. Temples were often built with 13 vaults to represent the 13 layers of Heaven of Maya cosmology.

Egypt and Rome

Ancient Egyptian death rituals reflected the roles of the Egyptian gods in guiding dead souls to the afterlife. Egyptians believed in eternal life and the rebirth of souls and of Duat, the underworld with its entrance only reachable by going through the deceased's tomb. Burial tombs varied through each different period of time, but they were always meant for one purpose—to house the body of the dead and help their soul to the underworld.

The Egyptians built pyramids as death chambers and practiced elaborate rituals such as mummification to preserve the dead so they could be reborn in the afterlife. Mummification protocols for the ancient Egyptians included magical spells and burial rites designed to reanimate the dead once

A papyrus from the Egyptian Book of the Dead shows the god Osiris at the gates of Aaru (paradise). The heart is weighed in the Duat (place of the dead) and judged to be worthy or unworthy. Anubis, the god of the dead, is at far right.

their journey through the underworld was complete. The Egyptians built pyramids as death chambers and practiced elaborate rituals such as mummification to preserve the dead so they could be reborn in the afterlife. Mummification protocols for the ancient Egyptians included magical spells and burial rites designed to reanimate the dead once their journey through the underworld was complete.

All Egyptians of any social class were buried with burial goods necessary to transport them safely into the next realm as well as sacred texts such as the Book of the Dead, which guided the soul. These might be simple trinkets or expensive jewels that often became the target of tomb raiders. Coffin texts were spells that were inscribed into the coffins to protect the deceased on their journey and provide them with the magic they might need in the form of spells.

Boats were used as passage to the underworld instead of coffins for pharaohs who had died. This was to mimic the travels of Ra, the sun god, who traveled to the underworld by boat as the sun set. The common people would build small model boats of different sizes to be buried near a pharaoh's final resting place.

From the coffin and boat passages of ancient Egyptians we move to the underground catacombs of ancient Rome, which housed the dead beginning in the 2nd century C.E. Like the Etruscans before them, the Romans cremated the dead and kept the ashes in urns and pots, but they eventually turned to inhumation, the burial of unburnt remains, which were kept in elaborate graves or sarcophagi (if one could afford them). The catacombs were carved through volcanic rock called *tufo*, soft enough to create the large subterranean burial chambers, sometimes built under roads named for martyrs thought to be buried below.

Around 380 C.E., when Christianity became the state religion, the practice of catacomb burial declined, replaced by the church cemeteries we still bury most of our dead in today. Inhumation replaced cremation in most cases, with burials taking place in coffins, pots, and even vaults. Roman middle-class dead were often buried in pots partially buried in the ground, which allowed families to leave offerings and libations at the grave site (something we still do today, usually in the form of flowers).

Aboveground, massive and elaborate mausoleums were built to house the urns of the dead, which were usually those of Imperial Roman families and emperors. Some of these massive structures have survived the ravages of time and can now be found in Rome and its environs. The Western world eventually carried on the tradition, with many of our most famous dead celebrities buried in mausoleums at cemeteries like the Forest Lawn cemeteries in Southern California, popular tourist destinations for those interested in viewing Liberace's lavish gravesite or seeing where Michael Jackson was laid to rest.

The Western world eventually carried on the tradition, with many of our most famous dead celebrities buried in mausoleums at cemeteries like the Forest Lawn cemeteries in Southern California....

MODERN CULTURAL TRADITIONS

Various civilizations have different beliefs regarding how to handle the deceased. The dead are spread out on a reef and left as food for sharks in the Solomon Islands, an Oceanian nation east of Papua New Guinea with close to a thousand islands. Similar to the Parsees of Bombay, India, who left their dead on the tops of towers to be eaten by vultures, the Aboriginal people of Australia would hang their dead bodies from trees. Another Aboriginal funeral ceremony entails family members and community members painting themselves white, cutting their own bodies, and performing rituals, songs, and dances to guarantee the deceased's spirit returns to its birthplace so it can one day be reincarnated.

The Maori of New Zealand place their dead in a hut in a sitting position, wearing nice clothes. The dead are viewed by mourners wearing green wreaths who cry out and cut themselves with knives. Then there is a feast, and the hut is burned down. In similar fashion, the Pygmies of the Congo pull the hut down on top of the dead person, then move their camp and never speak of the deceased again.

In Bali, Ngaben is a funeral ritual to send the deceased on to the next life. It is a Buddhist ceremony involving displaying the dead body as if they are sleeping. The family and loved ones treat the deceased as if they are alive and talk to them as such before the end of the ritual, the burning of the coffin. The fire frees the spirit from the body and allows the deceased to reincarnate.

Jamaicans celebrate the dead for nine nights to allow the deceased safe passage to the other side. There is dancing, singing, eating, and drinking plenty of good rum, signifying a less fear-based belief in the finality of death. Forty nights later, the relatives come back to sing again, celebrating the completion of the departed soul's journey.

Alaskan Inuit construct small igloos over the dead to leave them frozen in time. Other native traditions involve holding feasts with the dead present, then burning or burying the body in a secluded area. Native American tribal traditions involve a variety of rituals that speak of a reverence, even a fearful one, of the spirit world. The Navajo destroy the hut of the dead person and allow relatives to burn the body, then take an indirect route home so the spirit of the dead can't follow them. The Aztecs deliver a formal speech like a Eulogy to assure the dead safe passage. The Iroquois bury their dead in shallow graves that are later exhumed so that the bones, along with gifts left for the spirits, can be taken to a central burial site after a mourning feast.

Mongolians often cremate important and high-ranking officials and place their ashes into a monument. They also engage in sky burials, like the Tibetans, where the body of the deceased is left on a high place exposed to the elements to be eaten by birds and wildlife. While a Mongolian is in the process of dying, his or her valuables and jewels might be taken off and given away to prepare them for the next life. Cambodians, like Mongolians, honor Buddhist traditions and believe death is part of the cycle of reincarnation and rebirth. At the time of death, a Buddhist monk is called to be present to act as a guide for the soul as it leaves the body and prepares for the next incarnation. Family members may dress in white, and some shave their heads to honor the dead at the funeral. They do believe in cremation, and the ashes are usually brought to the nearest Buddhist temple.

An African mask used by shamans during ceremonies such as funerals. In some African cultures, death is treated with as much fear as veneration.

In many African cultures, the dead are treated with fear, veneration, and respect. In South Africa, the windows of a deceased person's house are smeared with ash, beds are removed from the dead person's bedroom, and an animal is used in a ritual sacrifice to the dead ancestors. Once the deceased person is buried, family members wash off the dirt from the graveyard before they enter the house to symbolize washing off bad luck.

OTHER RITES AND RITUALS

The Muslim tradition requires that the body of the deceased be placed on its sides and washed with soap and scented water. Like the Hindus, the Muslims must wash the body an odd number of times, and the teeth and nose must be cleaned out in a spiritual cleansing rite called ablution. The body is perfumed and wrapped in white cloth. Prayers are said facing Mecca, and a silent procession delivers the body to the burial grounds. One of the prayers is the Salat al–Janazah, which seeks pardon for the dead and is performed as a part of the Islamic funeral rituals. This is a series of complicated prayers and recitations performed at specific times in the ritual, during which the deceased is placed before an Imam, who stands in front of rows of people in odd numbers. Certain hand gestures accompany the recitations, which ask for God to bestow forgiveness on the dead and allow them passage into Paradise and protection from "the torment of the grave and the torment of Hell-fire." Throughout the ritual, a *dua*, or invocation, is offered for the deceased. One such final *dua* might be "O God, if he was a doer of good, then increase his good deeds, and if he was a wrongdoer, then overlook his bad deeds. O God, forgive him and give him the steadiness to say the right thing."

Iranian funeral rituals can go on for days and are very complicated, with strict rules for correct burial and mourning. The body must be buried within 24 hours of death and is prepared by being washed nine times, then wrapped in a white shroud with tie chords. It is considered holy to touch the coffin or help carry it, which is why funeral processions often involve crowds of people flocking around the coffin and reaching out to touch it. After the funeral, there are a number of days considered significant as part of the mourning ritual: the third day, seventh day, fortieth day, and one-year mark. Mourners must wear black until the fortieth day, when they can go back to wearing normal colors again.

In Sweden, a predominantly secular country, there is a tradition rooted in the Lutheran Christian church that burial or cremation occurs between one and three weeks after death. In the meantime, the body is placed somewhere considered special. Funerals are private and not for public viewing, and family members put local flowers on the coffin as they sing songs. Men will often don a white tie for the service. Other Nordic countries hold water burials as part of their traditions, laying the coffin on top of cliffs facing water or burying the bodies into the water directly. There is also the tradition of "death ships," where the body is placed into a boat that is set on fire as it drifts out to sea to signify giving the body of the dead back to the old gods for safekeeping and guidance to the beyond.

In the Philippines, many traditions honor the dead but vary depending on the region. The Tinguian people will dress the dead in fancy clothes and sit the body in a chair, maybe even with a lit cigarette in the mouth. The Benguet blindfold the dead before putting them in chairs at the entrance of the family homes. The Cebuano dress children in red to stop them from seeing the ghosts of the dead. In the Sagada region, coffins are hung from cliffs to bring the souls nearer to Heaven, and in Cavite, the dead are vertically entombed in a hollowed-out tree that they had chosen themselves before they died.

South Koreans turn the ashes of cremated loved ones into colorful beads that are then put inside glass vases or in dishes instead of an urn. These decorative items are a creative way to display the dead and turn their bodies into a family heirloom, similar to pendants made with small vials containing the ashes of the dead, a popular modern choice in the United States.

EASTERN DEATH TRADITIONS

On the first day of a family member's death, Buddhists call in a priest to come and recite a sutra based upon Buddhist scripture or teachings. On the second day, incense is burned in front of a butsudan, or family altar. On the third day, the body is burned at a funeral hall and the ashes are returned to the family home. The priest resides over the funeral while family members burn incense. The ashes are laid to rest in a graveyard, with family members visiting once a week for seven weeks. On the 49th day, a customary feast called the Shiju–ku–Nichi is given for friends and neighbors.

Tibetan Buddhists have death meditation traditions that recognize the impermanence, meaning, and preciousness of life. These traditions seek to bring understanding about the death process to remove fear from the time of death and ensure a good rebirth experience. It is believed that one's state of mind at death is a marker for how one will experience rebirth. There are two common Tibetan meditations on death. The first offers insight into the certainty and imminence of death and what will be of benefit at the time of death, so that we are able to make the best use of our lives. The second simulates the actual death process so we can become familiar enough with it to take away the fear of death and the unknown. Traditionally, in Buddhist countries, visits to a cemetery or burial ground are made to contemplate on and become more comfortable with death.

Hindus believe death is a continuation of the life cycle of birth, life, death, and rebirth. Souls of the dead move to another body after death. Hindus bathe the body of the dead and adorn it with garlands, wrapping the body in a pure white cloth. The body is then cremated upon a pyre. In the following

A funeral in Zhongdian, Yunnan, China is presided over by Tibetan monks. Buddhists believe that one's state of mind at death may influence how they experience the transition.

days, mourners remain inside and do not attend public events. In the 1800s, grieving widows in India practiced self-immolation (sati), burning themselves (not necessarily voluntarily) beside their husband's funeral pyre. This practice was banned in 1829 by the British, then again in 1956 and 1981.

Hindus chant a mantra at the moment of death that was used by the dying. But if they do not know what that mantra was, a family member will chant softly into the dying's right ear, "Aum Namo Narayana" or "Aum Nama Sivaya," as holy ash or sandal paste is applied to the forehead. Sometimes, water from the Ganges or other holy water will be dripped into the mouth of the dying.

Japan

In Japan, literate people would create a *jisei*, or "death poem," on their deathbed, a practice that dates from ancient times. Poetry was, and still is, revered in Japanese culture and allows for the dying to impart their final thoughts, feelings, and insights to leave behind, as in these two *jisei*.

Tokugawa Ieyasu (1542–1616)

Whether one passes on or remains is all the same.
That you can take no one with you is the only difference.
Ah, how pleasant! Two awakenings and one sleep.
This dream of a fleeing world! The roseate hues of early dawn!

Uesugi Kenshin (1530–1578)

Even a life-long prosperity is but one cup of sake;
A life of forty-nine years is passed in a dream;
I know not what life is, nor death.
Year in year out—all but a dream.
Both Heaven and Hell are left behind;
I stand in the moonlit dawn,
Free from clouds of attachment.

SKY BURIALS, FANTASY COFFINS, AND THE TURNING OF THE BONES

Tibetans once practiced sky burials, where a corpse was sliced up and left on the top of a mountain for the birds. Called "jhator," this giving of alms to the winged creatures involved monks chopping the bodies with axes into bite-size chunks

A sky burial site in Tibet. In climates where the ground can be frozen too hard for burial, the dead may be left out in the open to decay or be consumed by birds.

for the birds, laughing and joking the whole time. To the Tibetans who believed in this ritual, it was considered an acceptable custom.

In Ghana, people are buried in highly decorative coffins that celebrate their life passions. These are called "fantasy coffins" and come in many shapes, such as luxury cars, animals, or symbols that represent the deceased's hobby or profession. The people of Ghana do not believe death is the end but do believe that the afterlife is similar to life on Earth, so these coffins are vessels that allow the deceased to continue on with their interests in the next life. Families spend a lot of time and effort making these special coffins to please and show respect to their dead loved ones.

Famadihana is the name of the funerary tradition for the people of Madagascar. It is known as "the turning of the bones," where every five to seven years, the bodies of ancestors are removed by family members from their crypts and rewrapped in fresh cloths. The family members then dance to live music while holding the corpses above them. They believe that the spirits of the dead will only move on to the afterlife once the body is completely decomposed and all rituals and ceremonies have ended.

This is a way for Madagascar families to come together and celebrate the living as well as the dead. The exhumed bodies are often sprayed with wine or scented perfumes, and people tell the dead all the current family news and ask for blessings.

TRADITIONS YOU MIGHT NOT WANT TO TRY AT HOME

Smoked Mummies

In the Menyamya region of Papua New Guinea, the Anga tribe have their own special form of mummification that involves smoking the meat of the dead. Before smoking, relatives rub the guts and drippings of the dead body onto their skin. According to the Anga people, the bodies of people with high social status will roam the jungle as spirits if their bodies are not taken care of. These spirits can even destroy farming and hunting. The bodies are scraped with bristly leaves and kept in a smoke–filled hut for 30 days. The organs are extracted using a bamboo pipe, and bodily fluids are smeared on the villagers. Then the bodies are treated with ocher, which mummifies them, and the remains are used as cooking oil. After the smoking process, bodies are dressed in bright colors and taken to the edges of steep cliffs overlooking the village so the dead can look down upon and protect the living below.

The Dani people of West Papua, New Guinea, have an extreme ritual where the members of the family have a finger amputated when a loved one dies.

Finger Amputation

The Dani people of West Papua, New Guinea, have an extreme ritual where the members of the family have a finger amputated when a loved one dies. The process, known as *ikipalin*, is seen as a sign of mourning through physical pain. It is a voluntary process, and the people do this out of affection for the deceased. It is also thought that the pain keeps the dead's spirits away. A piece of rope is tied around the finger to cut off blood circulation and make it numb. Then a stone blade is used to cut off the finger, usually by a close family member. Although it is outlawed today by the Indonesian government, older members of the tribe still show signs of this practice that speaks of the connection between the emotional and the physical.

Drive-Through Funerals

Apparently you don't even have to leave your car to pay your respects. Drive–through funerals allow attendees to stay in their vehicles as they drive past the burial site where the body is being laid to rest. This might come in handy during rain or high winds but has not yet become commonplace throughout the world, perhaps in part because of the price of gasoline.

Endocannibalism

From eating the flesh to grinding bones, some cultures in New Guinea, Brazil, Australia, and other countries take part in ritualistic cannibalism as a way to become a part of the dead by consuming their flesh. The Yanomami tribe, for example, who live in 200 to 250 villages in the Amazon rainforest spread across Brazil and Venezuela, consume the remains of their deceased tribesmen as a sign of kinship. For the Yanomami tribe, death is an unnatural event caused by an evil curse of a rival tribe's shaman. To purge the evil spirit, the body is cremated after being left untouched for 30 to 45 days. After cremation, the ashes are mixed with fermented banana soup. The mixture is consumed in one sitting by everyone in the deceased's community.

Sokushinbutsu

This Buddhist custom of self-mummification was practiced by monks across Asia, mainly in Japan, up until the 19th century. It can take between eight and ten years to prepare for this, with the monk eating a strict diet of pine needles, resins, and seeds to reduce all body fat. The monks then gradually reduce and stop all liquid intake, which shrinks the internal organs. The monk then starves to death while meditating, completely preserved for mummification without chemicals.

Funeral Strippers

In Taiwan and eastern China, it is common to have strippers in funeral processions who dance on or in Electric Flower Cars, bright-colored neon-lit cars carrying the dancers. The dancers perform pole dances and stripteases during the funeral and at the gravesite. This tradition is thought to have begun in the 1980s among the mafia and then gradually spread to the general population.

Sati

In the sati (or suttee) tradition, the widow of the deceased sacrificed herself on the funeral pyre of her husband. It was common among the Hindus in India, especially among the upper-caste clans like the Rajputs. Sati was practiced beginning in prehistoric times in Asia and had deep roots in Hindu mythology. The word *sati* means "chaste woman." While the process was conceived as a voluntary one, the widow was usually reportedly drugged and forced to undergo this process. The sati was banned by the British government in 1829, mainly due to the works of re-

In this nineteenth-century illustration from India, a woman is burned to death after her husband dies as part of the sati tradition.

former Raja Ram Mohan Roy. Today, it is widely seen as an inhuman practice and is banned in India.

Totem Pole Burials

Native American tribes sometimes use totem poles or mortuary poles to honor the dead. Mainly used by the Haida people in the nineteenth century, these totem poles housed the remains of clan chiefs or other high–ranking members. The poles are made of red cedar logs etched with the family crests of the deceased. There is a small cavity at the top of the pole. One year after the death, the remains of the deceased are crushed and put in a box, which is then put in a cavity cut into the wide end. The package is kept hidden from public view by a large board bearing a drawing of the family crest.

Space Burial

Perhaps the wave of the future, the deceased might be cremated and their remains launched into space or one day spread on a distant moon or planet. Space burials today place the ashes inside sealed capsules in spaceships that burn up on reentering the Earth's atmosphere or upon reaching their destination. Gene Roddenberry, the creator of the *Star Trek* series, was the first person to be buried in space.

Zoroastrian Burial

The Zoroastrians consider everything that encounters a dead body as defiled. They cleanse the body with bull urine to get rid of bad spirits. After loved ones pay their respects (without touching), the body is placed in a location where it will be eaten by vultures so it can't spread diseases to the living.

Aboriginal Burial

Australian Aborigines leave the dead to rot in the open under layers of leaves and dirt. As the body decomposes, the liquid rot is rubbed onto the village children, which is believed to pass on the positive qualities of the dead. The bones are then displayed in a cave or worn around the family members' necks as keepsake jewelry.

CONCLUSIONS

No matter how the people of the world envision death or how they treat the body once it has died, one thing remains clear. The vast majority consider the process of dying to be of critical and profound importance–at least in the sense of freeing the soul within the body to continue its journey unencumbered by the weight of physicality. The belief that life goes on in some form other than the physical is as old as humanity itself and permeates every tradition and religion. Is it just wishful thinking that we continue long after our bodies are gone? Are we reincarnated? Will we be with our loved ones again on some different level of existence? Is there something inherent in all human beings, something embedded in instinct and intuition, that believes– that *knows*–that we are, in essence, eternal?

We expect to find out the answers to these questions at some point in the future. Death is not prejudiced or biased in any way. Everyone is affected, regardless of ethnicity, gender, culture, or socioeconomic status. It is said that we start dying the moment we are born. Knowing and possibly respecting our mortality should keep us from wasting our lives while we're still alive. Death is unavoidable, regardless of who we are, where we come from, or what religion we follow or do not follow.

What Is the Soul?

If you die, you're completely happy and your soul somewhere lives on. I'm not afraid of dying. Total peace after death, becoming someone else is the best hope I've got.
—Kurt Cobain

There is an eternal landscape, a geography of the soul; we search for its outlines all our lives.
—Josephine Hart

The hope of another life gives us courage to meet our own death, and to bear with the death of our loved ones; we are twice armed if we fight with faith.
—Will Durant

The concept of an afterlife begins with the question of whether we have a soul and, if so, what it is. According to Merriam–Webster, a soul is described as a noun, meaning:

1. the immaterial essence, animating principle, or actuating cause of an individual life

2a. the spiritual principle embodied in human beings, all rational and spiritual beings, or the universe

2b. capitalized, Christian Science: God

3. a person's total self

4a. an active or essential part

47

4b. a moving spirit: Leader

5a. the moral and emotional nature of human beings

5b. the quality that arouses emotion and sentiment

5c. spiritual or moral force: Fervor

6. Person: not a *soul* in sight

When a plane crashes, forensics and National Transportation Safety Board (NTSB) investigators may refer to the number of souls that were on board rather than how many people. Even before the plane takes off, the pilot knows how many people are aboard. Hearing a pilot refer to a passenger as a soul seems respectful of the fact that they are more than just a body in a seat.

The soul is the invisible essence of who we are, our emotional and spiritual nature that is eternal, even though our physical bodies have a shelf life. It is regarded as a separate entity from the body and is commonly thought to enter the body at conception and leave the body at death. The question of whether someone goes to Heaven, Hell, or somewhere else is really a question of where their soul goes. We know where the body decomposes–back to dust and ash and earth.

Most people believe that the soul is distinct from human consciousness, whereas others believe that the soul is the life force and awareness that we are alive and have a life force, as discussed in another chapter. Consciousness and soul may both be eternal, but the soul is the seat of feelings, emotions, sentiments, and morality, while consciousness is awareness of existence itself.

What, exactly, *is* the soul? Science, religion, and philosophy have argued for centuries what it might be or if, indeed, it even exists.

The soul survives death, according to some belief systems, and chooses the type of life it will have with each incarnation. Or it could incarnate once and never take on a physical body again. When it comes to the dead, we could say that the deceased's soul stays behind to haunt people, unable to cross over into the "light." More on that later as well.

The concept of the soul no doubt sprang from the existential fear of death and the finality of existence. It provides an opportunity for us to hold onto the idea of life continuing beyond death, even if on a different level. The idea that we die and that's it, fade to black, story over, is terrifying, so the belief in a soul that carries on afterward brings comfort, at least as much comfort as it can when we face our impending demise. Atheists and others who don't believe in any religious or spiritual faith suggest we do die and that's all, folks. The body rots and whatever made up our personality and emotions was nothing more than the firing of neurons in the brain. Once those stop, so do we.

The soul survives death, according to some belief systems, and chooses the type of life it will have with each incarnation.

ORIGINS OF THE SOUL

The etymology of the modern English word "soul" comes from Old English *sáwol, sáwel*, which means "immortal principle in man." The word is similar to the Gothic *saiwala*, Old High German *sêula, sêla*, Old Saxon *sêola*, Old Low Franconian *sêla, síla*, Old Norse *sála*, and Lithuanian *siela*. The soul is synonymous with the Greek *psyche* meaning "life, spirit, consciousness," derived from a verb meaning "to cool, to blow," referring to the breath, as opposed to *soma*, which means "body."

The ancient Greeks used "ensouled" to represent being "alive." This is the earliest Western philosophical view of the soul as what gives life to the body and was the incorporeal or spiritual breath animating a living organism (the Latin *anima*). Without the soul, the body would be like a robot or automaton, with no personality or life force.

Socrates, Plato, and Aristotle, three of the world's greatest philosophers, each had their own take on the immortal soul. They believed in dualism, which is the belief that reality or existence is divided into two parts: body and soul. The body is much easier to explain, but the soul elicits longstanding debate and discussion. Dualists believe that the soul is a real substance that exists independently of the body, and that while the body decays and decomposes after death, the soul does not. Some believe that the soul is the seat of the will, intellect, and human consciousness.

Socrates (470–390 B.C.E.) believed the soul was immortal and that death was the separation of the soul and the physical body. Plato (approx. 428–348 B.C.E.), a student of Socrates, believed that the soul was immortal, separate, and eternal, and it existed before the body and after it, when it finds another body to incarnate into, as in the concept of reincarnation. Plato believed the soul was imprisoned in the body, and he was the first great thinker to propose that the soul was the source of life.

Plato elevated the concept of the soul further, describing the psyche as the essence of a person and what decides how we behave. This essence was an incorporeal, eternal occupant of our being, and even after the body's death, the soul exists and is able to think and is continually reborn (*metempsychosis*) in new bodies. However, Aristotle believed that only one part of the soul was immortal, namely the intellect or mind (*logos*). Plato was the first person in the history of philosophy to believe that the soul was both the source of life and the mind as well as the bearer of moral properties.

Aristotle (384–322 B.C.E.) believed the body and soul were matter and form respectively, and that the body was a collection of elements, while the soul was the essence. The soul was "the primary activity" or full actualization of all living things. Aristotle, who wrote the seminal book *On the Soul* in 350 B.C.E., believed the organization between form and matter was necessary for any living thing to have functionality and identified three hierarchical levels of natural beings: plants, animals, and people. These had different degrees of a soul: *Bios* (life), *Zoë* (animate life), and *Psuchë* (self-conscious life) and three corresponding levels: nutritive activity of growth, sustenance, and reproduction shared by all life (*Bios*); self-willed activity and sensory faculties, which only animals and people have (*Zoë*); and "reason," which only humans have (*Pseuchë*).

The famed Greek philosopher Socrates believed that the soul and the body were separate and that the soul was immortal. This idea was built upon by his student Plato and then by Aristotle.

The purpose of the soul, according to Aristotle, was finding truth, a difficult task.

Thomas Aquinas (1225–1274 c.e.) believed the soul was the first actuality of the living body. He believed the soul was not corporeal and has a purpose that is not reliant on any bodily organ. It can therefore exist outside of a body and cannot be destroyed by any natural process. He supported the doctrine of the divine effusion of the soul in which the soul was judged after it leaves the body, and that the soul had three parts: nutritive, sensitive, and intellectual. Only the intellectual was created by God and given to humans. Borrowing from Aristotle's *On the Soul*, Aquinas attributed "soul" (*anima*) to all living organisms but believed only humans possessed immortal souls.

Immanuel Kant (1724–1804 c.e.) identified the soul as the "I" of our existence and stated that because it was an inner experience, we could neither prove nor disprove the soul. Russian philosopher George Ivanovich Gurdjieff (ca. 1872–1949) did not believe we were born with a soul but earned it through specific efforts. He taught that most humans do not possess a unified consciousness and live their lives in a state of hypnotic "waking sleep." The way to achieving a higher state of consciousness and full human potential is through the disciplined method he called "the work."

Other philosophers contributed to the broad debate over whether the soul existed, where it could be found, and whether only humans possessed a soul. These ideas found their way into religious beliefs and traditions, influencing our perceptions of the presence of an unseen force that represents our essence.

WORLD RELIGIONS AND THE SOUL

Most people believe we have a soul, and much of that belief stems from our religious upbringing. If we are Christians or Jews, we believe in a soul, but only for humans, though this is being challenged by pet owners who believe their pets have souls and go to Heaven. Hinduism and Jainism believe that all living things, from the smallest bacterium to the largest mammal, are souls manifested in their physical bodies. Animism and paganism believe that nonbiological entities such as rivers, oceans, and mountains have souls of their own.

The five "great" religions–Christianity, Judaism, Islam, Buddhism, and Hinduism–believe in a version of the self that survives physical death, but they differ in the origin, journey, and final destination.

Some Christians believe the soul is present at the moment of conception and therefore have passionate views against abortion. If the fetus has a soul at conception, it is a viable living entity and thus worthy of life. Like Plato's teachings, Christians believe the soul is immortal and the body mortal and that death is nothing but the separation of the two.

In Christianity, the soul exists after death and is judged by God to either receive the reward of Heaven or the punishment of Hell. Catholicism includes purgatory, a waiting or holding place for the soul where it can be purified of sin to enter Heaven, a sort of second-chance outpost. On Judgment Day, souls are to be reunited with their resurrected bodies and God confirms their final destiny, which coincides with the return of Christ.

Some Christian believers say they will inherit eternal life in Heaven or in the Kingdom of God on Earth, where they will experience followship with God, the Father.

Judaism teaches that the soul was created by God, then joined with an earthly, mortal body. There is uncertainty, though, as to whether this occurs at the moment of conception or later, but the soul does live forever. The dominant view is that the soul does retain a conscious state after death. Like Christians, Orthodox Jews await the Judgment Day when the souls and resurrected bodies unite and the saved enter into Heaven.

Judaism equates the quality of one's soul to one's performance of the commandments (*mitzvot*) as well as reaching a state of higher understanding and closeness to God. A person who achieves this is called a *tzadik*. Judaism celebrates the day of one's death, *nahala/Yahrtzeit*, as a festivity of remembrance, because it is at life's end that the struggles and challenges are what the soul will be judged on.

Kabbalah, the Jewish mystic tradition, separates the soul's attributes into five elements, corresponding to the five worlds:

1. Nefesh, natural instinct

2. Ruach, emotion and mortality

3. Neshamah, intellect and awareness of God

4. Chayah, a part of God

5. Yechidah, one with God

Kabbalah has its own concept of reincarnation, the *gilgul*.

More modern perspectives of both Christianity and Judaism have softened some of these beliefs, suggesting instead that the afterlife is a new spiritual life more so than a resurrection of the body.

Islam states the soul was breathed into the fetus by God, and when this occurs is under debate, but the modern consensus seems to be around 120 days after conception. Islam also states the soul is immortal and lives forever but awaits the day of resurrection while in a purgatory state. The good are at peace and will enter Heaven, but the sinful will suffer in the grave and are destined for Hell. The only exceptions are that those who die fighting for Islam will go directly to Heaven and those who fight against Islam will go straight to Hell. There is also a Judgment Day when the evil will be relegated to Hell and the righteous to Heaven.

The Quran, the holy book of Islam, has two distinct words to describe the soul: *rū* (translated as spirit, consciousness, pneuma, or "soul") and *nafs* (self, ego, psyche, or "soul"), with *rū* used to denote the divine spirit or "the breath of life," while *nafs* describes one's disposition or personality.

The Eastern traditions vary mainly in the addition of karma and reincarnation. In Hinduism, the soul exists eternally before and after a physical incarnation. Humans all have existed infinitely in the past and will do so into the future because of Samsara, the cycle of birth, death, and rebirth. At the time of death, our karma determines the status of our next incarnation. Good karma allows us to incarnate into a higher state, and bad karma sets us back to redo the lessons we should have learned in this life.

While Western religious adherents frequently believe in reincarnation, their beliefs

A soul represented in a 1717 manuscript by an Ottoman Empire scribe.

are more positive than those of Eastern traditions. It is the desired outcome in Hinduism to get off the wheel of reincarnation and be free of it. Hinduism has four different beliefs about the soul, which separate into different schools of thought:

- Samkhya-Yoga–the realization of the essential separate nature of the soul from the body so one can live in the present without attachment to material or worldly things. Upon death, the soul will exist forever with no attachments to the external world.

- Dvaita Vedanta–The soul is all about loving devotion to God to liberate the soul after death. This is the Hare Krishna philosophy.

Good karma allows us to incarnate into a higher state, and bad karma sets us back to redo the lessons we should have learned in this life.

- Vishishtadvaita Vedanta–True liberation occurs when the soul becomes one with God even as it keeps an individual identity.

- Advaita Vedanta–The soul is liberated upon the realization of its identity with Brahman.

In the Vedanta school, *atman* is the "Adam" or first principle. Atman is Sanskrit for inner self or soul. This is the true self that is the essence of the individual, and the person must acquire great self-knowledge to realize his or her atman.

In Jainism, the concept of *jiva*, a living entity possessing a life force, is similar to atman in Hinduism. Every living being, from the single-celled to the more complex, has a soul, forming the very basis of Jainism. There is no beginning or end to the existence of soul. It is eternal and changes form until it attains liberation from the samsara cycle of birth, death, and rebirth. Jains have an incredible respect for all living things and have been known to go out of their way to not step on insects so as not to kill them.

In Buddhism, consciousness is compared to the soul, and after death, the consciousness part of us enters a new body. Karma is also a factor, with our morality determining whether we level up or level down. In Hinduism, this is referred to as the soul.

For Buddhists, the goal is to become liberated from the cycle of endless rebirth and happens only when we realize that everything, including the self, is impermanent. This is called Nirvana and is the final release from all the worldiy suffering of the Samsara cycle. There are a number of different paths for achieving liberation according to each Buddhist tradition. In Theravada Buddhism, the awakened person enters a state of Pari–Nirvana upon death and their "flame of consciousness" or soul is extinguished, while in Mahayana Buddhism, liberation comes when the veil of illusion of reality is lifted.

Agnostics and atheists might or might not believe in the soul, but if they do they tend to quantify it more as a consciousness state without the religious attachments or promises of eternal life in a Heaven or Hell. Agnostics might believe there is a soul aspect to life that goes on past the death of the body, but not with all the usual religious trappings of reward or punishment or sitting at the right hand of a deity or angels. Atheists might embrace a more scientific concept of consciousness surviving physical death, but most do not believe in reincarnation.

In the Baha'i faith, believers affirm that the soul is a sign of God, described as "a Heaven gem whose reality the most learned of men hath failed to grasp, and whose mystery no mind, however acute, can ever hope to unravel." They believe the soul continues after physical death and is immortal. Heaven is a state of being near to God, and Hell is a remoteness from God, and it all depends on the consequences of individual behavior and level of spirituality. This belief system teaches that there is no existence before life on Earth, and the evolution of the soul is always toward God and away from the world of man.

Protestants believe the soul exists and is immortal, but there are two major camps about this in relation to the afterlife. The followers of John Calvin believe the soul lives on after death as consciousness. Martin Luther's followers believe the soul lives on when the physical body dies but remains unconscious or asleep until the resurrection of the dead. This same belief is mirrored in Seventh–day Adventists.

The Church of Jesus Christ of Latter-day Saints teaches that spirit and body make up the Soul of Man. The soul is the union of a preexisting, God-created spirit placed in a temporal body at physical conception on Earth. Upon death, the spirit lives on and progresses in the spirit realm until the time of resurrection with the body, resulting in the perfect, immortal soul.

In Taoism, ancient Chinese tradition teaches that every person has two souls, *hun* and *po*, which correspond to *yang* and *yin*. The yang is the light swirl and is associated with brightness, passion, growth, and masculine strength. The yin is the darker swirl and is associated with the feminine, shadows, weakness, and destructiveness. The two are bound together in that everything is a product of these two principles and their interactions.

Taoism teaches that each person has ten souls, *sanhunqipo*, made up of three *hun* and seven *po*. If a person loses any of them, he or she is said to be mentally ill or unconsciousness, and a dead soul may reincarnate to a disability, a lower desire realm, or choose not to reincarnate at all.

THE SCIENCE OF THE SOUL

Dr. Robert Lanza wrote in "Does the Soul Exist? Evidence Says 'Yes'," published in the December 21, 2011, issue of *Psychology Today*, that science has traditionally dismissed the soul as nothing more than human belief. Although science could explain the functions of the human brain, subjective experiences remained a mystery.

Lanza put forth the theory of biocentrism as a possible way to answer the question, Is there a soul? He explains that "the current scientific paradigm doesn't recognize this spiritual dimension of life. We're told we're just the activity of carbon and some proteins; we live awhile and die. And the universe? It too has no meaning. It has all been worked out in the equations—no need for a soul."

Biocentrism, a new "theory of everything," challenges the current traditional and materialistic model of reality. "Of course, most spiritual people view the soul as emphatically more definitive than the scientific concept. It's considered the incorporeal essence of a person and is said to be immortal and transcendent of material existence." When scientists

Shamanism and the Soul

A Tuvan shaman in Siberia consecrates a stone shrine. In the shaman tradition, we have two souls: a body soul and a free soul.

A common belief in shamanism is soul dualism, or multiple souls. When a shaman embarks on a healing journey, also called a soul flight, he or she has what equates to an out-of-body or astral travel experience between the body soul and the free soul. The body soul is linked to physicality, bodily functions, and awakened state awareness, while the free soul is able to wander around freely during sleep or a trance state and has no physical boundaries or limitations.

This soul dualism and concept of multiple souls is also found in the animistic beliefs of Australian, Chinese, Tibetan, African, Native American, Northern Eurasian, and South American peoples. Ancient Egyptians referred to the dual souls as *Ka* and *Ba*.

During a shamanic journey, the shaman, accompanied by rhythmic chants, rattles, and drums, gets into a trance state so that the free soul leaves the body and journeys to the spirit world to achieve knowledge for healing someone who is sick. In the healing traditions of Austronesian shamans, illnesses are said to originate from "soul loss," and to heal the sick, one must "return" the "free soul" (which may have been stolen by an evil spirit or got lost in the spirit world) and bring it safely back into the physical body. If the "free soul" cannot be found and returned, the sick person will die or go insane.

In the spiritual world or dimension, the shaman does his or her work by looking for the lost parts of the soul to bring back, called a "soul retrieval." They may also do a cleansing ritual to rid a confused or dark soul of negative energies. This work is done on the soul level because it is the belief that the body is a symptomatic expression of what occurs on the deep, soul level of existence, similar to the idea in modern medicine of bodily diseases linked to mental and emotional states. However, some of the wisdom the shaman brings back from a journey might require the sick per-

cont'd on next page

cont'd from previous page

son to eat or drink something or use a particular herb or concoction for physical reprieve, thus their earning the label of medicine men and women, or village healers.

This type of work is usually done by the wisest elders of a village who are experienced in the use of herbs and natural healing. They act as pharmacists and doctors by prescribing both physical and spiritual healing to the sick, understanding that the body and spirit are united; just covering up symptoms, which is what Western pharmaceutical-driven medicine is all about, does not cure the disease. They know which herbs and plants do what and which ones to avoid.

Some ethnic groups believe they possess many souls. The Tagbanwa have six souls, with the one free soul as the "true soul" and the other five as secondary in nature. Each has its own specific function. Some Inuit believe a person has various types of souls for different purposes, such as a soul for respiration, a soul for the shadow, or a soul for healing.

talk about the soul, Lanza explains, they do so in a materialistic way, or as a synonym for the mind.

Scientists focus on the functioning of the brain and hold that neuroscience is the only branch of scientific study relevant to understanding the soul. Science focuses on biological life and biological death; the animating principle we refer to as the soul is nothing but laws of chemistry and physics. "You (and all the poets and philosophers that ever lived) are just dust orbiting the core of the Milky Way galaxy," Lanza says.

Lanza concludes that none of his scientific books address the soul and that nothing, according to science, appears to outlive the body. However, science has yet to unravel the mystery of our subjective experiences or the nature of the self. Our existence has an "I" that lives our lives and defies our current worldview of reality and objectivity. The theory of biocentrism challenges the old physicochemical paradigm by placing life and consciousness at the center of a new cosmos reality.

Our current scientific paradigm is based on the concept that the world has an objective observer–independent existence, but real experiments suggest the opposite. Adding life to the equation, we can explain some of the more puzzling aspects of modern science, including the uncertainty principle, the observer effect, quantum entanglement, and the Goldilocks principle, the fine–tuning of the laws that create matter and the universe.

Science at the quantum level does seem to indicate that everything we experience is a representation in the mind. "Space and time are simply the mind's tools for putting it all together." These experiments at the quantum level also suggest that the mind and the soul may be immortal because they exist outside the limits and laws of space and time.

An adjunct professor at Wake Forest University School of Medicine and chief scientific officer of the Astellas Institute for Regenerative Medicine, Dr. Robert Lanza put forth the biocentrism hypothesis of a conscious universe.

Julien Musolino, a cognitive scientist, author of *The Soul Fallacy: What Science Shows We Gain from Letting Go of Our Soul Beliefs*, and member of the Psychology Department and the Rutgers Center for Cognitive Science at Rutgers in New Brunswick, believes the mind is a complex machine operating by the same laws as everything else in the universe. According to Musolino, there is no scientific evidence for the soul's existence, but there is considerable evidence indicating souls do not exist. Yet the search for the soul as part of our understanding of the human body continues to be driven by the primary question of the soul's existence.

The dominant ideas about the soul are that it is spiritual and immortal, or that it is material and mortal. There is ongoing debate over whether the soul is located in the entire body or in a specific organ such as the brain or the heart. Neuroscience considers human thought and behavior to be the result of physical processes in the brain, and it believes that we can study and comprehend cognitive processes that comprise the mind. Neuroscientists can study how the mind develops in tandem with brain development.

Is there physical evidence of the soul? According to Sean M. Carroll, a theoretical physicist who specializes in quantum mechanics, gravity, and cosmology as a research professor at the Walter Burke Institute for Theoretical

Physics in the Department of Physics at the California Institute of Technology (Caltech), the concept of a soul is incompatible with quantum field theory (QFT), which is a theoretical framework combining classical field theory, special relativity, and quantum mechanics. He suggests that for a soul to exist, "Not only is new physics required, but dramatically new physics. Within QFT, there can't be a new collection of 'spirit particles' and 'spirit forces' that interact with our regular atoms, because we would have detected them in existing experiments."

There is ongoing debate over whether the soul is located in the entire body or in a specific organ such as the brain or the heart.

THE WEIGHT OF THE SOUL

It may take some time for science to prove that the soul is a tangible, real thing, but scientists will keep looking for proof in the meantime. One notable previous experiment involved the weight of the soul. The idea was that when someone died, the soul left the body and should thus be measurable by weighing the body before and after death.

In 1901, Duncan MacDougall, a physician from Haverhill, Massachusetts, conducted what would come to be known as the 21 Grams Experiment. It involved making weight measurements of patients as they died. MacDougall claimed there would be varying amounts of weight loss at the time of death.

Because the soul was material, MacDougall reasoned, it should cause a weight loss when it left the body. Six terminally ill nursing home patients were placed on a specially constructed scale bed he built in his office, on top of an industrial sized platform beam scale sensitive to two-tenths of an ounce. He weighed them before, during, and after death. He specifically chose exhausted patients more inclined to remain motionless when they died. His findings were mixed, but he concluded that there was a very slight weight loss, 21 grams on average. This caused quite a stir, and he claimed it was proof of the human soul, but upon closer examination, his methods revealed major flaws. His findings were untrustworthy and inconsistent, the precise times of death were unknown, and his medical measurement methods were considered crude. He also allegedly discarded any results that did not match the 21-gram weight. He wrote of his experiment:

> The patient's comfort was looked after in every way, although he was practically moribund when placed upon the bed. He lost weight slowly at the rate of one ounce per hour due to evaporation of moisture in respiration and evaporation of sweat.

Dr. Duncan MacDougall aimed to calculate how much a human soul weighed by measuring the body just before and just after death.

> During all three hours and forty minutes I kept the beam end slightly above balance near the upper limiting bar in order to make the test more decisive if it should come.

> At the end of three hours and forty minutes he expired and suddenly coincident with death the beam end dropped with an audible stroke hitting against the lower limiting bar and remaining there with no rebound. The loss was ascertained to be three-fourths of an ounce.

> This loss of weight could not be due to evaporation of respiratory moisture and sweat, because that had already been determined to go on, in his case, at the rate of one sixtieth of an ounce per minute, whereas this loss was sudden and large, three-fourths of an ounce in a few seconds. The bowels did not move; if they had moved the weight would still have remained upon the bed except for a slow loss by the evaporation of moisture depending, of course, upon the fluidity of the feces. The bladder evacuated one or two drams of urine. This remained upon the bed and could only have influenced the weight by slow gradual evaporation and therefore in no way could account for the sudden loss.

He also checked into forcible inspiration and expiration of air but it seemed to have no effect. MacDougall noticed similar weight loss in his other patients, but the results were inconsistent. One patient lost weight but then gained it back, and two other patients had a loss of weight at death that increased over time. Only one patient experienced an immediate weight loss of three-fourths of an ounce, or approximately 21.3 grams, at the time of death. The results of the other two patients were ignored by MacDougall because the scales were "not finely adjusted."

MacDougall repeated his experiment with fifteen dogs. None registered a significant drop in weight, which MacDougall took as evidence that animals have no souls.

MacDougall took six years to publish his 21 grams finding, which was published in 1907 in the *Journal of the American Society for Psychical Research* and *American Medicine*. A story also appeared in the *New York Times*. Following publication in *American Medicine*, MacDougall and physician Augustus P. Clarke exchanged letters, with Clarke denouncing the validity of the experiment based on his knowledge that at the time of death there is a sudden rise in body temperature as the blood stops circulating through the lungs, where it is air-cooled. The rise in body temperature increases sweating and moisture evaporation and accounts for the missing 21 grams.

This would also explain why dogs did not lose weight after death. Dogs do not have sweat glands but cool themselves by panting. MacDougall argued that because circulation ceases at the moment of death, the skin would not be heated by the increase in temperature. Australian science author Karl Kruszelnicki criticized the small sample size and questioned how MacDougall was able to determine the exact moment a person died given the technology available at the time. MacDougall's 21 Grams Experiment received little credence from scientists at the time because his experiments were not replicable and his results were unreliable.

MacDougall moved on to photographing the soul at the moment it left the body. He found no evidence and died in 1920. Despite the unscientific nature of the experiments, the idea of the soul weighing 21 grams became a popular theme in pop culture, with songs, novels, and movies. The title of the 2003 movie *21 Grams* was taken from this belief.

There are physicists who believe that quantum physics will provide proof of the soul. Some suggest the soul has a quantum state as real as the wave-particle dualism. The late

German physicist Hans-Peter Dürr, former head of the Max Planck Institute for Physics in Munich, Germany, suggested that dualism of the smallest particles is not limited to the subatomic world but is omnipresent. He believed a universal quantum code exists in all matter, living or dead, throughout the cosmos.

Despite the unscientific nature of the experiments, the idea of the soul weighing 21 grams became a popular theme in pop culture, with songs, novels, and movies.

In the 2016 article "Scientists Say They Have Found Proof of the Human Soul," written by Sean Adl-Tabatabai for *News Punch*, Dürr was quoted as saying, "What we consider the here and now, this world, is actually just the material level that is comprehensible. The beyond is an infinite reality that is much bigger. Which this world is rooted in. In this way, our lives in this plane of existence are encompassed, surrounded, by the afterworld already.... The body dies but the spiritual quantum field continues. In this way, I am immortal."

His comments were seconded by Dr. Christian Hellweg, who believes spirit has a quantum state. He studied physics, medicine, and brain function at the Max Planck Institute for Biophysical Chemistry and was able to prove that information found in the body's central nervous system could be "phase encoded." He also researched phantom perceptions and hallucinations and suggests tinnitus–hearing a persistent buzzing, ringing, or roaring inside the mind–might be a phantom perception in the sense of hearing.

The grandfather of quantum physics, David Bohm, who was a student of Albert Einstein, believed that "the results of modern natural sciences only make sense if we assume an inner, uniform, transcendent reality that is based on all external data and facts. The very depth of human consciousness is one of them." Bohm believed in three orders of existence or reality: the explicate or material world, the implicate hidden world, and the super-implicate, which was an almost godlike world that transformed the implicate into the explicate. We can only perceive the reality of the explicate, but through intuition or a sixth sense, we might perceive the implicate, and during a spiritual or religious experience (or via the use of certain hallucinogenic drugs or mushrooms/ ayahuasca/peyote/LSD/DMT), we might get a glimpse of the super-implicate.

This is the point at which the soul and consciousness merge into one (more on consciousness elsewhere in the book). Some cutting-edge quantum scientists propose that consciousness/soul be considered a fundamental element of the universe.

Australian biologist Jeremy Griffith has his own biological explanation of the human condition, including good and evil. He suggests looking at the soul as instinctive memory of when our ancestors lived in a "Garden of Eden" state of cooperation and innocence. Neurobiologists and evolutionary psychologists suggest the soul, or belief in the soul, evolved to "bestow on the individual either an equanimity, or social trustworthiness that ultimately represented a competitive advantage," according to "Science at Last Explains Our Soul," written by Damon Isherwood on June 27, 2016, for ZMEScience.com.

Griffith explained our brains were made up of two different learning systems: One is gene-based, instinctual, and the system we share with all living things. The other is a nerve-based, conscious intellect that is unique to humans. As our intellect began to challenge our instincts for control, it became a battle between two different systems of learning, and the resulting behavior was competitive, selfish, and aggressive.

However, we also have the capacity for unconditional selfless behavior, an example of which is a mother's love for her child, which over generations becomes the new instinctive behavior, acting as our moral soul. This is a much different take than the idea that we are just a soul before we come into a body and return to being just a soul when we die, or that the soul itself can be seen or measured or, in the case of one man, weighed on a scale at the moment of death.

Australian biologist Jeremy Griffith is the founder of the World Transformation Movement, which seeks to discover biological reasons for human behavior.

Science may never be able to prove beyond a shadow of a doubt what a soul is and whether or not all living things have one, but that does not mean souls aren't real. We just haven't found the right way of working the soul into the existing scientific method of empirical, repeatable, tangible proof. Some people point to gravity as an example of an invisible force that cannot be held in a hand or put in a test tube, yet we know it exists mainly because of the effects we see of it working around us. The cause may be something occurring on Baum's implicate order, but we only see the effects in the explicate world. The soul may be like that. We don't see the cause, or even the soul itself, but we do sense the effects when we feel that incredible separation from the body during meditation, such as when the boundaries of reality seem to dissolve and we feel at one with everything and everyone.

DO PETS HAVE SOULS?

The animists of our primitive past believed all living things had a soul, but what about modern times? Do animals have souls? What about single-cell organisms? Fungi? Mold? Do only domesticated pets have souls? Or is the soul only afforded to human beings at the top of the food chain, a belief some might call arrogant and anthropocentric? When it comes to the hierarchy of the soul, religious leaders and scientists vary in opinion. When it comes to pet owners, the answer is usually a resounding "Yes."

Hundreds of people have shared their experiences with the ghost of a beloved deceased pet on social media. Cats, dogs, rabbits, horses—the species doesn't matter because these bereaved owners have seen, heard, or felt something that proves their adored fur baby is still alive, albeit in spirit form. Although these subjective, personal experiences do not constitute empirical proof, they occur far too frequently to be ignored. It's impossible to say that pets don't have souls, especially since we can't prove humans do.

A cursory glance at Facebook reveals at least a dozen stories of people who reported hearing the pitter–patter of a deceased pet's footsteps across the floor at night, or the depression on the bed right where the dog used to sleep. Hundreds more can be found in specific Facebook groups devoted to ghosts and the paranormal. Some people report seeing

Many people believe that animals have souls just as people do. Even Pope Francis has said that animals have souls and go to Heaven.

ghostly apparitions or hearing barks and meows when there are no living animals around. They see ghost dogs on ghost walks or sense the snuggly warmth of the cat that used to snuggle up against them on the couch. There are books and websites devoted to pet and animal ghosts. Is this all just wishful thinking or hallucinatory manifestations that come from the overwhelming grief and pain of losing a beloved pet? Or do animals have an eternal aspect like a soul that lives on past death just as humans do?

Dogs have a midbrain, or emotional section, that functions and is structured similarly to humans. They experience pain, happiness, and other emotions. They form attachments and bonds with their owners. They exhibit fear. They appear to have the cognitive abilities of a small child, and we would never say that children lack souls. Dogs and other animals will die to save a person's life, attack to protect a loved one, and cry when their child dies.

People who have had near-death experiences frequently report meeting a deceased pet on the other side. Unfortunately, some religions insist that animals, including our pets, are lowly and beneath us, even though they have the breath of life and experience many of the same states of being as we do.

The week of December 12, 2014, was memorable because Pope Francis publicly told a young boy whose dog had recently died that Heaven was open to all of God's creatures. It sparked outrage, particularly among Christians who may not have agreed with the Catholic leader's thoughtful response. Christians argue that man was created in the image and likeness of God to rule over all other creatures. For those other creatures, there is no mention of a soul or immortality. They suggest Christ only died to save other humans, not all living things, but Isaiah 65:25 says that "The wolf and the lamb will feed together, and the lion will eat straw like the ox" and suggests God will include animals in the new Heaven and the new Earth. The Bible is filled with such mentions of animals having the same fate as humans, but on a general level they are thought of as lower on the food-chain hierarchy. Psalm 145 states that God loves all His creation and has made plans for all His children and the lesser creatures to enjoy His eternal kingdom. It seems it is humans who discriminate against animals getting into Heaven, and not God.

A number of religions suggest animals have souls, although they differ on whether all dogs go to Heaven. Mormons believe animals can go to Heaven. Islam states that animal souls are eternal, but to go to Heaven, which they call Jannah, the animal must first be judged by God on Judgment Day. Animals are not to be judged in the same manner as humans, and some Muslim scholars debate on what happens after that judgment, but the Quran says you can have whatever you wish in paradise, so what if you wish for your dog, Fred, to accompany you?

When it comes to reincarnation, the consensus is that animals can be reborn as humans and vice versa. Buddhism has no concept of a Heaven or that there is such a thing as soul or self in the traditional sense, but it says that living things are all interconnected. In Hinduism, animals are said to have souls, but most souls will evolve into the human plane somewhere along the reincarnation process, which means they are a part of the same cycle of birth, life, death, and rebirth, except once they level up and become human, they no longer are on the same cycle. The end result for all living things is to become closer to God.

In Judaism, there are rabbis who say animals can go to Heaven and rabbis who say no way, but they do agree that animals have souls. Kosher law does not allow Jews to eat the blood of birds and mammals because they believe this is where the soul resides.

We can say that animals have souls if we define soul as self-awareness. If the soul is love and compassion, then so is the body. There will always be those who laugh at the idea that animals are on the same level as humans and thus deserving of a soul, to which we respond with those four punctuated words so often spoken in childhood when some smarty-pants said something stupid–"How do you know?"

Heaven and Hell and the In-Between

Go to Heaven for the climate, Hell for the company.
—Mark Twain

Religion is for people who are scared to go to Hell. Spirituality is for people who have already been there.
—Bonnie Raitt

Men long for an afterlife in which there apparently is nothing to do but delight in Heaven's wonders.
—Louis D. Brandeis

After death, many religious traditions believe the human soul resides in another place for eternity or that it sticks around for a while before hitching a ride in a new body and a new life. Depending on the tradition, Heaven is where people go who are being rewarded for a lifetime of good behavior. Hell is a place opposite of Heaven, where those who break the laws of God or the gods deserve eternal punishment for their sins. In the triadic worldview of Abrahamic religions, Heaven is located in the sky, and Hell is beneath or below the earth, an "underworld" filled with fire and the agony of tortured souls.

Not all traditions view the places our souls might journey to after death the same, just as they don't always agree on the existence of the soul or afterlife. Though we may wish

69

to end up in the right place, a life review might send us packing for the underworld unless, as some religions insist, we repent and beg for forgiveness. Those who make a lifetime of sin and brutality might not even get the chance to repent but get a one-way ticket to fire and brimstone. What about those who aren't exactly pure or evil, but somewhere in between? There's a place for them, too. In between Heaven and Hell is a place called purgatory, a sort of waiting room that some feel is life on Earth itself with all its pain and suffering, or outside a courtroom where you are about to go on trial and God is the judge.

It seems almost impossible to imagine ceasing to exist and having no conscious awareness of anything, even eternal blackness, so we humans like to imagine scenarios and places we will inhabit after we leave our bodies. Heaven and Hell also provide us with a moral compass to guide our lives, with Heaven pointing due North and Hell pointing due South, and our path toward one or the other is determined by the good or bad we did on Earth.

There is also a between-state, such as the Catholic concept of purgatory, or the "bardo" of the Tibetan Book of the Dead. More on that in the next chapter. We will start with Heaven and work our way down.

HEAVEN

The promise of eternal reward in a paradise-like place is what drives the behavior of many religious people who know that if they sin too much, they will end up somewhere else, as in Hell, suffering eternal punishment. Heaven has many names, as we shall see, but it is not attainable until we die and go on to meet with God, Jesus, angels, spirit guides, our dead ancestors, or other entities depending on the religious tradition we follow.

Heaven can be both a place and a state of mind, as in "Heaven on earth," which describes a beautiful location like Hawaii or a peaceful mountain lake, or the blissful, joyful state of mind a mother might experience while holding her newborn child. Heaven is associated with order and the absence of suffering, pain, ignorance, fear, and death. It is a place and a state of being unrivaled in terms of peace, communion with God, spirits, angels, joy, and fulfillment of the heart's desires.

Is Heaven a real place up in the sky? Is it a myth? Is it a state of mind? Something that exists in another dimension? Or, perhaps, something that we ourselves create?

In many cosmogenesis stories of the creation of the world, Heaven was an overarching realm that encompassed the sky and upper atmosphere far beyond the visible sun, moon, and stars. The triadic nature of physical existence found in many of these creation myths usually placed Heaven atop Earth and Earth atop Hell or the underworld, but there were in our ancient past concepts of Heaven as someplace far away from Earth, even a place only accessible on a spiritual level.

According to ancient Mesopotamian beliefs, the universe or entirety of existence is divided into three levels, with Heaven at the top, accessible only to the purest and most heroic of people. This was the domain of the high gods, who formed a heavenly council. Earth was created for mortal humans to serve the gods by providing food, tribute, and sacred dwelling places. Minor gods and magical demons were also present on Earth. Humans mostly descended into the underworld after death, with only a few brave souls ascending to Heaven.

Ancient Egyptians believed the soul was in the heart and upon death, they would be taken to Duat, which was the realm of the dead, similar to the underworld. They would be judged and their hearts weighed against a feather. Those found virtuous and light went on to a place called Aaru, the Egyptian Field of Reeds, their version of Heavenly paradise. The kings of the ancient Greeks would share with the sun god, Re, and the sky god, Horus, the responsibility of protecting the order of things against chaos. The kings would be given the privilege of renewable life as part of this cosmic cycle, and the mortals accepted this.

Ancient Egyptians had many visual depictions of this Heavenly concept: as the divine crow on whose back the sun god withdrew from the Earthly realm; as the goddess Nut arching her body over the Earth; and as the falcon–headed Horus whose glittery eyes formed the sun and moon. Originally an afterlife here was reserved only for the kings and royalty, but later in the Book of the Dead, an afterlife was accessible for all once they were judged by Osiris, ruler of the Underworld.

This tri–level concept of existence of the Heavens above, the underworld below, and Earth in the middle is mirrored in shamanism, with the lower, middle, and upper worlds a shaman travels through on a spiritual level to attain wisdom or perform a healing. The upper world is not so much a heavenly place as it is the realm of higher beings and wise, knowing guides.

A similar view is the designation of body, mind, and spirit, with the body representing the "underworld" or lower level of base drives and instincts; the mind as the middle level of intellect and reason; and the spirit as the upper level of oneness and higher consciousness.

This 580 C.E. drawing comes from a sarcophagus in China and depicts the Chinvat Bridge, which leads to the Sogdian Paradise. The story of the bridge is Zoroastrian in origin.

The ancient Persians coined the term "paradise," which referred to a walled garden or park. The Chinvat Bridge, also known as the Bridge of the Separator, is crossed by the righteous who were judged good by Mithra's scales to enter paradise in Zoroastrianism on the fourth day following death. A lovely girl who represented the righteous soul's good deeds on Earth welcomed them as they crossed the bridge and escorted them inside the House of Song to await the Last Day, when souls would rejoice and be purified. There is no mention of who the righteous female souls met, though the beautiful maiden is most likely a construct of male desire and nothing more.

Our popular Western concept of Heaven, and how you get there, comes from Christianity, which places it as the realm in the "Heavens" of God, Jesus Christ, and the angelic beings. The faithful and those who lived by grace would die and automatically ascend to Heaven until the second coming of Christ, and Christians believe this is where Christ went when he rose from the dead, to be at his father God's side. This act was considered to have closed the gap between Heaven and Earth so that all who were without sin or purified of their sins could be admitted through the "Pearly Gates." This idea of judgment clashes a bit with the teachings of Jesus Christ about not judging others and plays into Old Testament beliefs of God as a more punishing Father.

The Christian Heaven is also called paradise and a place for great rejoicing. Contained within this Heaven is the city of New Jerusalem, described in detail in the Book of Revelation as a city walled in with 12 gates. On each gate is the name of one of the tribes of Israel along with an angel. The wall, made of precious stones, is 200 feet high, and the city is 1,400 square miles in size. The river of the water of life flows through the city from the throne of God, and the trees along the riverbanks produce a huge variety of fruit.

Judaic texts don't offer a clear indication of a Heaven or an afterlife. The Pharisees believed in an implied concept of an afterlife, and the Sadducees claimed there was no biblical evidence to back that up. Over the course of a thousand years or so, Jews believed God alone could reside in Heaven, as in Psalm 115:16, "The Heavens are the Lord's Heavens, but the earth he has given to human beings," and that it was separate from Earth, or that some version of Heaven will occur when the Messiah brings the righteous dead back to life. Heaven was described as a vast realm that existed above the Earth and was supported by a hard firmament of dazzling precious stones. This firmament kept the upper waters from mixing with the waters beneath the firmament. In this firmament were the sun, moon, and stars, and rain fell when a window was opened, as well as snow, hail, and dew.

God sat in the highest realm of this heavenly place and intervened in the affairs of the living through his prophets and providential care. God was surrounded by a host of angelic and astral beings, which were similar to gods and goddesses of the Canaanite and Mesopotamian belief system. Later, when the Hebrew scriptures transitioned to monotheism, there was only one God, the Lord, who oversaw all heavenly and earthly powers.

Some Jews believed God ruled from his throne in Heaven and there was also an underworld, with Earth stuck in the middle. Souls upon death went to the underworld, but during the Hellenic period, this belief changed and humans were able to go to Heaven after death.

Muslims believe children automatically go to Heaven, no matter their religious upbringing. Adults must be virtuous to get into Heaven, where there is nothing but joy and bliss and loving family and friends. The best thing about paradise is being close to God, and those who were the most virtuous and blessed would achieve such closeness. Heaven is also described as a paradise where those who have done mostly good works can lie around on couches in a lovely garden surrounded by chaste, dark–eyed virgins (female, of course).

The best thing about paradise is being close to God, and those who were the most virtuous and blessed would achieve such closeness.

The Quran speaks of the Heavens as a sign of the sovereignty, justice, and mercy of God. When the Earth was formed, the sky was vapor until God commanded the earth and sky to join together. God then formed the sky into seven firmaments and assigned everything its measure and place. There were seven Heavens and one Earth where praise of God was to be celebrated as evidence that God had the power to raise the dead and judge all souls on the last day. Islam believes souls dwell in an intermediate or in–between state where they get to first see a preview of their future existence, which will be either misery and suffering, or bliss, depending on the judgment they receive.

On the last day, Heaven will split asunder and all souls will get their final test, with the most righteous moving through Hell easily and being accepted into the gardens of bliss.

Eastern traditions held a different viewpoint and did not believe in the concept of Heaven, Hell, and Earth in the Western sense. There are many "Heavens" in Buddhism (five main Heavens in Tibetan Buddhism), and the cycle of samsara, or birth/death/rebirth, continues as the soul moves up the ladder, so to speak, with the goal of achieving Nirvana one day. Nirvana is not Heaven but rather a state of being in which one's soul is free of the cycle of samara and enjoys the bliss of not having to reincarnate. According to one of the Buddhist four noble truths, all suffering is caused by desire, tanha, and the goal is to free ourselves from the illusions of ego and all desire to finally end our suffering. Enlightenment is regarded as the ultimate goal in terms of a state of being that frees one from the cycle of birth and rebirth.

There are, however, celestial beings in Buddhism who offer compassion and wisdom, such as Amitabha Buddha and the bodhisattva Avalokiteshvara, both of whom work to cultivate salvation in all sentient beings, but Heaven is not the end goal of Buddhist beliefs. It's all about becoming enlightened.

Hindus believe, as the holy Vedas tell us, that Heaven is not the ultimate resting place of a human soul but instead is the place where the gods exist, such as Indra, Soma, and Agni. The Upanishads of the Hindu Vedic texts state that one's actions connect us to the world of appearances and illusion. Brahman, which is the ultimate reality, transcends. In ancient times, ritual sacrifices and funeral rites assured a soul ascended to the "world of the fathers," and rebirth depended on having male descendants who would sponsor the rites. In the Upanishads, liberation required great spiritual discipline and was more the realm of devotional Hinduism. The Bhagavad–Gita and Puranas offered salvation as a personal union with the divine, and this opened up the path for more humans to enter by putting their trust in a deity who would protect them on their journey.

Confucianism is a belief system rather than a religion, with the emphasis on living in the present with kindness, harmony, and order. The emphasis is not on what happens after someone dies but rather on how they

As explained in the Hindus' holy Vedas, people don't go to Heaven (the place for gods only) when they die but instead ascend to the "world of the fathers."

live in the present, which is more important. Confucius was not a god but rather the teacher of this philosophy who aimed to combine ancient wisdom with modern daily life. Because death was thought to disrupt societal or community harmony, it was rarely discussed in the teachings.

Instead of a God figure portrayed by Western traditions, Confucianists rely on *tian*, a concept of Heaven as a more-than-mortal power that instilled morals and obligations. The word *tian* is often translated in Confucianism and Taoism as "Heaven," a cosmos that was complementary to *Di*, translated as Earth. In Taoism, the *tian* and *Di* are considered the two poles of the Three Realms of reality, with the middle realm as Earth. Early Taoism focused on this life instead of the afterlife and incorporated the notion of salvation as a matter of participation in the eternal return of the natural world, a never-ending cycle of chaos followed by spontaneous creation back to chaos again. True salvation was not escaping this world but becoming perfectly aligned with the natural world and its cosmic forces.

NATIVE AND INDIGENOUS AFTERLIFE BELIEFS

Native cultures have their own beliefs about what happens after death. When the Europeans came to North America, there were over 600 autonomous Indian nations with their own religions that usually focused on life rather than death or any kind of afterlife of punishment or reward. Some tribes did have afterlife beliefs of their own.

The North American Pueblo Indians saw life after death as the same as life before death, with the deceased joining a group of deceased people they knew in life. It is a continuation of the life–death cycle, with no Heaven or Hell. Unlike the Western tradition, Pueblo cosmology did not recognize a place of eternal punishment or reward by gods or deities.

In contrast, the Northern Plains Cheyenne Indians believed the souls of the dead travel along the Road of the Departed, aka the Milky Way, to the place of the dead. There is no Hell or punishment, and the spirits of the dead would all find a trail of footsteps leading them to a camp in the stars where their friends and relatives awaited them after death. They would continue to exist in this location.

This same lack of a place of punishment or reward is central to the vision of the afterlife among the tribes in the New England region, and one could find new opportunities after death and continue to flourish there. The souls would journey to the southwest where they could share in the joys of the wigwam and fields of the great god Kanta or Tanto with their ancestors after attending a welcome feast.

The Navajo Indians believed they would find out about the afterlife once they died and they should not waste their living moments thinking about it. To the Navajo, life was about life and making it harmonious and happier.

The Australian Aborigines believed in a "Land of the Dead," defined as the "sky world" where a deceased person's soul would go. There were certain rituals that had to be carried out throughout their lives and at their deaths that would allow them to enter the Land of the Dead. Souls could also go to places called the Braigu or the Uluru, which were sacred locations treated with great respect. Aborigines, like Catholics, believed in resurrection and that spirits or souls were resurrected into new living beings in their native land of Australia one by one.

Aborigines, like Catholics, believed in resurrection and that spirits or souls were resurrected into new living beings in their native land of Australia one by one.

To the Aborigines, life was a cycle that never ended. Both humans and animals were born, they died, and they were born again. They also ascribed to an idea called "eternal dreaming" in which death is seen as a rebirth from your previous life. Another belief is that the soul of a dead person would go to the land of the "Dreaming Ancestors" and unite with their gods and ancestors. Different tribes had different beliefs, and some believed you had two souls that merged during death.

Tribes often buried the possession of their dead with the bodies or destroyed them, and saying the dead person's name was forbidden. If someone in the tribe shared the name of a dead person, it would be changed for a year or more, during a period of avoidance.

World myths, like religious origin stories, speak of the original state of Heaven and Earth as being close or together, until some event occurred where they were torn asunder when the gods separated the two or withdrew one from the other. If you think about this, it is the perfect analogy for how human beings become separated from their own souls or spirits, and Heaven truly may be the return to a union of the body, mind, and spirit. Whether you believe in a god or gods or no gods, reuniting with these aspects of the self can lead to greater happiness, joy, fulfillment, and bliss even before your body leaves this realm, and isn't that really what Heaven is all about?

THE IN-BETWEEN: LIMBO, PURGATORY, AND THE BARDO

Some religious and spiritual traditions profess that the soul exists in a state between purification and judgment. This period of limbo goes by several names, such as purgatory and the bardo, but serves as a holding tank of sorts for the soul that has not yet either gone to Heaven, Hell, or been reincarnated or advanced along the cyclical wheel of birth, life, death, and rebirth.

Limbo is like an afterlife Grand Central Station where souls wait around for the next train to come. It also mirrors the human concept of holding someone in a prison cell while they await their court date and trial before a jury where they will be found guilty or not guilty. Another apt comparison is sitting in a doctor's waiting room before going in the back to find out whether you have a minor cold or full-blown pneumonia. In conversational language, we often use the word "limbo" to describe a state of not knowing or not yet deciding, as in "I'm in limbo until they tell me if I'm getting fired or not," or "I feel like I'm in limbo waiting to see if they love me back after texting them at 3 A.M. professing my love." It is the stage or location of waiting.

In Roman Catholic theology, limbo is like a borderland between Heaven and Hell where souls who are not yet condemned to punishment in Hell wait without the joy of eternal and heavenly existence. It's a neutral, dead zone with Teutonic roots, meaning "border" or "anything joined on." The concept of limbo may have developed in Europe during the Middle Ages but was never accepted as dogma, and after the official catechism of the church issued in 1992, references of limbo were removed.

There were two kinds of limbo in the original concept:

1. *Limbus patrum* (Latin: "fathers' limbo"), where the Old Testament saints were thought to be confined until they were liberated by Christ in his "descent into Hell."

2. *Limbus infantum,* or *limbus puerorum* ("children's limbo"), the waiting place for those who have died without sinful deeds but whose original sin has not been washed away by a ritual baptism. This "children's limbo" included dead unbaptized infants and the mentally impaired.

PURGATORY

The Merriam–Webster definition of Purgatory is a noun meaning:

1: an intermediate state after death for expiatory purification; *specifically*: a place or state of punishment wherein according to Roman Catholic doctrine the souls of those who die in God's grace may make satisfaction for past sins and so become fit for Heaven

2: a place or state of temporary suffering or misery

It describes a process or place of purification or temporary punishment where, according to medieval Christian and Roman Catholic belief, the souls of the dead enter a state of grace and are prepared to enter Heaven. Purgatory comes from the Latin *purgatorium*; from *purgare,* "to purge," and refers to a purging of uncleanliness and sin and temporary punishment in the afterlife.

The conception of purgatory as an actual location comes from medieval Christian beliefs. The living could offer intercessory prayers, masses, alms, and fasting on behalf of the dead trapped in purgatory to hopefully influence where they ultimately ended up. The early Christian practice of prayer for the

A painting at the Iglesia Catedral de las Fuerzas Armada de España in Madrid, Spain, depicts souls in purgatory.

dead appears in the story of Judas Maccabeus atoning for the idolatry of his fallen soldiers by providing prayers and monetary offerings on their behalf (2 Maccabees 12:41–46). Apostle Paul's prayer for Onesiphorus (2 Timothy 1:18), the parable of Dives and Lazarus in Luke 16:19–26, and the words of Jesus from the cross to the repentant thief Barabbas in Luke 23:43 also speak of an in-between period before the Day of Judgment when sinners can achieve redemption and the good see a preview of their coming Heavenly reward.

Some Christian writers refer to purgatory as a fire that tortures the damned, tests and purifies the mixed (e.g., 1 Corinthians 3:11–15), but does not harm the saints. Hebrews 12:29 of the Old Testament states that God himself is "a consuming fire." St. Augustine (354–430) made the distinction between the fires of purgatory that burn off stains and an everlasting fire that consumes those who refuse to repent and get right with the Church.

Purgatory can be a terrifying prospect by these standards because of the waiting, the judgment, and the possibility of not being found fit for redemption. "The waiting is the hardest part," as Tom Petty once sang, but the concept of this limbo or purgatory state no doubt offered those sinners who did not repent while alive another chance to avoid the eternal fires of Hell.

An illustration depicting the bardo, a purgatory-like place in which the dead experience hallucinations and visions through which only the more disciplined minds can navigate.

BARDO

In some schools of Buddhism, the bardo is considered an intermediate or transitional state between death and rebirth. This idea emerged after the death of Siddhartha Gautama, the Buddha, and some earlier traditions accepted it while others rejected it. The schools that accepted the concept of a limbo state for consciousness, which was probably introduced into Buddhism from the Vedic-Upanishadic Hindu tradition, later expanded the concept into six or more bardo states of consciousness for each specific stage of life and death.

In Tibetan Buddhism, this intermediary place is at the heart of Bardo Thodol, better known as the Tibetan Book of the Dead. The

Catholic Church Teachings on Purgatory

The *Catechism of the Catholic Church* defines purgatory as a "purification, so as to achieve the holiness necessary to enter the joy of Heaven," which is experienced by those "who die in God's grace and friendship, but still imperfectly purified" (CCC 1030). It notes that "this final purification of the elect . . . is entirely different from the punishment of the damned" (CCC 1031). The purification is necessary because, as Scripture teaches, nothing unclean will enter the presence of God in Heaven (Rev. 21:27) and, while we may die with our mortal sins forgiven, there can still be many impurities in us, specifically venial sins and the temporal punishment due to sins already forgiven.

What Happens in Purgatory?

When we die, we experience an individual judgment and receive our reward, for good or ill. We find out our destiny—Heaven or Hell. When Jesus returns at the end times, that is when the final judgment occurs, as in Matthew 25:31–32: "When the Son of man comes in his glory, and all the angels with him, then he will sit on his glorious throne. Before him will be gathered all the nations, and he will separate them one from another as a shepherd separates the sheep from the goats." At this time, our sins will be made public (Luke 12:2–5).

"Purgatory Not in Scripture"

The word "purgatory" is nowhere found in Scripture, but that may not disprove its existence or the fact that it has been a part of church teachings. By the same respect, the words "Trinity" and "Incarnation" aren't in Scripture either but are clearly taught to Christians.

Why Go to Purgatory?

The purpose of purgatory is to be cleansed, for "nothing unclean shall enter [Heaven]" (Rev. 21:27). Those who are not freed from their sin are considered "unclean." Even repenting one's sins doesn't guarantee a trip to Heaven. One must be clean for that. Though the teachings state that Christ died for the salvation of

cont'd on next page

cont'd from previous page

all, it is the long process of sanctification through which the Christian is made clean and ready for Heaven.

Nothing Unclean or Purged

Catholic theology states that "nothing unclean shall enter Heaven." A soul must be fully cleansed or "purged" of all imperfections. Hebrews 12:14 states that we must strive "for the holiness without which no one will see the Lord."

**From Catholic.com/tract/purgatory
IMPRIMATUR: In accord with 1983 CIC 827
permission to publish this work is hereby granted.
Robert H. Brom, Bishop of San Diego, August 10, 2004**

term translates to "Liberation through Healing during the Intermediate State" and is meant to guide the consciousness of a recently deceased person through the death bardo in order to be reborn and also to help their loved ones grieve.

The six bardos in Tibetan Buddhism are:

Kyenay bardo–the first bardo of birth and life that begins at conception until the last breath, when the mindstream leaves the physical body.

Milam bardo–the second bardo, the dream state and a subset of the first bardo.

Samten bardo–the third bardo of meditation, experienced by those who meditate but can sometimes be spontaneous.

Chikhai bardo–the fourth bardo of the moment of death that continues through dissolution and transmutation of the Mahabhuta, the five elements of air, water, fire, earth, and aether, until the external and internal last breath is complete.

Chonyi bardo–the fifth bardo of luminosity of the true nature that begins after the final inner breath.

Sidpa bardo–the sixth bardo of becoming or transmigration.

The bardo, then, is the limbo state of existence between two lives on Earth when a person's consciousness is not connected to a physical body. In the bardo, a consciousness experiences everything from a clear view of reality to terrifying hallucinations based on their karma from their previous impulse-based actions. If a person is prepared for this state by what they did while alive in terms of spiritual growth and insight, it can open the door to liberation and transcendental insights as they come to view reality as it is, minus the illusions of earthly perceptions.

In early Indian Buddhist texts, the bardo state is simply referred to as the "intermediate existence" that occurs in between the "birth existence" and the "death existence." There is thought to be no discontinuity between the moment of death and rebirth, so the three states of existence must be linked. The length of time a consciousness spends in the intermediate state will differ according to the tradition, with some claiming it lasts 49 days at most. Bardo is also equated with consciousness and that a particular consciousness can bypass the 49 days at any time and achieve a new life under any form in the six realms or bardos described earlier.

According to the Tibetan Book of the Dead, the failed consciousness will be reborn in the bardo after three days as an illusory body of the mind, with all the previous body and mind's possessions. It is also possible for a consciousness to exit the bardo and enter another existence too soon, impeding its ultimate liberation. Tibetan Buddhism also holds that death is not final. A person is not certified as medically dead until three days after the dissolution of the physical body's five elements and consciousness. This is due to the fact that Buddhism includes a more subtle dying process than the West, where the end of life is more explicitly declared.

DOING THE LIMBO IN MOVIES

Many books and novels have been written about the limbo state, but we are visual creatures, and nothing influences our perceptions like seeing a story play out on the big screen, or in the case of Netflix and streaming services, the small screen. Movies about purgatory run the gamut from fun and comedic to dark and horrific.

One of the most fun depictions of this limbo place comes from modern pop culture in the 1991 romantic

The Karmic Pebbles
of the Tibetan Book of the Dead

Folios 35 and 67 from the Tibetan Book of the Dead, housed at the Bodleian Library in Oxford, England.

In the Bardo Thodol (Tibetan Book of the Dead), there is a story of white pebbles and black pebbles relating to karma that speaks to the nature of the body and the nonphysical. This karmic judgment of sorts occurs in the bardo state:

The Good Spirit, who was born simultaneously with you, will come now and count out your good deeds with white pebbles, and the Evil Spirit, who was born simultaneously with you, will come and count out your evil deeds with black pebbles.

Thereupon you will be greatly frightened, awed, and terrified, and I will tremble; and you will attempt to tell lies, saying, "I have not committed any evil deed."

Then the Lord of Death will say, "I will consult the Mirror of karma." He will look in the Mirror, wherein every good and evil act is vividly reflected. Lying will be of no avail.

Then one of the executive furies of the Lord of Death will place a rope around your neck and drag you along; he will cut off your head, extract your heart, pull out your intestines, lick up your brain, drink your blood, eat your flesh, and gnaw your bones, but you will be incapable of dying.

Although your body be hacked to pieces, it will revive again. The repeated hacking will cause intense pain and torture.

Even at the time that the pebbles are being counted out, be not frightened, tell no lies; and fear not the Lord of Death.

cont'd on next page

cont'd from previous page

Your body being a mental body is incapable of dying even though beheaded and quartered. In reality, your body is of the nature of voidness; you need not be afraid. The Lords of Death are your own hallucinations. Your desire-body is a body of propensities, and void. Voidness cannot injure voidness; the qualityless cannot injure the qualityless. Apart from one's own hallucinations, in reality there are no such things existing outside oneself as Lord of Death, or god, or demon. Act so as to recognize this.

comedy motion picture *Defending Your Life*, directed by Albert Brooks, who also starred as Daniel Miller, a man who gets hit by a bus and dies. He enters the afterlife where he realizes he must now defend his life actions on Earth so he can ascend to a higher plane of existence. While he awaits his judgment, he meets and falls in love with Julie, played by Meryl Streep, whose own life was so close to perfect, she is assured ascension. Daniel, on the other hand, isn't such a cut-and-dried case. It's a fun movie that plays with the afterlife state of purgatory as a kind of way-station courthouse for those awaiting their trial to determine their fate.

There have been a number of movies and television shows that feature the idea of an afterlife or limbo, in every genre from fantasy to drama to horror to comedy. Here is a sampling:

- *Heaven Can Wait* (1978)–Warren Beatty plays Joe Pendleton, a quarterback for the L.A. Rams who is killed in an auto accident but discovers his guardian angel has taken him from his body a few years too early. He cannot resume his physical form, so he assumes the form of a greedy billionaire, tries a return to football, and finds true love with an activist played by Julie Christie.

- *Beetlejuice* (1988)–This Tim Burton masterpiece of comedic horror stars Alec Baldwin and Geena Davis as the Maitlands, who are killed in a car accident. They

Geena Davis (left) and Alec Baldwin (right) play a recently deceased couple stuck in a kind of limbo in the 1988 comedy film *Beetlejuice*. (Actor Simmy Bow is center.)

are stuck haunting their country home, and when a new family moves in, they try to scare them away. They fail and resort to "hiring" the services of a ghoul played by Michael Keaton, endangering everyone involved.

- *Ghost* (1990)–Demi Moore and Patrick Swayze star as Molly and Sam, who are madly in love when Sam is stabbed and killed outside of their new condo. He doesn't cross over but stays in a limbo state to protect Molly from his shady business partner and his goons. He gets some comedic assistance from Whoopi Goldberg as Oda Mae Brown, a psychic medium, in this '90s romantic classic.

- *Heart and Soul* (1993)–This fantasy/comedy stars Charles Grodin, Kyra Sedgwick, Alfre Woodard, and Tom Sizemore, who all die in a bus crash and become ghosts and guardians to a newborn baby born the exact moment they die. The baby grows up to be a businessman, played by Robert Downey Jr., who has memories of these ghostly playmates from his childhood. When the ghosts realize they can only move on with Downey's help, they must make another appearance.

- *What Dreams May Come* (1999)—Based on Richard Matheson's fantasy/romance novel, Robin Williams plays Chris, a doctor who dies in a car crash and is escorted into the afterlife by his spirit guide, where he sees his children. His wife, Annie, is left behind in the world of the living. She commits suicide and goes to Hell, and Chris begins the dangerous journey to find her.

- *Dead Like Me* (2003)—This Showtime dark comedy series focuses on an 18-year-old girl named George, who dies when she is struck by a toilet seat falling from a spacecraft. But instead of moving on to the afterlife, she must become a reaper, helping other departed souls move on. The show explores how the dead might be offered the thankless job of a Grim Reaper and can stay in their life, but with a different face, until they collect the number of souls required to free them from the job.

- *Corpse Bride* (2005)—This Tim Burton stop-motion animation classic tells the story of a young man who has an arranged marriage and is nervous about it. He is in the forest practicing his lines when a tree branch turns into a hand and drags him into the land of the dead. The hand belongs to the woman he was supposed to marry, who was murdered while trying to elope with her true love. Now he must get back above to the land of the living to straighten out who marries who in this visually eye-popping family fantasy based on Jewish folklore.

- *Hereafter* (2010)—The stories of three people who can communicate with the dead—including a professional medium, a woman who had a near-death experience, and a twin grieving the death of his brother. Clint Eastwood directed the film, starring Matt Damon.

- *The Good Place* (2016)—A television sitcom starring Kristen Bell, Ted Danson, and an ensemble cast focuses on Bell's character, Eleanor, who dies and ends up in the afterlife but wonders why she is in "the good place." The series follows her as she realizes she is there by mistake but that it is never too late to change for the better.

- *Happy Death Day* (2017)–A horror spin on *Groundhog Day* in which where a self-centered college girl is killed by a masked murderer on her birthday and wakes up to experience the same day over and over until she solves the crime.

- *Coco* (2017)–A beautiful and colorful animated tale of a young boy named Miguel who wants to prove his musical talents and finds himself in the Land of the Dead in search of his idol, an accomplished musician. Miguel's adventures in the Land of the Dead unlock the mystery of his living family history in this Oscar–winning and Golden Globe–winning animated feature.

HELL

It helps to have a good scare tactic if you want people to behave. The concept of a place where people who sinned, misbehaved, or committed crimes would spend their afterlife was as good a tactic as any, and it works to some extent in many religious traditions.

The word "Hell" in modern English comes from around 725 C.E. with the Old English *hel, Helle*, which means "netherworld, abode of the dead, place of torment for the wicked after death, infernal regions." This comes from the earlier Proto-Germanic *haljo* for "the underworld," and the Old Saxon *Hellia*, Norse *hel* and *Hellir*, which meant "cave, cavern." Hel in Norse mythology is the ruler of the underworld, also called Hel.

Our ideas about Hell are primarily influenced by Christianity, which depicts it as a place where bad souls go to burn in the fires of damnation alongside the Devil and his minions. Hell is the destination of criminals, killers, and rapists who, while on Earth, refused to accept Christ as their savior and beg mercy and forgiveness for their sins. The Christian Hell combines elements of the Jewish Gehinnom (eternal burning) and the ancient Greek Hades (eternal punishment).

In the New Testament, Hades is mentioned often, and Jesus uses Gehenna, a version of Gehinnom, to reference the place where sinners go where there is "an unquenchable fire and a worm that does not die." In the Book of Revelation, we are told that anyone whose name is not written in the Book of Life will be thrown into the lake of fire to burn–thus the

This fresco showing Hell can be seen on Brunelleschi's Dome at Florence Cathedral in Italy. Many of our concepts of Hell originate in Christian theology and lore.

popular saying when we hear of a serial killer or child rapist, that he or she will "burn in Hell."

In pagan belief, the underworld is the lowest of worlds, originating in Old Norse mythology and later merged with the Christian Hell. Referred to in the Old Testament as *Sheol*, Hell was a place of misery, horror, torment, and despair, hidden somewhere beneath the surface of the planet with entrances guarded by monsters and demons. No doubt these creatures were not guarding Hell from those who wanted in, but to keep those inside who wanted out.

Christianity and Islam both depict a fiery, agonizing underworld filled with eternal pain and suffering, but sometimes Hell is a place of ice-cold barrenness—think Dante's *Inferno* and the ninth level of Hell as a frozen lake of blood. The Catholic religion believes in four different depictions of Hell:

1. Hell is where damned men and demons go to be punished for their sins.

2. Hell is the limbus parvulorum or limbo of infants, where those who die of original sin without committing personal mortal sin are confined and punished.

3. The limbus partum, or limbo of the fathers, is where the souls of the just who died before Christ awaited their admission to Heaven since Heaven was closed to them as punishment for the sin of Adam.

4. Purgatory, where the just who die in venial sin or who owe a debt of temporal punishment for their sins are cleansed by suffering before they can enter Heaven.

The New Testament favors the name Hell, along with "lower Hell," "place of torments," "abyss," "everlasting darkness," "eternal fire," "unquenchable fire," "perdition," "second death," and others. Early beliefs suggested Hell could be everywhere, with the eternally damned wandering around at liberty, but the idea of Hell being a fixed location eventually replaced that belief, and the location was usually thought to be deep within the bowels of earth, where souls were kept far away from the divine light of the Heavens above.

During the 18th century, Englishmen suggested Hell was on the moon or even Mars, or possibly outside the confines of the known Universe. Before then, Hell was thought to exist on some deserted island, out at sea, or at either of the Earth's poles, before humans ventured to such locations and discovered it wasn't there.

The length of time a soul would spend in the Hellish underworld was up for debate. Conditionalists believe the soul is immortal but that the souls of the wicked are annihilated after a certain amount of punishment. Universalists believe that the damned will be saved. Some Catholics believe that if a sinner is not too wicked, he or she can achieve grace after death.

The finality and sheer terror of the promise of Hell was used as a tool of fear-based control by the church. The original idea was to provide a social and moral code to live by that would result in some semblance of order, but punishment has not made a mark on the continuous sins of humanity.

In Ancient Egyptian polytheism, sinful souls of the dead were either welcomed into the Two Fields, approved for good behavior by the Goddess Maat, or send to a "devourer" and thrown into a lake of fire if they didn't meet Maat's approval. The devourer took the poor soul and punished it before an-

Dante's *Inferno*

An engraving by Gustav Doré of Minos in Hell from Canto V of Dante's *Inferno*.

It is impossible to discuss any concept of Hell without bringing up the nine levels found in Dante's *Inferno*. The *Divine Comedy (Divina Commedia)* is a 14th-century Italian narrative poem by Dante Alighieri, which he began in 1308 and completed in 1320. He died one year later. Dante was a poet, writer, and philosopher and never lived long enough to see his creative masterpiece become one of the most important poems of the Middle Ages and the greatest Italian work of literature. Even today, it is considered one of the most important pieces of literature ever created.

This epic poem presents Dante's vision of the afterlife in three parts: *Inferno*, which is Italian for Hell; *Purgatorio*, which is about Purgatory; and *Paradiso*, or Heaven.

Inferno tells the story of Dante getting lost in the woods and meeting up with the ghost of the ancient Roman poet Virgil, who was sent to be his guide by Dante's lover Beatrice and two holy women.

cont'd on next page

cont'd from previous page

Hell is depicted in the poem as having nine concentric circles of torment, located within the Earth as a realm of all those who have rejected spiritual morals and values by "yielding to bestial appetites or violence, or by perverting their human intellect to fraud or malice against their fellowmen." The nine levels of Hell depict the horrors of each specific level or Circle and were said to ultimately lead to Heaven, where Dante would be reunited with Beatrice.

As Virgil leads Dante through the Gates of Hell, there is the famous inscription that warns, "Abandon all hope, you who enter here." The Circles of Hell are:

1st Circle—Limbo: Here resided the virtuous non-Christians and unbaptized pagans who are punished by being relegated into this inferior Heaven, where they live in a castle with seven green gates, each named for one of the seven virtues. Dante sees Socrates, Aristotle, Cicero, and Julius Caesar here.

2nd Circle—Lust: Here resided those overcome by lust and punished by being blown violently by strong winds so they can never find any peace or rest. This is where adulterers were found and the likes of Cleopatra and Helen of Troy.

3rd Circle—Gluttony: Here resided sinners who overindulged in food, drink, and other pleasures and were both selfish and cold of heart.

4th Circle—Greed: Here resided those who hoarded possessions and those who lavishly spent their bounty on things like jousting. Dante saw clergymen, cardinals, and popes.

5th Circle—Anger: Here resided the wrathful who fought each other on the river Styx and the sullen gurgling beneath the river's surface.

6th Circle—Heresy: Here resided those who were condemned to eternity within flaming tombs after being deemed heretics. Dante spots Epicurus, the Holy Roman Emperor Frederick II, and Pope Anastasius II.

7th Circle—Violence: This circle was divided into three rings. The Outer Ring housed the murderers and violent offenders, such as Alexander the Great and Guy de Montfort. The Mid-

cont'd on next page

cont'd from previous page

dle Ring was for those who chose suicide and were turned into trees and bushes with Harpies feeding on them. The Inner Ring was for sodomites and blasphemers who were forced to live in a desert of burning sand and rain.

8th Circle—Fraud: Here resided the fraudulent, seducers, were panderers who were divvied up into ten different ditches, depending on their offenses.

9th Circle—Treachery: Divided into four rounds according to the seriousness of the sins, those who resided here were frozen within an icy lake, with each round named after a particular representative sinner. The fourth round was named Judecca after Judas Iscariot, who betrayed Jesus. This Circle also included a three-headed, giant Lucifer who was half embedded in the ice and chewed on the four representative sinners of each round.

The story is vast and descriptive and has been portrayed in paintings and drawings throughout history and a movie by author Dan Brown, starring Tom Hanks. *Inferno* stands as a classic piece of literature and an allegory of Dante's own journey through the circles of Hell as a mirror of his spiritual journey and man's descent into sin.

nihilating it altogether. Those sinners who didn't commit the most heinous sins could be purified and reborn after overcoming evil rather than be forced into a total state of nothingness, or "nonbeing."

The Greek Tartarus was a pit or abyss, a dungeon–like place of torture and torment somewhere within the confines of Hades. This was where souls judged as deserving of punishment were sent. Mesoamerican cultures such as the Aztec had Mictlan, a place far to the north that took four years to get to. Along the way, souls overcame challenges and, aided by Xolotl, ended in a nine–level underworld. The Mayans also had a nine–level underworld called *Metnal* that could only be accessed via a dangerous, thorny, steep road.

Hell was thought to be a state of mind rather than the final destination of souls in Judaism. Sins and misdeeds bring great shame, and suffering atones for the sins. Hell became a place of punishment for nonbelievers in later forms of Judaism. There are references in the Torah and mystical Kabbalah to the Underworld of Sheol, Abbadon's doom and perdition, and Gehanna's purgatory, which clearly influenced later Christian/New Testament beliefs. Gehanna also refers to a real place called the Valley of Hinnom outside of Jerusalem where garbage, as well as the bodies of sinners and suicides, were burned. This fire never died, thus the eternal fire.

Similar to the Gehinnom of Judaism is the Jahannam of Islam, a fiery resting place filled with boiling water and tortures galore for those who do not accept God. After the Day of Judgment, unbelievers and sinners alike enter this hellish place when they die, passing over a bridge so narrow most fall into the hellfire. The suffering endured in Jahannam is physical and symbolic, with seven different levels depending on the actions of the sinner, one of which is made of ice and cold. The guardian to Hell is Maalik, an angel who oversees the Zabaaniyah, or guards of Hell.

Being a hypocrite or worshiping more than one God, according to Muslims, are the worst sins, sending a soul directly to the lowest pit, Hawiyah. The Catholic Church believes that Hell is the absolute and final exclusion of the self from communion with God. Hell could be avoided if you asked for forgiveness or mended your ways before death, accepting God's grace and mercy and accepting the ways of the Lord, but this had to be done while you were still alive.

Hades, the Greek god of the dead and ruler of the underworld, is depicted here with Cerberus, a three-headed, doglike monster that guards the entrance to the underworld.

Not all religious scholars agree on whether Hell is permanent or temporary. Some religions follow the belief in conditional immortality of the soul, which dies along with physical death and doesn't live again until postresurrection when it experiences a revival. Protestantism of the early Reformation period rejected the immortality of the soul, and Seventh-day Adventists support the idea of total annihilation of the soul, denying the concept of purgatory where souls wait their fate in a middle world between Heaven and Hell. Once you die, the soul is done.

Unitarians and Universal Reconciliationists believe the souls of the wicked will once again reconcile with God and get into Heaven. The Church of Jesus Christ of Latter-day Saints looks at Hell as an in-between state after death and before resurrection, where souls can either repent and move on, or not repent and suffer.

Remember the Bridge of Separation from Zoroastrianism? The one that would widen to allow the good and righteous to cross over and be met by a lovely maiden? The bridge would turn on its side and become as sharp as a razor for the sinful and evil. The souls of the sinful would be tormented by an old hag (what must she have done to earn this job?) and then fall off the bridge into Hell, where punishment was equal to the sins committed. Eventually all souls would become purified and get to leave this hellish place to join with the righteous with the god Ahura Mazda.

From Buddhism, we have five levels of rebirth that are divided into differing sublevels of agony and misery or pleasure. Suffering of souls can go on for a long time but is not permanent, as souls are reborn. The teachings of Buddhism emphasize the desire to escape the wheel of reincarnation and rebirth and the cycle of the soul, and to achieve a state of Nirvana, or being off the wheel completely. Hell could then be said to be staying forever on that wheel like Bill Murray's character in the movie *Groundhog Day*, living the same level of existence over and over and over again. Buddha also taught that desires of the ego were a flame burning inside of us that causes suffering and keeps us on that cycle, and only would that flame be extinguished when we put an end to suffering by achieving Nirvana. Much of Buddhism focuses on letting go of desires, especially in the context of materialism.

There is no traditional concept of Hell in early Hindu roots. Later Hindu texts mention a fourth realm called *naraka*. Sinners must accept punishment in accordance with their individual sins and face the Yamaraja, the god associated with death, before receiving punishment from the record keeper, Chitragupta. If a soul completes its punishment, it is reborn depending on its "karmic balance," and the way to Heaven is release from this cycle to achieve liberation or *moksha*. Jainism has a seven-level Hell that also holds souls accountable with karma carried over from a previous life and taken with them into a new life. Once karma has been used up, a higher level of rebirth is achieved.

Do We Ever Truly Die? The Brain and Consciousness

Of course, you don't die. Nobody dies. Death doesn't exist. You only reach a new level of vision, a new realm of consciousness, a new unknown world.
–Henry Miller

All goes onward and outward, nothing collapses,
And to die is different from what any one supposed, and luckier.
–Walt Whitman

There's also the issue of consciousness and whether it survives death when the brain stops working. We are still learning about the vast mysteries of the brain, perception, memory, and consciousness, and until we do, the debate between those who believe consciousness resides in the brain and ends with death and those who believe consciousness resides outside the brain and survives death will continue. It's the same argument as the one about the soul, and because we can't put a soul or consciousness in a jar and study it under a microscope, we can't find a winner.

WHAT IS CONSCIOUSNESS?

Merriam Webster defines consciousness as:

1a. the quality or state of being aware especially of something within oneself

97

1b. the state or fact of being conscious of an external object, state, or fact

1c. Awareness; *especially*: concern for some social or political cause. The organization aims to raise the political *consciousness* of teenagers.

2. the state of being characterized by sensation, emotion, volition, and thought: Mind

3. the totality of conscious states of an individual

4. the normal state of conscious life: regained *consciousness*

5. the upper level of mental life: of which the person is aware as contrasted with unconscious processes

The truth is that consciousness is a vexing enigma. Yes, it refers to a person's awareness of themselves and their thoughts, sensations, and surroundings. It is the awareness of the world around us and our existence within it, but it is not something we can hold in our hands or put on a shelf. It is a state of being, but one that changes when our perceptions and experiences change.

There are different states of consciousness we each experience regularly.

- Sleep and dreams
- Hallucinations
- Hypnosis
- Meditative
- Drug-induced

Altered states of consciousness can occur from a medical procedure, a spiritual ritual, or an ecstatic experience, and changes in our conscious awareness can result from a spiritual practice or spontaneously. We can also experience a sudden change in our consciousness when we have an aneurysm or brain injury, or from lack of oxygen to the brain and other medical causes that create a shock to the system. We might even lose consciousness when ill or injured.

But where does it fit in with death? American psychologist William James once compared consciousness to an unbroken and continuous stream despite life's constant shifts and changes. This might include one of the biggest shifts of all: death. French philosopher René Descartes proposed that "cogito ergo sum," or "I think, therefore I am," implying that being able to think demonstrates consciousness. Descartes introduced the concept of mind–body dualism, stating that while the mind and body are separate, they do interact. In this case, the mind and consciousness appear interchangeable, but modern research has given each their own "identity," with mind the functions of the brain, and consciousness something that drives states of being and awareness.

American psychologist William James once compared consciousness to an unbroken and continuous stream despite life's constant shifts and changes.

There are numerous theories that attempt to explain where consciousness is located and how it works, such as integrated information theory, which proposes that consciousness is based on physical processes and integrated information. According to the global workspace theory, the brain derives its experience of consciousness from a memory bank.

Then there is the Jungian concept of a collective unconscious, which is the home of archetypes and universal symbols understood by everyone, even as we possess our own individual consciousness.

Is consciousness an energy form? The human body is made up of matter and energy, which manifests itself as electrical impulses and signals as well as chemical impulses. However, the same can be said of plants. Humans have a more complex energy–generation process, with approximately 20 watts of energy coursing through the human body at any given time, enough to power a light bulb.

Energy, as the laws of thermodynamics remind us, cannot cease to exist. It changes states. It is not created. It is not destroyed. This means it always exists. When it comes to a human life, it existed before our birth in some state, during our lives in another state, and after death in another state. Could this chain of existence be linked to the past, present, and future by our consciousness?

Does Your Life Really Flash before Your Eyes before Death?

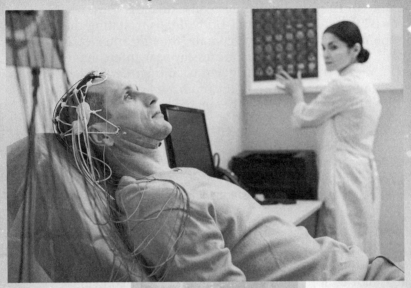

An electroencephalography (EEG) is a painless procedure that allows brain waves to be recorded and analyzed.

We see it in movies, television shows, even cartoons: someone on the verge of death sees their entire life pass by in a flash of memory after memory that lasts perhaps only a moment or two. In the 2001 movie *Vanilla Sky*, Tom Cruise's character leaps from a building and sees memories of his childhood, his parents, his dog, and the women he loved, and the years of his life pass by as he falls. The trope has become so popular, we now all expect to see this life review—a glimpse of the good times, the bad times, and those we loved and shared our lives with—in what some might say is a good-bye montage as we fade into the blackness of no longer ever remembering.

Science can now confirm that this flash life review occurs and what is going on in the brain. The phenomenon was investigated in a study published in *Frontiers in Aging Neuroscience* in February 2022 titled "Enhanced Interplay of Neuronal Coherence and Coupling in the Dying Human Brain." "The neurophysiological footprint of brain activity after cardiac arrest and during near-death

cont'd on next page

cont'd from previous page

experience (NDE) is not well understood. Although a hypoactive state of brain activity has been assumed, experimental animal studies have shown increased activity after cardiac arrest, particularly in the gamma-band, resulting from hypercapnia prior to and cessation of cerebral blood flow after cardiac arrest. No study has yet investigated this matter in humans."

The study, which had many coauthors, focused on an 87-year-old epilepsy patient who died during a brain scan. The scan, conducted by an international team of 13 neuroscientists, found that his brain appeared to replay memories in the 30-second period before and after his heart stopped beating. The patient had a heart attack and had a do-not-resuscitate order, so the scientists had the opportunity to track his brain waves during the final minutes he was alive.

The EEG brain scan found that the oscillatory brain wave pattern in which the activity of the brain's alpha, beta, and theta wave bands decreased relatively as the gamma band relatively increased, suggested memory recall was occurring. This was the first time this type of scan could be taken with a human but does correlate with the reports from those who have had a near-death experience that included some type of overall life memory recall and review.

There were challenges and problems that will require further study (including finding people who are dying to do the brain scans on!), if possible, but the study concluded: "Despite these caveats, the overall similarity in oscillatory changes between the highly controlled experimental rodent study and the present work suggests that the brain may pass through a series of stereotyped activity patterns during death. It may ultimately be difficult to assess this in a physiological environment, since gathering such data from 'healthy-subjects' is impossible by definition. We do not anticipate death in healthy subjects and therefore could not obtain uninterrupted recordings in the near-death phase in anything other than from circumstances involving pathological conditions in acute care hospital settings."

A similar study by Jimo Borjigin, a neuroscientist at the University of Michigan, found that rats displayed an unexpected pattern of

cont'd on next page

cont'd from previous page

brain activity immediately after cardiac arrest. The rats were clinically dead, but for at least 30 seconds, their brains showed strong signals of conscious thought. Borjigin posited that the final journey into permanent unconsciousness that we call death might involve a brief state of heightened consciousness and explain many of the phenomena reported in the classic NDE.

Human bodies are considered open systems that exchange energy with our environments. We gain energy through various chemical processes, and we lose energy via emitting heat or waste. When we die, the atoms that made us up are then repurposed, but the energy behind them has been around since the beginning of time and will be until the end of time.

However, one could argue that this only applies to the physical energy that makes up our bodies and bodily processes, rather than the consciousness that is infused in us. That could come from an external source and be "received" by the brain, or it could be a part of our physical source that dies along with the body, or it could be a combination of the two. Whatever the case may be, if it is energy, it will be repurposed elsewhere.

In "Consciousness: How Your Brain Creates the Feeling of Being" by Anil Seth for *New Scientist*, Seth, a professor at the University of Sussex and author of the new book *Being You—A New Science of Consciousness*, writes that "consciousness is, for each of us, all there is: the world, the self, everything. But consciousness is also subjective and difficult to define. The closest we have to a consensus definition is that consciousness is 'something it is like to be'. There is something it is like to be me or you—but presumably there is nothing it is like to be a table or an iPhone."

The question of how consciousness arises has yet to be adequately answered by scientists. "The orthodox scientific view today is that consciousness is a property of physical matter, an idea we might call physicalism or materialism. But this is by no means a universally held view, and even within physicalism there is little agreement about how consciousness emerges from, or otherwise relates to, physical stuff," Seth states.

Looking at the activity of the brain's 86 billion neurons and trillions of neural connections can provide clues to identifying the part of the brain associated with consciousness activity. Even though the cerebellum, located at the back of the brain's cortex, appears to house three-quarters of the neurons, the article claims it has nothing to do with consciousness. Neuroscientists know this because of research with people born without a functioning cerebellum who still manage to retain consciousness. There are parts of the brain such as the thalamus that, if damaged, can result in a permanent state of unconsciousness, but these regions might be nothing but a "power socket that simply allows whatever is plugged into it to work" and not the source of consciousness itself.

HOLOGRAPHIC BRAIN

The concept of a holographic brain suggests that consciousness resides outside the brain, and the brain is a conduit or transceiver of information outside of the physical, but also a transmitter of experience. Think of a holographic image, which is a piece of a whole image that also contains the whole

One of the theories about our consciousness is that it doesn't reside within our physical bodies but, rather, originates somewhere out in the universe, and the brain is merely like a television that receives a broadcast.

image within it. The holographic universe theory, which mirrors the holographic brain theory, posits that what we see in our 3-D reality might be a projection from a higher dimensional reality, and that our little piece we call the "universe" is but a smaller representation of the whole "universe," but not the whole itself. Likewise, consciousness is a holographic image our brains receive but is really a smaller piece of a greater consciousness that exists outside of the physical brain.

As early as the early 2000s, studies proposed that the brain functioned more like an access device for information in the form of memories stored outside of the brain. The work of Simon Berkovich, professor of engineering and applied science at George Washington University at the time, wrote a paper titled "On the Information Processing Capabilities of the Brain–Shifting the Paradigm" for the Department of Electrical Engineering and Computer Science. He wrote that a new paradigm of the brain and its functions was needed and suggested that research began with the holographical mechanism of information processing in the brain done by Stanford University neurophysiologist Karl Pribram, combined with the quantum mechanics interpretation of David Hohm, to create, as he stated, "an integrated view on the transcendental phenomena of Nature."

Pribram's work, documented in the seminal book on the holographic theories of the universe and brain, *The Holographic Universe* by Michael Talbot, focused on whether holography could explain the brain's ability to store massive amounts of information in such a small space. Pribram worked with rats in several experiments and became convinced that memory was stored not in a specific part of the brain but rather all over it, when he would remove specific parts of rats' brains to see how it affected their ability to navigate a maze they had been in and recall their way around.

The rats were able to navigate the maze regardless of which part of the brain he removed. Even after having parts of their brains removed during surgery, human patients were able to retain specific memory functioning. This altered our understanding of memory and the brain as being focused in a single area and suggested further research into the possibility that memories could be stored elsewhere, and our brains simply tapped into that larger field.

Berkovich published another intriguing paper in 2008 titled "A Note on Science and NDE: A Scientific Model Why

Memory, aka Consciousness, Cannot Reside Solely in the Brain," where he compared the brain with DNA and posited that it might be more of an "information marker" while the information itself was stored elsewhere. He compared it to a library card catalog, where one could look up something and find out which aisle or area of the library contained the book or magazine in question. He also compared it to the Internet, in which millions of personal computers were linked together to form a massive, universal computer. His final thoughts were telling: "In other words, the human brain is not a stand-alone computer but rather a terminal on the Internet of the physical universe."

In his book, Talbot wrote that this holographic theory of the brain made sense in that "holograms possess a fantastic capacity for information storage.... When we are unable to recall something, this may be the equivalent to shining various beams on a piece of multiple-image film, but failing to find the right angle to call up the image/memory for which we are searching."

This theory also mirrors the universal or collective unconscious taught by Carl Jung that all human consciousnesses could tap into to access archetypal information and wisdom. Jung believed there was an individual unconscious that was linked to this deeper collective, and we accessed it via intuition, dreams, and psychological analysis, just as each human brain might be linked to a deeper, universal brain. Many people who claim to have psi abilities, particularly remote viewing (the ability to "see" a distant object or location in one's mind), argue that they are simply tapping into this collective or holographic field of all information to see into the past or the future, or to see a building or a piece of paper at a remote location, far beyond the confines of the human eye.

Thus, the long-standing debate and search for theories and, ultimately, proof continues in the quest to determine whether consciousness is a field or supercomputer that we can tap into to access information and memories, or an individual state that can apply to a human as well as to an electron. The quest to fully define consciousness, like that of the soul, is at the heart of proving whether or not some part of us continues on another plane of existence after the death of our physical body and brain, just as it may have existed before we incarnated into our current body.

*The quest to fully define consciousness,
like that of the soul, is at the heart of proving
whether or not some part of us continues on
another plane of existence after the death of our
physical body and brain....*

IS DEATH JUST ANOTHER LEVEL ON THE GRID OF REALITY?

With quantum physics and theories of parallel universes, multiworlds, a quantum field of all potentiality, and alternate dimensions and timelines, we might speculate that reality itself is similar to a giant three–dimensional cubelike grid with multiple levels that each represent a timeline or individual "level" of reality. We can, via our consciousness and maybe upon death, move up and down, side to side on this grid to experience other realities, even other timelines. Therefore, we don't die, we just level up or down, or jump to the side and find ourselves experiencing a whole new world.

A great visual of this concept might be removing the exterior of a skyscraper so that we could see all the floors and rooms. Each floor is a different level of reality, ascending or descending, but each floor also has many rooms, so travel can go horizontally as well as vertically. Add to this many ways of traveling floor to floor, room to room, such as elevators and escalators, fire escapes, taking the stairs, and walking door to door, and we can get an idea of what the entirety of reality might look like if there are, indeed, multiple universes, timelines, and dimensions.

Is there any real proof that death is the end of our entire existence? Does the fact that the body returns to ash and earth imply that our consciousness, personality, soul, and essence will as well? We can begin by considering the thousands of subjective and personal experiences of people who have had near–death experiences as hopeful "circumstantial evidence" that life not only continues, but also has a purpose, and that we will one day be reunited with loved ones as we return to the Source. We can also look at the millions of people who have had a paranormal experience that they couldn't prove but that hints at the interaction of energy and even beings from another part of the grid with ours. Is a déjà–vu experience or the ability to remote view working with the grid to see into the future or beyond distances the eye can see? Are ghosts and entities nothing more than physical beings we glimpse on another level of the grid? Did Nostradamus reach into another timeline on the grid to make his predictions? Do mediums and channels pull their information from living beings in the grid? So many questions.

When we get to that next level, we might get another physicality and be reincarnated, as many Eastern spiritual traditions believe, into another soul journey on another plane, a journey that really is nothing but a new stop along the highway of our conscious evolution. Think of a road trip with friends, and how leaving one town can seem like an ending but entering another brings a whole new range of experiences.

Scientists continue to look to neuroscience and the study of the brain and consciousness to determine if there really is a way to prove that death is not the final destination. Right now, we are at the mercy of our limitations, but with each and every research study, and with personal experiences by respected people in the scientific and medical fields, we get closer and closer to one day determining if a part of us continues on.

According to the First Law of Thermodynamics, energy does not cease to exist. Energy within a system can change form or be transferred into or out of the system, but it cannot be reduced or disappear. Energy is conserved in some way. If we are all made of energy, then we must also be conserved in some way, in order to live on another level of this grid.

An idea or theory is only as good as it is useful to us in our daily lives, though. The grid concept suggests that when certain triggers and mechanisms line up that allow us to experience those other realities, whether upon death, via a hallucinogenic mushroom, or in a deep meditation, our own perception of existence itself is changed forever. We get a more expansive and grander sense of who we are and what life has to offer.

If we are energy and not our body, and if the First Law of Thermodynamics that energy always exists is true, then our energy essence should also always exist.

Parallel universes, multiple realities, or a multidimensional grid could one day explain

The Afterlife Book

both the quantum and the cosmic, as well as how they interact. We assume that because we are alive in this reality, it is the only one.

Science may beg to differ. Each point along each level of the grid may be a whole kind of life in and of itself, or at the very least, a whole other perception of it. But can we walk the grid ourselves, or must we wait until death or some bizarre paranormal event knocks us out of this particular reality like a smack to the head with a two-by-four? The truth is, we are already walking the grid, whether we are aware of it or not.

One of the most profound ways to experience another state of conscious reality is to dream. During dreams, our brains and bodies react and respond to stimulus as if it were just as real as anything in the waking state. Many people have dreams of past lives they know they did not live—or did they? Others dream of future events that prove to be precognitive, and still others get guidance and answers in these other realms of existence from beings that don't exist in our own realm.

During the waking state, where we feel reality is "really real," we often find ourselves experiencing shifts in perception of time and space that make us question our own fixed beliefs about what we think is real. Whether we are having some kind of anomalous or paranormal experience such as seeing a ghost or having a psychic knowing that comes true, or we are listening to music that puts us in a trance and completely changes how we perceive time, or running out in the woods and losing all sense of our own physical bodies, we are walking the grid.

Meditation, dancing, chanting, drumming, and a host of other activities can easily change our brain wave patterns and alter our consciousness enough to allow us access to that greater, grander landscape of potentiality. Sometimes, we have an out and out direct, head-on encounter with another reality in the form of a UFO sighting or a glimpse of a strange, cryptozoological creature crossing our path at night. We might even experience a shift in reality during orgasm, which has been called the "little death." The sensation of being elevated or expanded, of the loss of ego constructs and limitations, could in fact be what we have to look forward to in death.

When we die, what happens to time for us on the other side? Maybe time does not exist in death. We might not know how long we've been dead, or even care.

For the living, time slips and time shifts allow us to step out of the linear confines of the arrow of time and exist with a distortion of that structure. Time is one way we can traverse the grid and experience levels of reality because time can slow down when we are engrossed in an activity or speed up when we are experiencing an adrenaline rush. Time can even disappear and "go missing" as it has for the thousands of people who have experienced a missing time event.

Time can even disappear and "go missing" as it has for the thousands of people who have experienced a missing time event.

We enter another level of the grid whenever we are outside of our normal brain wave patterns or conscious waking reality. It doesn't always take ayahuasca, a strange contraption that stimulates the frontal lobes, or an earth-shattering out-of-body or near-death experience to realize that we are immersed in a sea of realities that offer us an infinite number of experiences.

Death may just be another level of the grid that intersects this life and the one before it, and this life and the one after it. Perhaps we exist on the death level and don't go into a new life but rather continue on as a different form of energetic expression, one that appears to those still incarnated as a ghost or apparition.

Intuitively we sense there are more worlds than the one we live our day-to-day lives in. Death might be just one of many of these worlds awaiting us on the other side, and not the ending we all fear and expect.

ANIMATE VERSUS INANIMATE

Either an object is alive or not alive. It is animate or inanimate. We can look at our surroundings and easily identify one from the other, but understanding what makes something alive is a different animal—er, argument. A chair is not an animate object, for it is not alive and never had life. A goldfish is animated, alive. Both are made up of energy, but what is that spark of life that, when added to something made up of atoms and energy, animates it? Soul, consciousness, something else entirely?

"Animate" is often considered to mean, simply, alive. "Inanimate" means not alive. When used as an adjective, "animate" implies something that has the ability of motion. "That frog is animated." A chair is not animated. But a robot has the ability of motion and is inanimate, so motion alone is not the qualifying factor. We use the term "to animate" when we mean "to bring life to" something, even if only a way of doing something, as in "He is an animated coach who inspires people."

People, animals, plants, and organisms are all assumed to be animate. We all agree that a rock or a telephone pole is inanimate. A telephone pole, on the other hand, is made of wood, which was once part of a tree, which is an animated, living thing. It's worth noting that the word "animate," when used as a verb, means "to give spirit or vigour to, to stimulate or enliven, to inspirit." Inspirit. In spirit, that is. As a result, this implies the existence of a spirit, such as a breath or force that gives life to an object.

Our planet was once uninhabited of life–a big, round rock that, when various natural forces such as storms, volcanoes, mighty quakes, or asteroids struck, suddenly resulted in the appearance of microbes and single–celled lifeforms that over the course of evolutionary history became the vast array of life we share the planet with today. We know that life is made of carbon, nitrogen, oxygen, hydrogen, phosphorus, and sulfur, and these elements are present in all things alive. These elements form bonds and building blocks of organic molecules that serve as the first complex forms of life, and it just keeps getting more complex as other things such as amino acids, lipids, and nucleobases create the foundations for RNA and DNA. Things are metabolized and catalyzed, and the end result is considered alive.

It's a pretty basic concept: the sculptor in this photo is animate, and the bust he is working on is inanimate. But the inanimate object was never alive, while the sculptor will one day become inanimate.

Add to this constant organic soup the fact that our planet was just the right distance from the sun to allow for life to form as we know it and describe it today, including things like viruses that have some of the properties

Can Animals and Robots Possess Consciousness?

Animals are alive, have sentience and feelings, and appear to be aware of their surroundings, but humans are divided on whether this equates to consciousness. We may never know unless we first figure out what consciousness is for humans and compare notes. When it comes to robots and artificial intelligence, the idea of a machine having consciousness appears impossible, if not terrifying.

With the addition of AI and advanced engineering, robots are becoming very human in appearance and actions, but can they possess true consciousness?

Philosophy Weighs In

Two final areas of interest involve animal and machine consciousness. In the former case it is clear that we have come a long way from the Cartesian view that animals are mere "automata" and that they do not even have conscious experience (perhaps partly because they do not have immortal souls). In addition to the obviously significant behavioral similarities between humans and many animals, much more is known today about other physiological similarities, such as brain and DNA structures. To be sure, there are important differences as well and there are, no doubt, some genuinely difficult "grey areas" where one might have legitimate doubts about some animal or organism consciousness, such as small rodents, some birds and fish, and especially various insects. Nonetheless, it seems fair to say that most philosophers today readily accept the fact that a significant portion of the animal kingdom is capable of having conscious mental states, though there are still notable exceptions to that rule. (Carruthers 2000, 2005)

From the Internet Encyclopedia of Philosophy
https://iep.utm.edu/consciousness/

of living, animated things, and others that make them more mechanical, driven by their interior chemistry. This leads us to ask whether matter itself, which we are all made up of, animate or inanimate, is a soul or consciousness that takes matter and animates it. Perhaps matter requires a system such as the body of a human or animal to interact and engage with to become animated. We are animate objects, but if we cut off our finger, would our finger be animated? Unless it were quickly attached back to the original hand, it would die and rot, but the hand would live on as long as it was still attached to the still-living body (the system).

Perhaps what determines life is more than elements and chemical reactions but rather a larger, bigger picture involving things we cannot measure or see–that "spirit" that is infused like the breath in our lungs to animate the inanimate.

THE SCIENCE OF DEATH IS NOT SETTLED

There are others in the scientific field who believe differently and point to the current laws of physics as denying the persistence of consciousness beyond death. Physicist Sean M. Carroll wrote in a May 23, 2011, guest blog, "Physics and the Immortality of the Soul," for *Scientific American* magazine, that "claims that some forms of consciousness persist after our bodies die and decay into their constituent atoms face one huge, insuperable obstacle: the laws of physics underlying everyday life are completely understood, and there's no way within those laws for the information stored in our brains to persist after we die. If you claim some form of soul persists beyond death, what particles is that soul made of? What forces are holding it together? How does it interact with ordinary matter?"

Carroll maintains that quantum field theory provides no reasonable answers to these questions, and that for a soul to exist in the way most people imagine it, "dramatically new physics" would be required to explain the form this soul energy would take and how it would interact with its environment.

Sean M. Carroll, Ph.D., is a theoretical physicist who has written on subjects as varied as cosmology, quantum mechanics, and philosophy. An atheist, he maintains that the laws of physics do not support the idea that a soul somehow survives death.

Rocket engineer Wernher von Braun, who graduated from the Berlin Institute of Technology and University of Berlin and designed the deadly V–2 rocket, later assisted the Americans and became the director of the U.S. Army's ballistic weapon program. He also helped the United States beat Russia in the space race as NASA's chief rocket scientist. He believed in life after death and stated in the 1967 book *The Third Book of Words to Live By* that the fundamental laws of the universe supported the existence of the afterlife and God. The engineer claimed that belief in the afterlife gives people the moral strength to become more ethical and that "in our modern world many people seem to feel that science has somehow made such 'religious ideas' untimely or old-fashioned.… But I think science has a real surprise for the sceptics. Science, for instance, tells us that nothing in nature, not even the tiniest particle, can disappear without a trace."

Von Braun believed in a continuity of spiritual existence after death. He also quoted Benjamin Franklin, who stated, "I believe that the soul of man is immortal and will be treated with justice in another life respecting its conduct in this."

Sam Parnia, M.D., Ph.D., director of critical care, and resuscitation research director of pulmonary, critical care, and sleep medicine at New York University Langone Medical Center, was interviewed by Robert Birchard for the New York Academy of Sciences in September of 2019. Parnia talked about death, which occurs when the heart stops beating. He was asked about the nature of consciousness, and he stated that traditionally, researchers proposed that the mind or consciousness, the self, is produced from organized brain activity. However, nobody was ever able to show how brain cells, which produce proteins, could produce something as complex as consciousness. Newer research raised the prospect that consciousness, the thing that makes you you, might not be produced by the brain, and the brain might be an intermediary.

Parnia said, "The fact that people seem to have full consciousness, with lucid well-structured thought processes and memory formation from a time when their brains are highly dysfunctional or even nonfunctional is perplexing and paradoxical. I do agree that this raises the possibility that the entity we call the mind or consciousness may not be produced by the brain. It's certainly possible there is another layer of reality we haven't yet discovered that's essentially beyond what we know of the brain, and which determines our reality."

Sounds like the idea of the grid.

Other researchers believe that quantum effects in the brain could explain consciousness. This is a decades-old theory that has sparked much debate, but new research may lend it more credence. In August of 2021, Thomas Lewton reported in his *New Scientist* article "Can Quantum Effects in the Brain Explain Consciousness?" on new research suggesting that quantum states in tiny proteins inside brain cells, called microtubules, might hold the key to what consciousness is and where it resides. The theory, called "orchestrated objection reduction," or Orch OR, was originally proposed by physicist Roger Penrose and anesthesiologist Stuart Hameroff in the 1990s. They wanted to bridge the gulf between matter and felt experience and showed that consciousness arises "when gravitational instabilities in the fundamental structure of space–time collapse quantum wave functions in tiny proteins called microtubules, which are found inside neurons." These tiny, hollow tubes could break down the space–time structure that interrupts quantum superposition and suggests a physical system can exist in two states at the same time.

If this research proved to be true, it could merge quantum mechanics, gravity, and consciousness in one theory. Critics of Orch OR believe that any quantum coherence inside microtubules would fall apart in the brain's warm, noisy grey matter before it could affect the workings of neurons.

Respected physicist Dr. Roger Penrose (pictured) and anesthesiologist Dr. Stuart Hameroff came up with the "orchestrated objection reduction" (Orch OR) theory that microtubules within neurons could exist in two states simultaneously, breaking down the barrier between matter and experience.

In 2020, Jack Tuszygarński of the University of Alberta and Aristide Dogariu of the University of Central Florida conducted an experiment that found when a light was shone on the microtubules, it was slowly re-emitted over the course of several minutes, which is a hallmark of what they stated were quantum "goings–on." Their reaction was that it was crazy, but additional research by Gregory Scholes, a Princeton biochemist, pointed to "long-lived, long-range collective behavior among molecules in the structure." Both teams of researchers planned to continue studying whether anesthetics, which work by switching consciousness on and off, have an impact on microtubules.

Jump to the April 18, 2022, *New Scientist* where Thomas Lewton now reported in "Quantum Experiments Add Weight to a Fringe Theory of Consciousness" that this theory passed a "key test" with experiments showing that anesthetic drugs reduce how long tiny structures found in brain cells can sustain suspected "quantum excitations." Again, these structures, known as microtubules, may open the door to our understanding of consciousness and its relation to quantum mechanics and how a system can exist in multiple states simultaneously.

More research is needed to determine whether the delay is due to quantum or classical physics, but it is clear that scientific understanding and knowledge change over time as new discoveries enter the fray and theories are proven or dropped and replaced with new ones. Perhaps the soul and/or consciousness will never be explained by today's scientific minds and methods because they transcend our level of understanding. Scientists and physicists may find it easy to dismiss the idea that when life ends, some part of us lives on, but this ignores a massive database of subjective, personal experiences that science struggles to fully explain.

The answers do exist. Unfortunately, we just won't know them until we die.

And Death Shall Have No Dominion
Dylan Thomas

And death shall have no dominion.
Dead men naked they shall be one
With the man in the wind and the west moon;
When their bones are picked clean and the clean
bones gone,
They shall have stars at elbow and foot;
Though they go mad they shall be sane,
Though they sink through the sea they shall rise
again;
Though lovers be lost love shall not;
And death shall have no dominion.
And death shall have no dominion.
Under the windings of the sea
They lying long shall not die windily;
Twisting on racks when sinews give way,
Strapped to a wheel, yet they shall not break;
Faith in their hands shall snap in two,

And the unicorn evils run them through;
Split all ends up they shan't crack;
And death shall have no dominion.
And death shall have no dominion.
No more may gulls cry at their ears
Or waves break loud on the seashore;
Where blew a flower may a flower no more
Lift its head to the blows of the rain;
Through they be mad and dead as nails,
Heads of the characters hammer through daisies;
Break in the sun till the sun breaks down,
And death shall have no dominion.

Near-Death Experiences, Prebirth Experiences, and Reincarnation

I felt the question of the afterlife was the black hole of the personal universe: something for which substantial proof of existence had been offered but which had not yet been explored in the proper way by scientists and philosophers.
—Raymond Moody

The chief problem about death, incidentally, is the fear there may be no afterlife—a depressing thought, particularly for those who have bothered to shave. Also, there is the fear that there is an afterlife but no one will know where it's being held.
—Woody Allen

Death is not extinguishing the light; it is putting out the lamp because dawn has come.
—Rabindranath Tagore

Belief does not equal fact. Even though there is no scientific proof of life after death, many people choose to believe in it for a variety of reasons. It provides them with solace. It alleviates some of the anxieties associated with death. It provides the opportunity for redemption, or the opportunity to get it right on another level, even returning to this plane of existence to do it all over again and possibly be reunited with loved ones.

Those who have died and come back have stories to tell. Those who have lived before have stories to tell. While

117

stories are not proof according to the scientific method, until science catches up, there is still so much we can learn about what might happen on the other side of life. Prebirth and near–death experiences suggest, if they are real, that we come from somewhere and go to somewhere when this current incarnation is over. They also speak of the concept of past lives and reincarnation–that we have lived before not as we are now but in other bodies and as other genders or races, in other times doing other things, and that we will continue to do this until we achieve some kind of liberation from the wheel of birth, life, death, rebirth.

When we are children, most of us have no recollection of a life prior to this one, but there are those who can and do recall a previous life, or an experience of being in the womb before birth and traveling down the birth canal until we pop out and get gently slapped by a friendly doctor. It makes sense to proceed in chronological order, so we'll begin here, with prebirth experiences and the possibility of previous lives we've lived before this one, the one in which we're reading this book.

PREBIRTH EXPERIENCES

A prebirth or near–birth experience is not a past–life recall. Prebirth experiences are memories or visions of what occurred before or during the act of birth, sometimes even as far back as being in the womb during a pregnancy. These are memories of preexistence and often involve going down a dark tunnel toward a light, then being born into that light, which no doubt represents the lights of a hospital or birthing room.

It might also include a memory of being connected by a cord to the mother's womb and involve memories of who was in the hospital room while the birth was happening. Skeptics state there is no way that an infant could be aware of their own birth or have infantile memories of the cord cutting or coming out of a tunnel into the light, but again there are many stories of those who years later not only remembered exactly that but more.

Even further back, some prebirth experiences involve being in a bardo or waiting state between the previous and current lives, where they choose the next incarnation, who they will be born to, and under what circumstances. Interestingly, Carl Sagan stated in 1979 that the near–death experiences that so many people report are memories of birth, an idea that was echoed by psychologist Barbara Honegger, who wrote in 1983 that out–of–body experiences (OBEs) could also be rebirth process memories or fantasies, particularly the symbolism of the umbilical cord of birth and the cord that is attached to the body while it travels during an OBE.

On the website *The Last Frontier: Exploring the Afterlife and Transforming Our Fear of Death*, research studies done with children show an awareness of their preconception existence regardless of their backgrounds. An article titled "Are We Hardwired to Believe We're Immortal?" by Barbara Moran of Boston University states that the idea some part of us will live forever is one that transcends race, religion, and culture. The article, written on January 29, 2014, pointed to a study that year published in the journal *Child Development* that examined the profound questions about children's ideas of a prelife before conception.

Researcher Natalie Emmons, a postdoctoral fellow at Boston University, interviewed 283 Ecuadorian children from an indigenous Shuar village in the Amazon Basin and two distinct cultures in Ecuador who did not have any cultural prelife beliefs or traditions. These children were exposed regularly to farm life and death and would have a more biologically based view of preconception. What she and the other researchers learned is that our bias toward a belief in immortality is something that emerges naturally early in life. Children believed, as did many adults, that when people died, their mental capacities and emotions continued in some form, even though their bodily needs ended upon death.

Emmons focused on the prelife period prior to conception since few cultures had any beliefs on this. "By focusing on prelife, we could see if culture causes these beliefs to appear, or if they appear simultaneously," she said. The Ecuadorian children, those from the Amazon Basin, and another group from an urban area near Quito were showed drawings of a baby, a young woman, the same woman pregnant, and then asked questions about the baby's abilities and memories in the womb and before birth. The results surprised her as

Astronomer Carl Sagan, who was famous for popularizing cosmology for the masses, believed that NDE's were merely memories of one's birth.

both groups gave similar answers despite different cultures and geographic influences. All the children reasoned that their bodies did not exist before birth and they were not able to think or remember, but both groups said their emotions and desires did exist before birth. Some children reported being happy about coming into the world and meeting their families, and some stated they were sad being apart from their families.

Perhaps the body dies, but feelings and emotions, especially desires, live on.

The prebirth experience can be felt by those who have already been born, including adults, and includes things like "announcing dreams," in which someone has a vivid dream with someone who announces they have not yet been born but will be soon. A person may have a persistent vision of someone they do not know, or hear a voice announcing a name, or receive a telepathic message from someone who is about to incarnate. A woman or man who wants to be a parent may have a vision of a baby or hear the name of a baby called out and then discover they are pregnant.

In the 2022 Disney movie *Soul* part of the plot involves a musician named Joe who dies accidentally and discovers that there is a world of pre-born souls waiting to get their personalities and assignments on Earth. This is not a new idea as many believe something like this does happen.

This brings up an interesting point. Are all ghostly sightings of those who have passed on, or could some be of those about to enter this realm as they navigate the in-between world? According to "Summary of Pre-Birth Experience Research" by Elizabeth and Neil Carman for *Cosmic Cradle*, "Pre-conception communications with the unborn portray the soul's desire for birth and highlight a remarkable process that begins to unfold before pregnancy. Creation of each human life begins to transpire on the level of a parent's cognition of the child's soul." Many people believe that a life begins at birth or even conception, so the idea that the life in question may begin long before either of these events may upset them.

The writers claim that preconception contacts have existed for as long as there have been people, and they claim that children's souls have been announcing their impending advent from a heavenly dwelling for months or even years. They suggest that talented people, even children, remember making plans for their existence on Earth and selecting their parents before assuming a physical form or growing a brain that can store information.

People who recall their own prebirth existence might, through hypnotic regression, journaling, or dreams, recall being escorted to Earth by a light being telling them of their mission. They might also experience flashbacks and visions of the womb or the tunnel of the birth canal, or of a "waiting area" before they were even conceived, where they chose their next mission and what body and family they would be born into. This speaks to the topic of soul contracts.

SOUL CONTRACTS

Before birth, our souls make agreements. These "preincarnation" contracts are between the individual and perhaps one or many other individuals about to incarnate that will create specific learning scenarios where all souls will benefit. These early agreements provide the soul with the kinds of learning experiences that they might not choose when already born because they may not understand the ongoing evolution of their own souls. There is a theory called Gaia philosophy, created by James Lovelock, that is based on the Greek Earth goddess Gaia and the belief that the organisms on the planet interact with their surroundings to affect their own nature and make their environments more hospitable to their own life conditions.

The general idea behind soul contracts is that a specific soul agrees to go through certain experiences with specific other souls. A woman might agree to meet and marry a man who will abuse her in order to learn to stand up for herself and discover her inner worth. A child may agree to be born to poor parents who love and care for their child and help him or her grow into a more compassionate person. A man may enter into a soul contract with two other souls in order to be born into a situation where they all become extremely successful in order to experience friendship, betrayal, failure, and resilience.

The general idea behind soul contracts is that a specific soul agrees to go through certain experiences with specific other souls.

These behind–the–scenes, or perhaps before–the–scenes, agreements serve a purpose for all involved, but the individuals do retain free will when they have incarnated and can choose to ignore the urgings and intuitions of their souls. Because the goal of said contracts is growth and evolution of the soul, it behooves everyone involved to stay attuned to their soul intuitions and promptings when meeting people or being given an opportunity where it just feels right or they feel they've known the person before, even if they've never met.

Soul agreements don't always lead to a positive outcome or lesson, and meeting up with someone you have a soul agreement with might not be the most pleasant of experiences. Often, the greatest lessons come from the most difficult challenges, and those involved have agreed to be a part of the process, even if it leads to your suffering. Couples might have a contract to marry and then divorce, if only to teach each other how to be better communicators or more empathic partners for their next loves. Someone might keep attracting narcissists into their lives as part of their contract to learn to stop being codependent.

However, discovering your soul contract and who is involved is not required to fulfill the agreements made before you incarnated. It may even impede your progress, but many people claim they simply know who they are in a contract with based on the patterns or experiences they encounter, sometimes repeatedly, and the feelings that arise that "this was meant to happen" or "this was meant to be." The most fertile ground for a soul's evolution may be with their families, and soul contracts with their families can be the most challenging and rewarding.

Once the purpose of the soul contract has been fulfilled, the people involved may leave your life for good, depending on their next spiritual evolution goals, and yours, too. This might explain why some people come into our lives for a short period of time, have a profound effect on us, then vanish. Others may stay for a longer period, or until "death do you part," as with long marriages or family members.

There is an argument that believing in soul contracts absolves you of much of the responsibility for making choices and acting on those choices in your life. When everything you do or everything that happens to you is accepted as part of a soul contract, it can remove the element of choice from the equation, especially when used as an excuse for laziness or inaction. Believing that everything was planned does not imply that everything was predestined. A soul contract is usually so compelling that you feel drawn to someone or something, and it helps to be in tune with your intuition and inner guidance so that you don't float along the river of life like a wine bottle cork with no volition of your own.

Having a sense of predetermined destiny is similar in that you feel as though you made choices and decisions before being born that were meant to guide you in a specific life direction. Those who are a part of your fulfillment of your destiny are most likely, then, people you have a soul contract with just as you are a part of the fulfillment of the destinies of others.

Aside from all the philosophical arguments for destiny or for free will, this all implies that you have existed before. If prebirth experiences show us what happened before conception and during birth, then we can go back even further to past lives we may have lived.

REINCARNATION

Have we lived other lives before this one? If so, can we recall those lives? Beyond the time of a soul's decision to in-

Reincarnation has become a familiar concept these days. It goes all the way back to ancient India, the Greeks, and the Celtic Druids, groups that had no communication with one another. Perhaps there is an innate sense in us that it is true.

carnate via birth, was there just a void from whence came the soul, fresh and virginal, ready to experience its first rodeo? Or did the soul exit stage left on one life and step into another one entirely, with different people and experiences, in a different city or country, and with a different body, gender, or ethnicity?

The religious or philosophical notion of reincarnation holds that our soul or spirit transfers from one incarnation to the next, taking a new physical body each time we go through life. According to certain philosophies, we can return as a person or an animal, and much of our new life is determined by the teachings or morals we retain from our previous life. Reincarnation is a major component of Eastern and modern traditions, including many indigenous cultures, but it is not an accepted concept in Christianity, Judaism, or Islam, all of which believe we can achieve immortal life with God but do not return to try again.

The word "reincarnation" comes from the Latin term for "to take on the flesh again" and has been discussed in the traditions of India and ancient Greece from as far back as the sixth century B.C.E. The idea of leaving one life and taking on another is centered on the growth and evolution of the soul. This suggests the soul or individual essence stays the same even as it takes on a new physical form or, as some traditions believe, a spiritual form without a body. Other words for reincarnation are "rebirth," "transmigration," and "metamorphosis."

Our cells die every seven to ten years, implying that we are constantly being reborn even while we exist in the body we have now. It is the consciousness, or what some refer to as the "I consciousness" part of us, that remains constant and unchangeable throughout this life, as well as previous and future ones.

Hinduism

Hindus believe in karma and the cycle of death and rebirth, which is samsara, and that your new incarnation is dependent on the type of karma you accumulated in the life that came before. A life of service will allow you to incarnate differently than a life of greed and violence. Hindus believe even the Gods or Devas can be reincarnated, and Lord Vishnu himself experienced ten incarnations. The Bhagavad Gita states, "Never was there a time when I did not exist, nor all these kings; nor in the future shall any of us cease to be. As the embodied soul continuously passes, in this body, from childhood to youth to old age, the soul similarly passes into another body at death. A sober person is not bewildered by such a change." It goes on to later state that "worn-out garments are shed by the body; worn-out bodies are shed by the dweller within the body. New bodies are donned by the dweller, like garments."

> *The Bhagavad Gita states, "Never was there a time when I did not exist, nor all these kings; nor in the future shall any of us cease to be."*

What a powerful visual image of reincarnation as a change of clothing on an ever-existing being, where the "embodied soul" keeps going beyond physical death.

In Jainism, the soul and matter are eternal and perpetual, uncreated and always in existence. The two are in a constant state of interaction leading to different manifestations in the physical and spiritual worlds. Change is not death to the spirit or matter, which is more of a transmigration and rebirth concept. After death, the life we know now moves into another form of life dependent on karma-like merits and demerits we earned in our current incarnation.

Jains believe the soul transmigrates within four *gatis*, or states of existence: *Deva*–demigods; *manussya*–humans; *naraki*–Hell beings; and *tiryanca*–animals, plants, and organisms. Each gati has its own corresponding realm in the vertically tiered universe of Jainism. These are also considered the four destinies of the soul depending on its karma, which decides how it will transmigrate and reincarnate within the whole universe. These four gatis are subdivided into still smaller categories, and there are, in Jain texts, a cycle of 8.4 million birth destinies souls can incarnate within during samsara.

Buddhism

Buddhism does not have a concept of an eternal soul or spirit or self. Instead, Buddhists believe in a consciousness stream that moves from one life to the next. This process of changing life is called *punarbhava* in Sanskrit, which means "becoming" or "becoming again." In early Buddhist texts, there is discussion of how to use meditation as a tool for recalling previous births, but there are warnings of the challenges of interpreting these experiences. Buddha taught that there is no self that ties these lives together, which is the opposite of what Hindus believe.

The expanding consciousness stream can be a contributing factor to the new life after death, and one way to image this is to imagine a candle flame that can be utilized to light another candle before it burns out. Awareness, rather than being a soul or spirit, becomes the continuation of birth and death, such that each new consciousness is not the same as the old but does include aspects of it to carry on the stream.

Western Traditions

All three of the monotheistic religious traditions do not in general accept the concept of reincarnation, at least as it is understood from an Eastern perspective. However, modern Sufis, Orthodox Jews, and gnostic Christian sects do embrace the concept, along with modern Spiritism, Theosophy, and followers of the mystical Kabbalah. For those who follow traditional Islam, Judaism, and Christianity, there is no concept of the soul going from one body to another and another along a line of soul evolution as there is in Hinduism. There may be eternal life in Heaven or Hell, depending on one's actions, similar to karma, but the soul doesn't jump into a new body as a new person in a new setting.

In the Buddhist tradition, there is no concept of a separate soul, a self. Instead, there is a consciousness stream that moves from life to life.

With the growing number of people in the West who identify as spiritual rather than religious, and the impact of the New Age/metaphysical community, which often blends the knowledge of the East with the wisdom of the West, believing in reincarnation has become significantly more acceptable and popular in Western cultures.

Reincarnation in the West was popularized by the work of Edgar Cayce (1877–1945), who became known as the "sleeping prophet." Cayce is perhaps the most documented psychic of the twentieth century, and for over 40 years he gave readings to thousands of people while in a "sleeping" or unconscious state. He was able to reveal past lives, diagnose illnesses, and even make future prophecies. The Association for Research and Enlightenment (A.R.E.) was founded in 1931 to spread his teachings, and it exists to this day.

According to the A.R.E. website, Cayce, who was born in Hopkinsville, Kentucky, in 1877, had psychic abilities since childhood and often claimed to see his grandfather's spirit, among others. He also had the strange ability to memorize the contents of a book by sleeping on it. He would put himself into a sleep-like state lying down on a couch and close his eyes, and in this meditative stage, he claimed he could put his mind into the universal consciousness to access all points in time and space and get the information he sought. He was also a devoted churchgoer and taught Sunday school.

Cayce's beliefs on reincarnation, which appeared over 2,000 times in his many readings, were, as he described it, "life readings that read the person's soul and look for relations with the universal energies latent in the person," which he referred to as the entity. However, his concentration was on discovering practical ways to better deal with current life by learning how past acts affected current conditions, and how to use that wisdom to find chances and overcome problems. He also believed in karma but viewed it as a soul memory rather than a "bank of information that the subconscious mind draws on and can use in the present." Cayce believed that when we die, our soul has an opportunity to take stock and determine what lessons it wants to learn next, choosing persons we may have known before (a soul group) but who will not be the same in the future incarnation. We can choose our gender to best serve the goal of our next existence.

PAST-LIFE RECALL

If we have lived many lives before, why do we not remember them in detail? Some people claim they have glimpses of a past life when they travel to a place they have never been before and know for sure they were there hundreds of years ago. Others might meet someone for the first time and get a vision of themselves with that person, albeit in clothing from a hundred years ago living in a village they've never been to. Children frequently recall memories that astound their parents because they appear to be recollections of things the child could not possibly know, such as a foreign language, a specific historical location, or a figure in the family's history they never met or were told about.

Spontaneous past–life recall occurs when we have a sudden insight or vision that seems to be real but involves things we couldn't possibly know or have experienced. This again might occur during travels or meeting new people but also as a persistent knowledge of a place or historical period of time that we have no explanation for. We might be obsessed with Scotland in the 1800s or the Civil War period beyond just normal curiosity or interest and feel like we are from that place or that time, despite any proof to back those feelings up. We just know we've been there before or have known that person before.

Most people access past lives through hypnosis, and past–life recall sessions were popular decades ago. The use of hypnosis allows for the retrieval of lost or suppressed memories from the subconscious mind and has been used to assist victims of violent crime in identifying a suspect and releasing trauma, as well as with those who claim to have been abducted by aliens but cannot remember the experience. Hypnotic regression can bring out lost memories in incredible detail that further research can later confirm. It's not proof of past lives, but it's an intriguing possibility for those who want to investigate it.

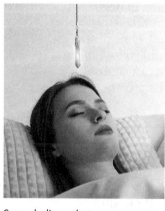

Some believe that we can access past lives through the technique of hypnosis.

There is the argument that past–life recall is more fantasy than reality. This may stem from people doing a hypnosis session and finding out they were a queen or king or pharaoh in a past life but rarely discovering they were a maid or maintenance man. You might argue that only the "great" past lives are worthy of being recalled, but if we accept the notion of reincarnation as the evolution of our souls, then shouldn't each life and the position or job we held matter? There is also the idea that accessing your past life can explain current phobias, illnesses, or fears. If you are terrified of water, you might find out you drowned in a tidal wave in a past life and use that information to process through the old trauma and finally release it.

One major argument against past–life recall is channeling, the idea that people might be channeling the spirits of someone and not their own past self. Like spirit communications, séances, and other methods of talking to the dead, a person could possibly be used as a vessel or conduit through which a spirit might come forth. This doesn't address the many stories of people seeing themselves, or at least recognizing that the person they are seeing IS themselves, in another place and time.

There are hundreds of fascinating stories in books and on the Internet of intriguing past–life recall, including those experienced by children. The most famous past–life recall comes from a woman named Virginia Tighe who recalled a past life as a woman named Bridey Murphy. Tighe underwent hypnosis between November of 1952 and August of 1953 and told her therapist, Morey Bernstein, an amateur hypnotist at the time, that over 100 years earlier she was an Irish woman named Bridget Murphy with the nickname Bridey. Over the course of their sessions, Tighe offered detailed conversations as Murphy, speaking with an Irish brogue and telling specifics about her life in nineteenth–century Ireland.

She gave a birthdate of 1798 and talked of her childhood in Cork with a Protestant family and her marriage to a man named Sean Brian Joseph McCarthy. She even talked about her own death in 1958 at the age of 60. When Tighe would come out of the hypnotic state, she would remember nothing, but many of the names, dates, and locations she provided were proven to exist. Despite this, no one could ever find a historical record of a Bridget or Bridey Murphy, but some say this could have been the result of poor record-keeping. It was discovered later that Tighe had grown up living near an Irish woman named Bridie Corkell who may have inspired her recollections as Bridey Murphy.

Then there is the case of a boy named Sujith in Sri Lanka who began at an early age telling his family he had a previous life where he was a man named Sammy. He gave specifics as to where he lived at the time and that he was a railroad worker and a dealer of bootleg whiskey known as arrack. He recalled that Sammy was killed by a truck after getting drunk and walking along a highway. Even when he was young, Sujith wanted to smoke cigarettes and drink arrack. His family didn't know anyone who fit any of the descriptions young Sujith gave. An investigation by a professor at the University of Virginia later confirmed up to 60 of the details of a man named Sammy Fernando who lived and died just months before Sujith was born, and when Sujith went to meet Sammy's family, he knew a great deal about them, including their pet names.

There are dozens of stories of parents who have a child who says something strange, if not downright eerie, that smacks of a past-life memory.

There are dozens of stories of parents who have a child who says something strange, if not downright eerie, that smacks of a past–life memory. In "Tales Told by Children Remembering Their Past Lives," Phylameana Iila Désy writes about a few of these for *Learn Religions*. One story comes from a mother. "Christian is my youngest, but he was born wise beyond his years. I can tell he is a very old soul. When my son was 4, I was making him a peanut butter and jelly sandwich one day for lunch. He said to me, 'That's not how my other mommy used to make my sandwiches. She did them differently.' A few days later he told me how he remembered coming down from Heaven with all the other babies, and God sent him to me."

Another person tells the story of his four–year–old brother, who told him that he missed his "old mom." Throughout the week, he would cry and say how much he missed his family. He claimed they were killed in a fire. He even remembered walking across the street to find his house on fire. When the brother was seven years old, he was unable to recall such memories. Do children arrive in this world with memories that fade quickly, allowing them to better assimilate into their current incarnation without confusion?

In 2014, a four–year–old boy named Andrew Lucas would not stop crying and asked his parents over and over again why they let him die in a fire. His mother, MicHelle, asked him about it, and Andrew recounted details of his past life as a Marine. MicHelle looked into the details her son gave her and suspected he was once Marine Sergeant Val Lewis, who died of a bomb attack in Lebanon in 1983. She and Andrew appeared on a television show called *The Ghost Inside My Child* during which Andrew was presented with several photographs of men in the military. He was able to pick out the photo of Lewis and later visited his gravesite with flowers.

Another intriguing story involved a girl named Barbro Karlén, who was only nine when Anne Frank died. From an early age, Barbro would insist that was not her real name and asked to be called Anne. She told her parents they were not her real parents. At the time, her parents did not know the story of Anne Frank and assumed their daughter was playing make-believe. When she was 10, her family visited Anne's home, and Barbro had no trouble navigating the area on her own, and after entering Anne's room, she resisted leaving. By the age of 12, Barbro had published a collection of poems that was well-liked throughout Sweden. She kept on writing despite always feeling that she wasn't who people believed she was. Years later, when Barbro met Buddy Elias, Anne's cousin, she learned that he thought she was Anne's reincarnation.

Barbro Karlén believed that she had the spirit of Holocaust victim Anne Frank (pictured) within her. Incredibly, when her family visited Frank's home, Barbro had no trouble finding her way around it.

One of the most well-known cases comes from Ian Stevenson, the world's foremost expert on reincarnation and past lives. In his book *European Cases of the Reincarnation Type*, he documented many cases, including the story of Laure Raynaud, who was born in Aumont, France, in 1868. She was born into a Catholic family but insisted there was no Heaven, Hell, or purgatory and that after death, people reincarnated in different bodies. At the age of 17, she moved to Paris to study medicine and become a healer, marrying in 1904.

While working at a Paris clinic she began talking about memories of a past life in a large, two-story house with arched windows in a place with a lot of sunshine. She described the location in detail and said that she was a 25-year-old over a hundred years earlier. She claimed to be plagued with a chest disease and coughing. Later, on a trip to Genoa, Italy, Laure felt a strange familiarity even though she had never been there. She found a house in the country that matched the one she spoke of years before and became convinced she once lived there as a Giovanna Spontini, who died in 1809 from a chronic illness. Stevenson did admit in his investigation that Laure could not recall specific names in her past–life memory until after she had done some research and that her knowledge of the house's architecture was common to Italian Renaissance mansions.

Are these people seeing glimpses into their own pasts, or are they seeing visions of the past based on a collective pool of memories? Can they be channeling people who lived before them, whose memories are now stored in a vast storehouse of information in a kind of quantum field to which we all have access but not all of us have the skills to tap?

Just as intriguing as past–life experiences are those that happen in the moments before, during, and after death.

DEATHBED VISIONS

Hospital workers and hospice nurses are close to those who are on their deathbeds. In "Life after Death" for the March 16, 2015, *Guideposts*, hospice nurse Trudy Harris wrote of her experiences with those about to pass over, including one 54–year–old woman who had inoperable cancer. The woman had her family around her and suddenly addressed Trudy, saying, "Ms. Nurse, this big angel comes and stands by my bed. Right there. He's always smiling at me." The woman pointed to a corner of the room and asked if the angel might be real. As a hospice nurse, Trudy had encountered other people at the end of their lives claiming to have seen something, and she was aware that it might be the effects of medication and exhaustion. But to these people, perhaps they truly were seeing someone, like her patient Frank, who was dying of lung disease and told her one day that his son was there with him, sitting in the chair by his bed, except that his son had died years before in Vietnam.

Another dying patient claimed he had been visited by his son, who was in prison and could not have possibly been there. Trudy realized that the closer her patients got to dying, the more, as she wrote, "their eyes and spirits seemed to open to a reality I glimpsed dimly. One after another, patients recounted not just visits from absent loved ones but an extraordinary awareness of God's presence."

One might think these deathbed visions are a result of end–of–life drugs, but in *At the Hour of Death: A New Look at Ev-*

idence for Life after Death by Karlis Osis, a physics professor, and Erlendur Haraldsson, a clinical psychologist, the authors studied over 5,000 cases of death–bed visitations culled from observations by 17,000 nurses and physicians and found that those on painkilling drugs were no more likely to have such visions. A history of psychoactive drugs did not increase the likelihood of these visions. They found that brain malfunctions were likely to reduce visions.

They also discovered that belief in the afterlife was not required for someone to have a deathbed visit, and that some patients who had these visits were unaware they were dying. "The visions frequently did not fit with the individuals' religious preconceptions," the authors wrote. "There was no evidence of Hell for Christians, and no visions for Hindus confirming their rebirth."

In the April 2018 LiveAboutDotCom article "Visions at the Hour of Death," Stephen Wagner documents the experiences of 13 people who had visions on their deathbeds. They included the experience of a mother who was dying and stared out the door of her room into the hall, asking, "Don't you see them? They walk the hall day and night. They are dead." Moments before her death that night, she said, "I have to go. They're here. They're waiting for me," as her face glowed and she tried to stand up. Her final words were "It is beautiful."

Another reader reported that while his brother–in–law was ill, he woke up from a nap and asked his wife if she had seen who had pinched his toe. His brother–in–law was ill and was now dying. He asserted that his mother, who had passed away, had pinched his toe despite his wife's insistence that she was the only person in the room. The man's mother used to wake him up like that for school. Shortly before he died, he claimed he saw his mother leave the room with the same long, black hair she had when he was a child. Another vision took place in 1979 when a woman's dying father was upset during breakfast. He said, "They came to get me last night," and pointed to the ceiling. When she asked who, the father yelled, "THEY! They came to get me!" He refused after that to sleep in his room.

Studies have shown that it doesn't matter whether someone is religious or not, or whether they are on painkillers, for them to have visions when they are close to death.

Other stories include a man who knew he was dying and requested a final beard trim and haircut. The majority of the visions appear to have provided some comfort to those left behind and involved the dying patient seeing one or more loved ones who had passed on or some type of angelic being ready to accompany them to the other side, but one has to wonder who the "They" were who so agitated the dying father in 1979, or if he simply didn't want to go with them.

These visions do bring up a good point for skeptics. If we see dead loved ones upon the moments of death or after we die, does that mean they refused to cross over into the light, or go on to the next level, until we died so they could greet us? This presents some logistical problems because if they are waiting for us, then it would imply they stay in a sort of waiting room until we show up, but what about the next to die, as in our children and children's children? Do these spirits wait forever and become a huge crowd of deceased ancestors who greet each person who dies? Or are they visions in our brains meant to make the process of letting go of the final gasp of breath and life a little easier?

Their eyes glowed, they had beatific smiles, and they frequently appeared to be seeing something out there that the others in the room couldn't see.

Nurses and doctors who care for the dying frequently report that the patient's face changes after death. Their eyes glowed, they had beatific smiles, and they frequently appeared to be seeing something out there that the others in the room couldn't see. They appeared to have had a deep sense of peace wash over them, which is a comforting thought for the rest of us, that our final moment will evoke such a deep sense of peace. Perhaps it doesn't matter whether the experience is a brain trick or something much deeper, as long as our transition leaves our eyes bright and our faces smiling.

Deathbed visions are not the only intriguing subjective and experiential proof that life goes on after the moment of death. People who see things when they are clinically dead for some period of time and then come back tell of their visions after being revived. These are called near–death experiences (NDEs) and have baffled the minds of scientists and researchers alike who debate on the origins and meanings of such events. For those who experience them, they are life-altering and profound.

NEAR-DEATH EXPERIENCES

With modern medical advances and technologies, we are living longer and surviving diseases and accidents that long ago would have meant certain death. It has become common to hear of someone who died on the hospital bed but was revived moments later and, while clinically dead, had visions and experiences of a reality beyond the one they momentarily slipped away from. That these visions and experiences have occurred all over the world and share some incredibly common traits furthers the debate between those who suggest this is just the brain going through its chemically reactive motions as it loses access to oxygen and begins to cease functioning and those who believe these are real and tangible glimpses of the afterlife.

The term "near–death experience" was coined by physician and psychologist Raymond Moody Jr., who wrote the seminal book about the phenomenon in 1975, *Life after Life*. Moody's book featured many cases of patients who had been pronounced clinically dead but were later revived and claimed that during their "death" they saw and heard things that defied known reality. The patient might have a specific interpretation of the events that transpired, and there were many differences, but there were also many similarities that ran across the board no matter the patient's age, gender, creed, or religious belief. Moody's research spanned thousands of cases and was continued by the Dr. John Dee Memorial Theater of the Mind in Alabama, among other organizations and scientists seeking the answers to this puzzling phenomenon.

Moody's initial work identified some common stages of an NDE:

- The sense of dying and being released from pain and suffering.

- The sensation of rising out of the body and looking down on it from above in the hospital bed or room.

- Passing through a dark tunnel toward a light at the end–similar to the birth process reported in prebirth experiences.

- Greeted by beings of light at the end of the tunnel, often the patient's deceased loved ones or a person understood as the founder/leader of the patient's religion, such as Jesus Christ.

- Life events flash before the patient's memory as if in a life review–some later cases stated this happened on a large screen like watching a movie.

- Wanting to stay in this place because it felt like Heaven but being told they must go back and return to life and that it "is not your time."

- Consciousness returning into the body and surprising the medical personnel or family members who thought they were dead.

A common experience among many of those reporting an NDE is being in a dark tunnel at the end of which is a bright light toward which they are drawn.

- Making life changes to account for the wisdom and understanding learned in the afterlife and becoming a more loving, better human being.

Thousands of Moody's cases matched this pattern, but skeptics were quick to point out that this could be the patient's own ideas, imaginings, or misinterpretations or expectations of the death process, and/or the effects of any drugs in the system at the time. In *Recollections of Death: A Medical Investigation*, Dr. Michael Sabom posits that these experiences were hallucinations due to heightened brain activity and happened more often in those patients who had been unconscious for at least 30 minutes, resulting in reduced neuroactivity. He also believed that these patients were accurately describing what they saw and that they were most likely hearing medical personnel discussing their deaths. Sabom compared a group of patients who reported NDEs with a control group of patients who had not had NDEs and discovered that the NDE patients' accounts of their own resuscitations were highly accurate, whereas the non–NDE patients' descriptions were far off from what actually happened.

A 2001 study in *The Lancet* medical journal reported that NDEs could not be explained by lack of oxygen to the brain, medications, or even a fear of death. But many medical professionals remain skeptical, while others become more open-minded as more research is done and more people experience an NDE. Some accept that NDEs might be a combination of the brain's chemical activity at death along with a true transcendent experience and that both are real and a part of the death process. Truth is, just because we cannot yet scientifically prove NDEs exist or don't exist or all of the mechanisms that cause them, it does not mean they are not real to those who experience them. Just as birth is the portal from the womb to external life in the world, death might also be a portal experience through the dark tunnel and into the light of what comes next.

THE OBE CONNECTION

Pam Reynolds of Atlanta, Georgia, underwent surgery for a brain aneurysm in 1991 and had blood drained from her brain. She was kept in a brain–dead state for 45 minutes during the surgery before being resuscitated. Reynolds was able to fully describe parts of the surgical procedure, including the bone saw used to remove part of her skull, while brain dead.

Was she having a true NDE and seeing the procedure from a higher vantage point, or could she perceive the sights and sounds of the surgery in an altered state of consciousness in her brain–dead state? Or did she have an out–of–body experience, which is frequently confused with an NDE?

Out–of–body experiences (OBEs) do feature similarities in that a person is able to leave their physical body to "astral travel" to other locations. They can happen spontaneously or through practice and effort, and involve getting into a relaxed state where an altered state of consciousness is achieved. Experienced OBEers report a silvery cord or string that attaches their traveling "self" to their physical body, a sort of anchor that, if broken, can result in trauma or death. This is not a feature of a classic NDE.

OBEs are also grouped in with things like lucid dreaming, where the dreamer is aware he or she is dreaming and has some control over the dream's outcome. Olaf Blanke, a Swiss–German neurologist at two university hospitals, worked with his team to study the brain activity of an epileptic woman who was having seizures for over ten years. His team found some interesting links to both NDEs and OBEs while conducting research to find the cause of the 43–year–old patient's epileptic seizures. Blanke did a brain mapping using electrodes planted on the brain to try to determine what part of the brain controlled which function and why when one region in particular was stimulated, the patient had a sudden OBE. She told Blanke she could see him from above working on her body.

If the information entering this part of the brain is disrupted during the sorting and filtering process, the result appears to be a misfire in the form of an OBE or even a déjà vu experience....

The angular gyrus, which is part of the temporal parietal junction, was stimulated at the time. He could then induce more OBEs by electrically stimulating this region, and the patient had an OBE each time. The temporal parietal junction oversees filtering information that enters the brain through our senses and converting it into a coherent form. This part of the brain is also in charge of our understanding and awareness of our bodies as well as where we are "located" in the space around us, which is referred to as "spatial awareness." If the information entering this part of the brain is disrupted during the sorting and filtering process, the result appears to be a misfire in the form of an OBE or even a déjà vu experience in which the person feels as if they have "been there, done that before." Many studies have found déjà vu to be a side effect of brain stimulation experimentation done on the same parts of the brain active during a grand mal epileptic seizure, as well as studies done with dimethyltrypamine (DMT) where the subject had a spontaneous déjà vu experience even though that was not the study's goal.

This study and its results mirrored earlier research done in the 1950s by American–Canadian neurosurgeon Wilder Penfield, who succeeded in eliciting OBEs using electrical stimulation on the part of the brain known as the sylvian fissure, which divides the temporal lobes from the rest of the brain lengthwise. This became known as the Penfield Effect. However, these studies and purposeful stimulations did not explain how such experiences could arise spontaneously such as most déjà vu and OBE experiences, or in the case of OBEs, at the will of a person seeking to experience one by going through their own process that does not involve electrodes on the brain in a clinical setting.

Other cases of OBE are documented in *Journeys Out of the Body* by Robert Monroe, which was based on his own OBE during an experiment where he described his spirit going into a hallway where he was able to accurately report that a lab technician who was supposed to be monitoring him was busy talking with another person instead.

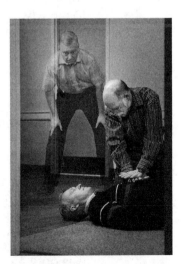

The silvery cord is not always mentioned in medical or spontaneous OBEs. Perhaps this is something more often utilized by people who actively engage in out-of-body travel who "imagine" the cord as a way to keep themselves safe and connected to their physical body during the process. Both OBEs and NDEs share the concept of being separate from one's body or a sense of detachment from the physical. Another similarity is that in some studies with critically ill patients who

People have reported observing their body from afar, watching doctors or others trying to revive them, and later, when they have been revived, could accurately report what went on while they were dead.

were removed from life support, there was a visible spike in neural activity at the moment of death, and seizures in the memory regions of the brain may have been responsible for the NDEs. There have also been numerous cases of NDEs in which the patient later stated that they did leave the body and hover over the operating table and could describe the process below, as if they had an OBE that then led to an NDE, implying that the two may be working in tandem.

While this helps to shine light on the brain activity during OBEs, it does not answer the question of how a brain-dead patient could travel out of the body to see her own surgery. It does, though, offer further subjective and circumstantial evidence for the belief that the body is not the home to our consciousness but rather to a vessel or conduit through which it flows.

In his article "The Enigma of the Near-Death Experience: A Survivor's Reflections on the Afterlife" for the July/August 2015 issue of *New Dawn* magazine, author Timothy Wyllie recounted his own death in the fall of 1973, when he was quite ill and took a bath to relax. It was then that he felt "plucked up and out of my pain-wracked body. Looking down, I could see my body lying in the tub about five or six hundred feet below me. There was no panic at all. I was completely at ease and fascinated by what was happening to me. My perception and thought processes were far clearer than anything I had ever experienced."

He had a few moments of "extraordinary clarity" and chose to return to his life but not before having incredible encounters with beings such as angels....

Wyllie saw the familiar blinding white light and sensed a form within it before hearing a male voice tell him he was dying. He was then given the option of continuing his journey or returning to his life, and he was told that he had completed his mission in this lifetime. At the time, he was only 33 years old. He had a few moments of "extraordinary clarity" and chose to return to his life but not before having incredible encounters with beings such as angels, which he later described as "more deeply meaningful than anything experienced in everyday life." He also stated that

Shot to Death and Lived to Talk about It

Author Marie was first exposed to the concept of NDEs back in 1978, when she was asked to come and talk to a teenage boy who had been shot in a violent crime, died, and came back from the dead after almost a half an hour. Names and locations are changed here to protect privacy, but the boy's story was different than most of the NDE experiences we read about where people feel a sense of peace and calm and reluctantly return into the bodies to continue their life's mission with more passion and love in their hearts.

This boy's experience was dark and violent and involved him passing through a dark tunnel toward a light, but never reaching the light. Instead, he entered an almost hellish state he could not wait to get away from. There were no angels or deceased relatives to greet him, and once he was resuscitated, he remained angry, fearful, and at times, violent. His mother was beside herself and hoped to get some advice and help, and she even let her son's story be told in a book that Marie would write, but he proved to be so difficult to work with that the book never happened.

Years later, they seemed to be doing better, and eventually Marie lost touch with them both. Still, the question remained, why was his NDE so different and so dark, even violent to an extent, compared to others? Was the violence of his own "death" a part of his experience or interpretation of what would happen to him after death? Marie later connected with the mother and learned that even before the incident, her son had been involved in some street crime and drugs, was an "angry young man," and had tried to take his own life once or twice. The family was not religious, so the taint of suicide that some religions believe will send you "straight to Hell" was not a factor.

It is a case that haunts Marie to this day because it goes against so much of what we have come to know about NDEs and their outcomes. Was he lying for attention? Or did this young man really experience something that was on the same level of his consciousness while alive?

the lucidity of the experience was difficult to convey to someone who had not had an NDE, which is echoed in many NDE stories. The experience's profound nature and incredible sensory aspects appear to push up against the limits of our vocabulary.

He was encouraged by more medical research on NDEs opening the door to people coming forward more freely to share their experiences and be taken more seriously.

More NDE Studies

Someone once said that understanding life was like trying to quickly put a jigsaw puzzle back into a box with one hand. You take a handful of pieces, but by the time your hand reaches the box, most of them have fallen back onto the table, leaving only three or four in the box. But if you do this enough times, you'll eventually get all of the puzzle pieces back into the box.

That is also how scientific research works, as more studies are carried out to fit more pieces into the box. Radiation oncologist Jeffrey Long wrote a book about the largest NDE study ever conducted, which revealed proof of life after death. *Evidence of the Afterlife: The Science of Near-Death Experiences*, coauthored with Paul Perry in 2010, examined the work of the Near–Death Experience Research Foundation (NDERF), where Long and his wife, Judy, gathered thousands of accounts from all over the world. With over 4,900 current cases, their website, NDERF.org, has become the largest NDE database in existence.

Jeffrey Long, M.D., is seen here being interviewed for the documentary *Hidden Beyond the Veil*, which examines NDEs from both religious and scientific perspectives.

The book documented Long's goal of compiling as many NDEs as he possibly could, and he did this via a questionnaire that allowed him to separate and study key elements of the experience. Even though he was in the scientific community, he realized that getting proof of NDEs was a different kind of animal. "In science, confirming the reality of a concept generally comes not from a single observation or study but from many independent studies with different methodologies. This cross–checking among scientific studies has always been the foundation for validating scientific discoveries. Thus, it is vitally important to note that the NDERF study findings are corroborated by hundreds of prior NDE studies conducted by scores of NDE researchers."

Even though these were personal experiences, the presence of such repeatability led Long to state that before embarking on this study, he asked one question: What is the key to understanding near-death experiences? When he was finished, he knew the solution was to listen carefully to people who had experienced an NDE. "They are, without a doubt, one of the best sources for understanding what awaits us on the verge of death and beyond." Long stated that once he realized this, he never looked back, and he believed our questions about our own mortality could very well be answered by these stories and the answers they provide.

NDERF Cases

This is a tiny sampling of the many thousands of cases on the Near-Death Experience Research Foundation website at NDERF.org.

- 2191. Paul C NDE 4/6/2010 & 4/22/22. NDE 4404/ 9383. I was surrounded by a very, very intense white light, and it seemed to crackle, almost "electrically," so to speak. The light encircled my form; it wrapped around the contour of my body, as I recall. NDE from heart attack.

- 5029. Dave C NDE 4/12/2022. NDE and Others 9380. From the United Kingdom. I remember being above my body, but still in the car, fully conscious of all around and with no fear, this kept me in good stead for future experiences.

  NDE following car crash, and several other experiences described.

- 5028. Lisette SL Probable NDE 4/12/2022. Probable NDE 9378. I felt only Love and joy and wanted to stay there. I felt entirely peaceful where I was in whatever state of consciousness that was outside of space and outside of time. Probable NDE at time of urgent caesarian section.

- 5024. Isaiah J NDE 3/26/2022. NDE 9368. This energy began to take form. I believe this was my guardian angel. We did not exchange words, but I knew so much information instantly. My guardian angel wanted me to return back to my body. I remember that I did not want to return.

NDE due to car accident.

- 5021. ErinRae G NDE 3/20/2022. NDE 9365. After looking at all that was below me, I looked up because I saw the brightest light I have ever seen but it didn't hurt to look at it. I saw what looked like clouds swirling around the light, almost like I was about to move towards the light, I felt something carrying me and I tried to look behind me, and as I did, a huge white (maybe an angel?) wing lifted in front of the light

NDE at age 4 due to drowning.

Long was especially intrigued by some of the cases reported in Raymond Moody's book *The Light Beyond*, which involved very lucid experiences by those who were brain-dead or whose hearts stopped on the operating table. A woman's experience was shared:

I found myself floating up toward the ceiling. I could see everyone around the bed very plainly, even my own body. I was fine and I wanted them to know that, but there seemed to be no way to let them know. It was as though there were a veil or a screen between me and the others in the room.

I became aware of an opening, if I can call it that. It appeared to be elongated and dark, and I began to zoom through it. I was puzzled yet exhilarated. I came out of this tunnel into a realm of soft, brilliant love and light. The love was everywhere. It surrounded me and seemed to soak through into my very being. At some point I was shown, or saw, the events of my life. They were in a kind of vast panorama. All of this is really just indescribable. People I know who had died were there with me in the light—a friend who had died in college, my grandfather, and a great-aunt, among others. They were happy, beaming.

I didn't want to go back, but I was told I had to by a man in light. I was being told I had not completed what I had to do in life.

I came back into my body with a sudden lurch.

This woman's experience covered all the elements Moody wrote were part of a classic NDE, and she told them in detail. Long was surprised because if she were dead as death is traditionally described, it should have been a permanent cessation of all functions, yet she and others like her were clearly recounting lucid events, even if they were unconscious or clinically dead.

Other NDEs Long recounted involved things like heightened senses during the experience, such as vivid vision and sound that were much clearer than in normal life. "Many NDEers indicate they have 360-degree vision during their experience, sometimes even more than that. The term '360-degrees' refers to two dimensions only, while NDEers often report spherical, three-dimensional spatial awareness simultaneously in all directions—forward, backward, right, left, above, and below." Long offered one example of a child named Ray who was knocked unconscious on the playground. Ray later stated, "I still had a 'body,' but it was entirely different. I could see in three dimensions as if I had no body at all but was just a floating eyeball, for lack of a better explanation. I could see all directions at once, yet there were no directions or dimensions as we think of them."

Other NDEers experienced a peaceful total silence, while others recounted sounds unlike anything they had ever heard in life. "I heard a sound and it wasn't like the sound we hear with our ears," one NDEer wrote. "It didn't seem to be coming from anywhere; it was just there. It did not seem to be there because of vibration or wind or anything. I can't describe it."

The inability to fully describe the NDE is a common one, suggesting these experiences truly transcend anything our limited waking-state consciousness is exposed to.

Long discussed and provided examples of the life review stage. One of these came from a man named Roger, who had died in a car accident:

> I went into a dark place with nothing around me, but I wasn't scared. It was really peaceful there. I then began to see my whole life unfolding before me like a film projected on a screen, from baby-

hood to adult life. It was so real! I was looking at myself, but better than a 3–D movie as I was also capable of seeing the feelings of the persons I had interacted with through the years. I could feel the good and bad emotions I made them go through. I was also capable of seeing that the better I made them feel, and the better the emotions they had because of me, the more credit (karma) I would ac-cumulate and that the bad emotions would take some of it back … just like a bank account, but here it was like a karma account to my knowledge.

This karma connection was found in numerous other cases. Long examined, as if there is a squaring up of our lives after death before we can move on to the next. However, Dr. Susan Blackmore, a leading NDE skeptic, attributed these life reviews to "a psychological defense mechanism at the time of a life–threatening event that involves a retreat into a time-less moment of pleasant, prior memories." Long states that this might be a good explanation until one begins encoun-tering NDE memories that are not pleasant. "Such content would not be expected if the life review were simply a pleas-urable psychological escape from unpleasant circumstances."

Dr. Susan Blackmore, a parapsychol-ogist, broadcaster, and lecturer, is a leading researcher in memetics. She has been a vocal critic of NDEs, be-lieving they are a psychological de-fense against trauma.

When it comes to children, Long looked at many convincing cases of all ages and stated that "very young children have every NDE element that older children and adults have in their NDEs." He also quoted Dr. Cherie Sutherland, an NDE researcher, who reviewed 30 years of scholarly research on NDEs in children, especially very young children. "It has often been supposed that the NDEs of very young children will have a content lim-ited to their vocabulary. However, it is now clear that the age of children at the time of their NDE does not in any way determine its complexity." She continued by stating that age did not appear to alter the content of an NDE and that prelinguistic youngsters were later able to recall complicated experiences.

Long's findings offer the promise of hope for those who want to believe in the af-terlife, that there is a place of peace, comfort, and joy that dissipates fear of death but also transforms the current life into something more vibrant and makes those who have been on the other side far more appreciative and grateful for their loved ones and life choices. As one NDEer, Lauren, stated, "I am no longer afraid of death. I know now in my soul that there is so much more after life. I feel that once I have learned what it is I am supposed to learn or a task that I must complete, that I will be rewarded with a life after death!" Another woman, Sharla, stated, "The most significant part of the experience is that there is (to me) nothing to fear of death."

On the NDERF.org website, there is a plethora of updated information, including an FAQ that answers many questions about NDEs, case studies in every language imaginable, resources, and a form to submit an NDE.

DR. EBEN ALEXANDER'S STORY

It's one thing when an NDE occurs in someone who isn't a scientist or doctor, and quite another when it occurs in someone who is. One of the most well-known NDE cases in modern times is that of neurosurgeon Eben Alexander, who wrote about it in his *New York Times* best-selling book *Proof of Heaven: A Neurosurgeon's Journey into the Afterlife*, which was published in 2012. Alexander experienced his own NDE in 2008, when he became ill with microbial meningitis and fell into a seven-day coma.

Alexander had been an academic neurosurgeon for 25 years when he wrote his book about his amazing NDE, including 15 years at Brigham & Women's and Children's Hospitals in Boston, as well as Harvard Medical School. During his illness, he, like any other scientist, was skeptical of the NDE phenomenon. But, while his brain was shutting down and he was in a coma for seven days, he had a profound experience. He had always believed that NDEs occurred primarily in people whose hearts had stopped. Here he was, with no neocortex functioning at all, experiencing something far beyond the physical brain's boundaries.

He wrote, "As a practicing neurosurgeon with decades of research and hands-on work in the operating room behind me, I was in a

Dr. Eben Alexander is shown here giving a talk on the Theosophical Society's YouTube channel titled *Eben Alexander: A Neurosurgeon's Journey through the Afterlife.*

better-than-average position to judge not only the reality but also the implications of what happened to me. Those implications are tremendous beyond description. My experience showed me that the death of the body and the brain are not the end of consciousness, that human experience continues beyond the grave. More important, it continues under the gaze of a God who loves and cares about each one of us and about where the universe itself and all the beings within it are ultimately going."

Alexander stated that the location he visited was real, making waking life appear dreamlike in comparison. Like many others who have had NDEs, it made him appreciate life even more when he returned to it. He described his experience as "dream-like," but he knew it wasn't. He remembered beautiful music unlike anything he'd ever heard before, as well as a light that spun closer. He couldn't quite focus on something in the center of the light, but he ended up passing through it and moving quickly upward. He was in a beautiful new world after passing through the opening, which he described as "brilliant, vibrant, ecstatic, stunning...."

He felt as if he were being born, and he flew over streams and trees and waterways, seeing children playing below him, people singing and dancing, beautifully dressed and filled with joy. He described it as a "beautiful, incredible dream world.... Except it wasn't a dream" and he flew along, then realized there was a presence next to him, that of a beautiful girl with deep blue eyes. They rode along together on "an intricately patterned surface, alive with indescribable and vivid colors...." The girl spoke to him without words and gave him a message he immediately understood as true. The message had three parts:

- "You are loved and cherished, dearly, forever."
- "You have nothing to fear."
- "There is nothing you can do wrong."

He felt a wave of relief wash over him and was then told that after seeing many things, he would have to return. But first, he came across a place of clouds and flocks of transparent orbs, shimmering beings, and entities he couldn't quite describe but knew were of a higher realm. He also encountered an enormous void that was completely dark but infinite in size, which brought him comfort. As dark as it was, he claimed it was also filled with light from a nearby orb. He was aware of the presence of a God or Being, as well as unconditional love. His experience was one of positivity, joy, and light, and when he returned, he wrote his book and became something of an NDE celebrity, offering hope and comfort to millions of people.

His NDE contained many of the typical NDE elements, except one. He did not recall his earthly identity. He believes this allowed him to go deeper into his NDE without the hesitation of remembering his real life.

Depending on whom you talk to, consciousness is either the greatest mystery facing scientific enquiry or a total nonproblem.

Having a medical scientist or researcher witness such a profound event lends the subject credibility that a common Jane or Joe does not have. This is similar to the field of ufology, where sightings of UFOs by captains, pilots, and military officials carry more weight than those of ordinary people driving down the street on a Sunday evening. Alexander, later in the book, states that his experience changed his thoughts on consciousness, too. "The further I dug, the more convinced I became that my discovery wasn't just interesting and dramatic, it was scientific. Depending on whom you talk to, consciousness is either the greatest mystery facing scientific enquiry or a total nonproblem. What's surprising is just how many more scientists think it is the latter. For many–maybe most–scientists, consciousness isn't really worth worrying about because it is just a by-product of physical processes. Many scientists go further, saying that not only is consciousness a secondary phenomenon, but that in addition, it's not even real." He went on to state that we have lost touch with the "deep mystery at the center of existence–our consciousness."

Nonetheless, for the majority of his career, he refused to consider anything outside of accepted science, such as the soul, God, the afterlife, and Heaven, as well as paranormal and psi experiences such as ESP, remote viewing, and psychic phenomena. That is, until he had his own profoundly deep experience with something ordinary science couldn't explain.

Healthy skepticism is necessary for truly understanding NDEs because it does no one any good to throw out a theory with too many holes and gaps to fill. Men and women of science who conduct research on this topic must avoid the bias of proving or disproving but rather look for evidence of both. As much as we all want to believe that Alexander's experience is what we can all expect, we want to believe it not because of false hopes and promises but because there is something tangible that says life after death exists.

THE PSYCHOACTIVE LINK TO NDES

An article by Robert Martone in the September 10, 2019, issue *Scientific American* titled "New Clues Found in Understanding Near–Death Experiences" found interesting parallels between NDEs and the effects of psychoactive drugs, including having one's life flash before the eyes and the sensation of leaving the body, seeing one's own face and body, and moving through a tunnel toward a light, feeling "at one" with something universal.

Because these experiences are universal, regardless of region, religion, or creed, it is possible that NDEs are linked to brain functions and chemical reactions at the moment of death. Many cultures use drugs to produce the same sensations and experiences as an NDE, but it is nearly impossible to study those who are having an NDE in real time ethically because it would involve someone having to die and hopefully come back from death without brain damage. In many states, using drugs to induce religious states is illegal.

Use of psychoactive drugs—synthesized, for example, from psylocibin mushrooms (pictured)—can provide visions that prove therapeutic to some, and these experiences have been compared to NDEs.

We do have NDE stories that can be studied for linguistic analysis. In a new study that compared 625 NDE stories with those of over 15,000 people who had taken a psychoactive drug, linguistic analyses showed similarities between the recollections of NDEs and the experiences of those who had taken a specific class of drug. Ketamine was the most successful in creating similar experiences to an NDE, suggesting that ketamine creates the same chemical changes in the brain.

The article states, "To compare NDEs with drug experiences, the researchers took advantage of a large collection of drug experience anecdotes found in the Erowid Experience Vaults, an open–source collection of accounts describing firsthand experiences with drugs and various substances." The recollections of those who experienced NDEs and those who took drugs were compared linguistically. Their stories were broken down into individual words that were sorted according to their meaning and counted. "In this way, researchers were able to compare the number of times words having the same meaning were used in each story. They used this numerical analysis of story content to compare the content of drug–related and near–death experiences."

There were very few similarities reported between the NDEs and stimulants and depressants. The experiences most similar to NDEs occurred with the use of hallucinogens, psychedelics, antipsychotics, and deliriants, with hallucinogens and psychedelics showing the most similarities, and the hallucinogen ketamine with the highest similarity to NDEs. Two other hallucinogens, LSD and DMT, have been linked to similar NDE experiences.

These studies, though subjective, give us intriguing insights to the connection between brain chemical activity, induced or natural, and the sensation of having an NDE and suggest that what people experience when they die may be some kind of brain "high."

OTHER NDE DESCRIPTIONS

Those who have NDEs see and hear many of the same things while they are clinically dead, but some veer from the norm. There are the usual "I was floating above my bed and saw the doctors talking over my body" reports, and the dark tunnel leading to the light, but some variations are quite interesting. In Lorenzo Jensen III's August 9, 2017, article "24 People Who Were Clinically Dead Describe What They Saw Before They Were Revived" for *Thought Catalog*, he lists some intriguing variations, many of which involved seeing lots of stars or a darkness that was comforting. Others involve a heightened sense of vision or perception of sound.

"I had a dream I was flying all over us. There were so many pretty people. So many pretty faces. I talked to some birds. I fell in love again...."

"I remember the feeling of falling down into a small spark of light that got bigger. It fractured into an infinite number of stars."

"An indescribable blue–white light.… No sensation of a physical body … it's like my essence was distilled to its original, perfect concept."

"All I saw was blackness, followed by many lights, lights became stars and stars turned into something I cannot describe."

"I felt nothing but unspeakable peace and joy for a second.…"

People clearly see and feel different things during an NDE, as shown by the huge difference between being in complete darkness and seeing millions of stars. Could it have something to do with their own chemical makeup in their brains or whether they were on drugs at the time? Could the cause of their death have played a role? Were they truly dead, or were they having an OBE and alive in another reality or state of consciousness? The majority of NDEs appear to share some commonalities, such as messages from the other side confirming that life does go on and we will see our loved ones again. The proliferation of discussion groups on sites like Facebook, Reddit, and Quora, where people have their own stories to tell, is a telling sign of how many people have had an NDE or want to know more about the afterlife. People who post on these sites frequently have recently lost a loved one and are reaching out in grief and sorrow. They want some solace and hope that their loved one is in a better place and that they, too, should not be afraid of death when the time comes. Others have had their own unique experience and want to share it with the world, or they want to ask questions and compare notes.

Hopefully one day science will definitively prove one way or the other what these experiences really are, but for now, they do provide hope and comfort as we all face our own mortality. Like the paranormal and UFOs, NDEs and life after death, the existence of the soul, the location of consciousness, and so many other related factors might continue to come down to personal experience and faith.

Then there's the question of whether we're really meant to understand all of life's and death's mysteries.

NDES AND THE MOVIES

There are dozens of documentaries about NDEs and a number of recent movies that tackle the subject. Here is a sampling:

- *Dragonfly* (2002): Dragonfly tells the story of a doctor who is contacted by his dead wife through his patients' near-death experiences.

- *Afterlife* (2011): Director Paul Perry allegedly used real research into NDEs for this documentary that includes interviews with near-death researchers, case studies of people who have had NDEs, event re-creations, and spiritual artwork by NDE experiencers.

- *Heaven Is for Real* (2014): The true story of a four-year-old child who dies and enters Heaven during emergency surgery. When he regains consciousness, he tells his story about life beyond death. Based on the book by Lynn Vincent about her own son's NDE.

- *Garnet's Gold* (2014): The story of a man who had an NDE and the mysterious stick he discovered before he was rescued and who now seeks to find it again.

Connor Corum (right) plays a four-year-old child who sees the afterlife during surgery, much to the amazement of his father (played by Greg Kinnear) in *Heaven Is for Real*.

- *The Channel* (2016): A horror offering in which a teenager becomes a channel for an evil spirit after she experiences an NDE.

- *Let There Be Light* (2017): An atheist has an NDE after an auto accident and reverts to Christianity. Starring and directed by Kevin Sorbo.

- *Surviving Death* (2021): A Netflix documentary series with interviews and re-creations of stories of those who have had NDEs and who believe they have been reincarnated.

Ghosts in the Afterlife

In sorrow we must go, but not in despair. Behold! We are not bound for ever to the circles of the world, and beyond them is more than memory.
–J. R. R. Tolkien

What happens after death is so unspeakably glorious that our imagination and our feelings do not suffice to form even an approximate conception of it. The dissolution of our time-bound form in eternity brings no loss of meaning.
–Carl Jung

Death is the greatest illusion of all.
–Osho Rajneesh

Have you ever seen the ghost of a loved one who has passed away? If so, you are not alone. Ghostly sightings of those we loved and lost have become the norm, and people are no longer mocked when they admit to a visitation from a deceased relative or pet. They are usually met with, "Oh, that happened to me, too." Even those who have never seen the ghost of someone they loved are likely to wish to do so. Why? Because seeing the apparition of someone who has died again would instill a strong belief in the afterlife and provide hope for what is to come after we die. A ghost, at the very least, represents someone caught in limbo who has not yet passed over into the light or, depending on one's religious beliefs, received their ticket to Heaven or Hell.

155

According to Merriam–Webster, the word "ghost" means "a disembodied soul; especially: the soul of a dead person believed to be an inhabitant of the unseen world or to appear to the living in bodily likeness." The word has been inextricably linked to the concept of the essence or spirit of a dead person. Ghosts have not accepted death and crossed over into the light, instead choosing to haunt their old hangouts and loved ones, trapped between worlds. The English word "ghost" has roots in the Old English "gast" from the common Germanic "gaistaz." In Old Norse, the word "geisa," which like the pre–Germanic "ghoisdo-s," meant "fury, anger ... to rage." The word "ghost" is synonymous with the Old English "spiritus," which means "breath, blast," which then became the more modern "soul of the deceased" or "spirit of the dead." By looking at the original association with anger and rage, we might get the impression most ghosts are not happy being caught between the worlds of life and death or harbor anger and resentment from their time on Earth that may end up as negative, even destructive hauntings in an attempt to exact revenge on the living.

Ghosts are a universal phenomenon that have been reported for thousands of years in every culture, religion, and nation on Earth.

Every culture, religion, and belief system have a place for ghosts and spirits of the dead within their myths, traditions, and rites. Ghosts are a universal phenomenon that have been reported for thousands of years in every culture, religion, and nation on Earth. People of all walks of life, ages, genders, races, and social status have seen or had encounters with ghosts. The idea that we somehow transcend death is a global and primitive one. Literature, movies, novels, operas, and every other possible form of entertainment are filled with ghostly tales, whether frightening, comedic, or tragic. We love a good ghost story, no matter how it is told.

In 1882, the Society for Psychical Research (SPR) was founded in England to focus on collecting data of such phenomena for the purpose of presenting scholarly investigation and discourse. After four years, the society published its first report, a two–volume, 1,400-page summary of 700 cases later updated by Eleanor Sidgwick in 1923 in a revised edition,

Phantasms of the Living. These reports included cases of ghostly hauntings from all over England and could be considered the precursor to the current ghost hunting phenomenon.

Still, we might ask, what exactly is a ghost, and is there more than one fitting explanation?

1: *Ghosts are spirits of the deceased.* This is the most popular and widely accepted explanation and the concept that guides most paranormal research. There is an overwhelming amount of anecdotal and experiential evidence recorded throughout the ages, not to mention pop culture with hundreds of ghost-related movies, novels, and television shows, that suggest a ghost is a dead person's spirit. We are obsessed by ghosts and ghost stories as proof that life beyond death exists even when presented as horror movies or scary tales told over a campfire.

Many people have their own personal experiences where they believe they have seen, heard, smelled, or felt the presence of a departed loved one. Some even report seeing a ghostly figure of a loved one in their home or at their bedside at a particular time, only to find out later this was the exact time of death. These hauntings may be prescient or precognitive in nature, as many of these experiences impart or transfer vital information to the living or are meant to calm the living, maybe even say goodbye one last time, a common report among those who claim to have been visited by loved ones at the time of their deaths.

We know from quantum mechanics theories–specifically, Einstein's "spooky action at a distance" and quantum entanglement–that two objects, once entangled, can still influence each other even when separated with no known intermediary. Is it a stretch to believe that humans can also become "entangled," possibly as a result of some unknown form of emotional bonding, while continuing to influence each other across vast physical (or even etheric) distances? Is there a grid-like infrastructure connecting us, and could this connection transcend life itself, with each level of the grid simply another level of existence we experience before or after this incarnation's death?

Ghosts don't have to be scary and malevolent beings as in many horror movies and TV shows. Many people say they have been visited by the spirits of their departed loved ones.

According to the first law of thermodynamics, energy does not cease to exist; rather, it changes form within a system or transfers to another system. If ghosts are the essence of the dead, they could be energy manifesting itself to us from within the framework of another system. There is so much about energy and matter that we still don't understand before we can truly determine what happens to our "soul" and even consciousness after death.

This law of physics might also help explain ghostly apparitions of inanimate objects, such as cars, trains, and mysterious ships that have appeared to people for centuries. Physical objects, such as cars, do not have life, but they do have energy, and these objects that continue to appear could be stored or imprinted energy, or even a holographic projection that has "looped" into the environment from another, higher dimension.

2: Ghosts are caused by things in the environment such as electrical, magnetic, or electromagnetic fields and weather conditions. For years, ghost hunters have used technology as a means to measure and analyze environmental factors such as weather, barometric pressure, humidity, and electromagnetic field levels that might be conducive to a paranormal event. The most popular tool used by ghost hunters is an electromagnetic field meter (EMF). This device, originally designed for measuring AC or DC electromagnetic field strength, is often used to "prove" that a ghost is nearby, even though there is no scientific evidence for such a claim. While most consumer grade meters on the market measure the electromagnetic radiation flux density of DC fields, or the difference in an AC field over time, they essentially function as a type of simple radio antenna, albeit with distinct detection abilities. Interestingly, most meters are calibrated to measure 50hz or 60hz, which is the frequency of U.S. and European AC mains electricity. There are no legitimate scientific studies that conclusively link EM fields to the detection of ghosts or other paranormal phenomena, although admittedly there is no legitimate scientific study being conducted, as there should be. Electromagnetic fields certainly might play a role in the *perception* of ghosts as we do know they effect the human brain.

3: Ghosts are trapped emotions and energy playing back in a loop that is present in a location and "recorded" into the environment. This is called a *residual haunting*, the most common type of haunting. A residual haunting is a visual or auditory signature that has somehow been imprinted (or recorded) into the environment, which can be a room, a wall, or an outdoor grave site and played back in a continuous loop. This phenomenon is usually attributed to a visual manifestation appearing to replicate the same actions continually as if watching the same movie clip over and over. The second law of thermodynamics states that although the quantity of matter and energy remains the same, the *quality* deteriorates over time. This could explain countless reports of faded or semitranslucent apparitions that appear to blink in and out of view, as if the energy behind the apparition is not consistent in strength. Furthermore, this theory begs the question of whether human emotion may be a form of energy powerful enough to be imprinted onto the environment.

4: *Ghosts are alive and active in alternate dimensions or realities.* If the universe is infinite in size and scope, who knows what is out there? Who knows if our universe is the only universe? In 1895, American philosopher and psychologist William James coined the term *multiverse* when referring to the hypothetical set of possible universes and realities. According to the theory, these multiple universes comprise the entirety of time, space, energy, and matter, and each one has its own set of physical laws and constants. The multiverse theory was later expanded by cosmologist Max Tegmark, who believed there are many other universes beyond the observable universe and helped pave the way for other theories such as the M-Theory and Hugh Everett's "many-worlds interpretation."

A ghostly apparition may not be the essence of someone who is dead but rather a real, live person we witness in another dimension or parallel universe. We may also see time travelers, or people from the past or future, who appear to us as erratic, flickering, fuzzy, and ghostly images of what is, on the other side, a perfectly solid person. This theory could also apply to ghost trains, planes, and automobiles, all of which could be active in other levels of reality.

5: *Ghosts are figments of our imaginations.* This theory is also known as the "is it all in our heads" theory. Considering the thousands of reported incidents as well as the similarities among them, this suggestion seems silly on the surface, particularly because ghosts and other anomalous phenomena have been documented and described since the dawn of time. Have every single one of these reports simply been fanciful imaginings or hallucinations?

Are ghosts just illusions, the result of your imagination? Or perhaps they are strange weather phenomena. Spookier yet would be that they are images of people from other dimensions of time or space.

What role does preconception and expectation play in this equation? If you are told that a location you are in is haunted, or if you are grieving the passing of a loved one, would that make you more likely to have a paranormal experience? Perhaps the trauma and emotion of dealing with death might be the trigger that allows someone who wants to see a ghost so badly to actually see one.

6: Ghosts are generated by the right blend of brain chemicals. Dopamine, serotonin, acetylcholine—these are but a few of the chemical substances present in the incredibly complex human brain. Some researchers believe that the perception of ghosts can simply be explained as a chemically induced hallucination or delusion. Peter Brugger, a neurologist from the University Hospital in Zurich, Switzerland, conducted studies showing that a direct correlation exists between increased levels of dopamine and paranormal beliefs. In the experiment, Brugger recruited 20 "believers" and 20 "nonbelievers" and asked them to distinguish real faces from scrambled faces that were briefly shown on a screen. They then repeated the process by distinguishing between real and fake words. Not surprisingly, "believers" were much more likely than "nonbelievers" to see a word or face where none existed. What about the "nonbelievers"? They were far more likely to overlook the genuine faces and words displayed.

Rick Strassman, M.D., a psychiatrist from the University of New Mexico School of Medicine, conducted an 11-year study using dimethyltryptamine (DMT), one of the principal ingredients found in ayahuasca, the shaman's brew that causes hallucinogenic trips and visions among both natives and curious tourists eager to see beyond the veil of normal perception. DMT has also been associated with experiments discussed earlier that induced NDEs. The human brain contains a trace amount of DMT, and if triggered by some internal or external event, it could lead us to perceive a ghost, have an NDE or OBE, or experience déjà vu, as Strassman discovered. This doesn't quite explain how a person's DMT is activated in a natural setting without a source of stimulation.

Ghosts can be exactly what we think they are: the essence or spirit of a deceased person who is still in limbo and has not yet passed on to the light, or they can be something entirely different. Our belief in ghosts is directly related to our desire for proof that we do not simply fade to black after death, but that we continue to exist in some form–any form. Perhaps our belief in ghosts is what causes them to appear because they represent one of the most profound of questions: what happens after we die?

If you are fortunate enough to see the ghost of a loved one, hopefully it is a pleasant ghost, or at the very least a ghost who is unaware of your presence. There are various types of ghost reports that seem to indicate that not everyone in the afterlife is overjoyed to be there!

Another possible explanation for ghosts is sleep paralysis. Sleep paralysis "is like dreaming with your eyes open," explains neuroscientist Baland Jalal, who did studies of sleep paralysis at the University of Cambridge in England. During rapid eye movement (REM) sleep, our eyes dart around under closed lids. Our eyes can move, but our bodies are paralyzed. Jalal believes this is to stop us from acting out our dreams. In this in–between state, your consciousness can make you believe you are experiencing things that do not occur in your normal waking state.

David Smailes, a psychologist at North Umbria University in Newcastle–upon–Tyne, England, thinks misinterpretations of normal things that occur to all of us could give the impression we are seeing ghosts. One of these examples of misinterpretation is pareidolia, which is seeing patterns or objects where there is chaotic disorder, such as a wild wallpaper on a wall where you insist you see a face or a lion, or clouds in the sky that look like sheep or a child's wagon. The brain is bombarded with information and seeks patterns that are recognizable as a way to make sense of the environment.

This is known as bottom–up processing. We sometimes find meaning in the most insignificant things. The brain also processes information from the top down. It adds to our understanding of the world. The reticular activating system (RAS) of the brain is in charge of taking in all that information and filtering out what is important, and when a pattern is detected, it often becomes important. If the RAS did not do this, our brains would malfunction from overuse. As a result, the brain finds the most important information, filters out the rest, and fills in any gaps that may exist. The brain fills in

Optical illusions are good examples of how our brains try to fill in information that is not there. In this Kanisza triangle (pictured), for example, shapes are arranged in a way that fools the brain into perceiving there is a triangle in the middle even though nothing is actually there. We might be doing something similar when we "see" a ghost.

the gaps in our perception so that what we are experiencing makes sense to us.

What we see out in the world is our perception of reality filtered through our own RAS and not necessarily what is really out there. It's our perception based on the images our brains painted based on signals captured by our eyes and our other senses. Sometimes, the brain adds things in that aren't there but thinks should be.

For example, when you mishear the lyrics in a song, your brain will fill in the gaps with its own lyrics, even if they don't make sense.

This may play into the electronic voice phenomena (EVP) recordings captured by ghost investigators who hear what they expect or want to hear in a sea of static and garbled chaos. The recording could be nothing but random white noise. If you listen to it without knowing ahead of time what was supposedly said, you probably won't hear any specific words (although there certainly are some believable and clear EVP captures). However, if someone tells you what you're supposed to hear, you'll almost certainly hear it. This is also true for visual images, such as when someone shows you an ink blot and asks if you see the shape of a billy goat crossing the bridge. Your brain will now look for the goat on the bridge pattern in the blot, whereas if the person said it was just an ink blot, you might never have seen a goat at all.

If our brains have the capacity to pick out specific information from a barrage of what it is presented with, it begs the question of what it is not picking up, and what aspects of reality we may be missing entirely until they become relevant to us, such as death.

GHOSTLY ANIMALS

If animals also possess conscious awareness and possibly even a soul, it makes sense that they, like humans, can be ghosts. Just as books are filled with stories of human ghost sightings, there are hundreds of reports of people encountering not only their own dead pets but also animals of all shapes and sizes from the great beyond. Some are just

Haunted Animal Legends

London's Newgate Prison was said to be haunted by a killer black hound.

When it comes to famous animal ghost reports and legends, Morris the Cat of Eureka Springs, Arkansas, stands out. Cats are a popular guest at many hotels because they are great for keeping the rodents at bay. Fifty years ago, an orange tabby cat named Morris would greet visitors in the hotel lobby of the historical Crescent Hotel, which is popular for being haunted and has been featured on many ghost-hunting television shows. After he died, the staff buried Morris in the hotel's rose garden, but guests continued to report seeing Morris greet people as he sat perched upon his favorite chair or while walking through the rose garden.

Leona, a rat terrier, is the ghost dog of the Holly Hotel in Holly, Michigan. In 1989, famed parapsychologist Norman Gauthier visited the haunted hotel and claimed it was "loaded with spirits," one of which was Leona, who could be heard running down halls. Visitors reported feeling a dog brushing against their legs, and the morning chef crew heard her bark for breakfast, just as she did when she was alive.

One of the oldest ghost pet legends comes to us from Port Tobacco, Maryland. In the 1700s, a man named Charles Thomas Sims walked into a bar and was attacked by bandits after claiming he had a ton of gold when he got a little too drunk. Sims had a dog with him, a loyal Bluetick Coonhound that battled the thugs, protecting his owner until they both fell on a rock along the road and perished together. The thugs got the gold, but they didn't much enjoy their booty, because after they came back for the buried treasure, a large Bluetick Coonhound appeared and chased them off. They all fell ill and died, and to this day, there are reports of the faithful hound spotted in the area.

The Capitol Building in Washington, D.C., is home to a demon cat that walks the halls at night. During the post–Civil War era, night watchmen allegedly saw a mysterious black cat that got bigger as it came toward them. One man said the cat became the size of

cont'd on next page

cont'd from previous page

a tiger and leapt at him. When he fell to the ground, he felt no weight and realized the cat had vanished into thin air. After a gas explosion in 1898, concrete filled in the damage and there were six to eight perfect paw prints found indented in it.

On a cold day in 1626, Sir Francis Bacon was riding with a friend in a carriage. As they passed Pond Square in London, Bacon brought up a new method of preserving food by keeping it so cold that it wouldn't rot. His friend, who was the king's physician, disagreed, prompting Bacon to experiment on a local chicken that he plucked, cleaned, and packed with snow. Bacon then came down with pneumonia and died.

Soon after, witnesses were reporting a half-plucked chicken running around Pond Square that would vanish when anyone approached it. This occurred for many years, including during World War II, when it ran through a wall to escape being captured. It was allegedly seen in the 1970s by a couple kissing in a nearby doorway.

The supernatural black hound of Newgate Prison in London was first written about by a prison inmate in 1596, who reported that during a terrible famine, inmates resorted to cannibalism to survive. A scholarly inmate was accused of witchcraft and eaten by the stronger men.

Soon after, the inmates noticed a large, black dog roaming the dark corridors. The beast hunted down each man who had eaten the scholar one by one. When there were only a few men left who had cannibalized the scholar, they panicked and broke out of the prison to escape, though it is believed the ghost dog tracked them down and ate them all.

passing through, but others interact with those lucky, or unlucky, enough to see them.

Most pet ghost stories are reported by loving owners who claim to have seen, heard, or sensed the presence of a beloved dog, cat, or other critter. This ghostly presence frequently behaves exactly as the animal did when it was alive, such as jumping up on the same spot on the bed they once slept on or roaming the hallway at a certain time of night. A pet can appear as an apparition or simply as a presence. An owner may hear a bark or a meow that sounds exactly like his or her dog or cat, only to discover that the house is empty. The pet ghost appears for a short time after death, then fades away or stops, as if it has finally found its way to the other side. Unfortunately, for most owners, this sense of finality is almost as painful as the initial death.

Skeptics claim people see the ghost of their dead pets because they are immersed in grief and wishful thinking, but they fail to explain the many cases of people seeing other people's dead pet ghosts, to which they would have no emotional connection, or why some witnesses were doctors and psychologists who might be thought to possess a more objective viewpoint about the subject matter. Nor can skeptics explain the pet and animal ghost reports that involve the reactions of other animals in the vicinity that appeared to acknowledge and respond to the ghost, which removes the "wishful thinking" and "it's all in your imagination" aspects. Unless, of course, the animal witnesses also had wishful thinking and overactive imaginations. As one such story on Quora's Afterlife forum claimed, "Our cat had passed away and we saw him running across the living room now and then, and what made it even spookier was seeing our other two cats react and follow his ghost with their eyes."

Internet forums are filled with such touching stories and accounts that it would be difficult to believe that everyone who reports one is a complete liar or has a wild imagination.

And another: "Jonas was our bulldog and passed of cancer two weeks ago. Our boxer, Fredo, loved Jonas and has been in a depressed state, not eating or wanting to play.... But the night we saw Jonas sitting on the couch where he always did when he was alive, Fredo became so animated and excited and jumped up on the couch and kept rolling around right where we saw Jonas.... After that, Fredo started to eat again and got back to being himself again...."

Internet forums are filled with such touching stories and accounts that it would be difficult to believe that every–

one who reports one is a complete liar or has a wild imagination. Maybe, just maybe, just as our human loved ones make ghostly appearances from time to time, so do our beloved animal companions.

HUNTING THE GHOSTS OF THE DEAD

Ghost hunting has grown in popularity because of the proliferation of television shows featuring paranormal groups and individuals actively investigating alleged haunted locations such as local hotels, restaurants, mental institutions, prisons, and cemeteries since the early 2000s. While the goal of these shows has always been entertainment, they helped to popularize the belief in ghosts and inspired thousands of local and regional groups and organizations to follow in their footsteps.

The use of equipment to detect ghosts has spawned its own cottage industry, with many people inventing or modifying existing devices. Most equipment serves another purpose entirely, but it can be useful in documenting environmental changes that occur during a ghostly encounter.

Using everything from digital cameras to digital tape recorders (to record EVP), thermal imagers, EMF meters to detect electromagnetic field anomalies, barometers, infrared thermometers, K2 meters, and more, those who hunt ghosts will take baseline measurements before an investigation, then compare them with data obtained during the investigation. Other types of equipment include Faraday cages, ghost boxes, dowsing rods, infrasound monitors (infrasound is associated with experiences of paranormal phenomena), flashlights, and motion sensors.

According to *Ghost Hunting: The Science of Spirits*, the five most common types of evidence sought after are:

- EVP

- Noises–Knocks, creaks, any noises not accounted for

- Moving objects–Objects that move of their own accord

- Shadow figures–The shadowy presences that appear on video or out of the corner of the eye

- Temperature changes—Spots of extreme heat or cold with no other explanation

EVP is hugely popular. It involves using a digital recorder and turning it on to run as the investigator poses questions such as "Who are you" or "Is there someone here?" The investigator pauses after each question to give the ghost time to "answer." After the EVP session, the tape is played back to listen for vocal responses during the pauses. There are many EVPs on the Internet, with the highest and clearest of those considered proof of ghost talk from the other side.

There can also be video and photographs of ghostly activity that cannot be debunked as digitally altered. While none of the above alone or together prove ghosts are real, they are different tools that are used to try to pinpoint anomalous activity and hopefully record it on audio or video to be further analyzed. More on this in the next chapter.

Regardless of the number of ghost hunters and investigators working alone or in groups, many people will be skeptical of even viable evidence and data. Personal experience may be the only evidence that matters in this case. The following insight is provided in *Ghost Hunting: The Science of Spirits*. "There are scientific tests to measure psi, but none that conclusively prove the existence of ghosts." While paranormal investigators collect evidence and frequently rely on equipment to take the most scientific, evidence-based approach possible, their methods lack a set of standards to measure against in the same way that parapsychological studies do."

Yet paranormal researchers are dedicated to more than just finding or recording a spirit as proof to offer the wider community at large. Most truly want to know for themselves if ghosts are real, and they continue to seek to understand if there is a science to ghosts—what they are, how they manifest, where they come from. For many in the field, it is also about helping the ghosts of the dead to find peace and cross over, to make the transition into the light or the other side and out of the limbo they are trapped within.

The existence of ghosts may never be proven scientifically because, like the afterlife, ghosts cannot be placed on a glass slide or replicated at will in a laboratory setting. This is not to dismiss the millions of people who have claimed to have had paranormal experiences or to assume that they are all liars or

Is There a Science to Ghosts?

English physicist Paul Davies is a professor at the Institute for Quantum Studies in Chapman University.

Experiments with photons and other quantum particles have revealed that the observer alters the outcome of the results. There is no real particle to observe until the moment of observation. In his book *Superforce*, physicist Paul Davies writes, "In the absence of an observation, a quantum system will evolve in a certain way. When an observation is made, an entirely different type of change occurs. Just what produces this different behavior is not clear, but at least some physicists insist that it is explicitly caused by the mind itself." This statement was made in 1984, and more scientists have since admitted that the mind plays a role in creating the physical reality we "observe" on a daily basis. Every day, new research emerges that confirms that the outcomes of quantum phenomena can be altered by consciousness. What is consciousness? A quick look at the dictionary turns up a variety of answers. "Awakened state; the awareness of self and of what one is doing and why; the totality of one's thoughts, feelings and experiences; a state of knowing the self; cognizance." Consciousness, then, is a state of awareness, of knowing that one exists. We possess consciousness when we are awake and aware of our own existence.

Consciousness is also described as the ability to think and perceive. Thoughts, perception, and consciousness are the key players in understanding the connections between the paranormal and the normal, just as they are the key players in determining the outcome of a quantum physics experiment. The nonlocality experiments of Alain Aspect and his team in 1982 proved that space is "nonlocal" and that the world is not made up of separate objects that, when put together, make the universe as we know it. Instead, these groundbreaking experiments showed that the "observer" and the "object being observed" were connected and part of an indivisible whole, with everyone and everything affecting and influencing everything else.

cont'd on next page

cont'd from previous page

Some physicists believe that the realm of "superspace," or the Zero Point Field, is the home of the cosmic consciousness that witnessed and continues to witness the creation of the universe. This cosmic mind is linked to the mind of the individual human, who observes his or her own reality come into being on a microcosmic scale. And the synchronization of vibrations and frequencies, whether in the electromagnetic field or in the human brain, can undoubtedly result in an experience of something other than normal, waking consciousness.

Consciousness is the key, and the observer chooses the branch of experience. Physicist Brian Josephson states in his paper "String Theory, Universal Mind and the Paranormal" that "some aspects of mentality involve a realm of reality largely, but not completely, disconnected from the phenomena manifested in conventional physics." He believes life is based on information, with a biological character that is behind the informational processing of organisms, and makes a living thing "able to shape its environment in a partnership with it." When a mental state is shared between two different living things, this could explain such phenomena as ESP and telepathy.

Many serious parapsychologists suggest greater levels of psi phenomena are reported under laboratory testing conditions when the research subjects have a *vested interest in the outcome of the experiments.* Implied meaning can often make a big difference. Richard S. Broughton, scientist and former president of the Parapsychological Association, wrote in his presidential address in 1987 about the importance of meaning when working with test subjects. He proposed that researchers ask "Whom does psi serve?" when working with subjects, pointing to the "need-serving" nature of psi phenomena and how it might affect the skill levels of individuals.

Obviously, if there is a greater need, often survival-based, for psi, then the psi will show up in a greater amount in the subject. Broughton stated, "Quite a few experiments in ESP and PK can be read as providing support for both the need-serving character and its operation at an unconscious level." Test results seem to imply that there are psychological and biological implications to paranormal phenomena, and that their functioning significance must be considered.

cont'd on next page

cont'd from previous page

Thus, if one person has a greater need to display PK, they will display it. But that does not mean psi only shows up when there is a desperate need for it, Broughton continues, but that researchers must keep in mind that "probably the primary function of psi is to help the individual survive when faced with serious threats to health and safety, and to gain a competitive advantage in the struggle for survival."

So, do we have a choice between being psychic or seeing ghosts? Maybe we do, but only subconsciously. And, once that decision is made consciously, can our brains "synch" with the precise frequency required to perceive what is considered beyond normal perception? The human brain functions as an incredible filter, accepting and rejecting information and stimuli based on our survival requirements. You could say we operate on a "need-to-know" basis, with our brain acting as a sentry at the gate, refusing entry to anything we don't need to understand. People who are able to shift their perception thus shift their "need-to-know" basis to include *things they did not perceive before.* If you don't need to see it, you won't see it.

On the other hand, phenomena such as ghosts, UFOs and other entities that take on a nearly physical form may be coming into our consciousness without our consent, simply because they have found the operating mechanism for being able to do so. And, on some level, we must be consenting to perceive their presence, just as we tend to see, or not see, what we want to see in daily life.

Excerpted from *Celebrity Ghosts and Notorious Hauntings* by Marie D. Jones. Detroit, MI: Visible Ink Press, 2019

have overactive imaginations. So, why aren't there ghosts of every dead person we know roaming around? According to ghost hunters, only some of the deceased fail to cross over to the other side for a variety of reasons, and they sometimes require assistance to let go of this life and move on to the next.

These and other questions add to the frustration for scientists seeking answers that fit into their methodologies, but for those who have had these ghostly experiences, they are as real as the noses on their faces.

Talking to the Dead:
Devices of Ghost Communications

Spiritual and psychic investigators have traditionally taken the lead in addressing the question, but the popularity of "paranormal investigation" television series like *Ghost Hunters*, which reveals that the general public is heavily interested in the topic, has spawned a whole new breed of research. There are currently over 3,000 paranormal investigation teams in the United States, with many more around the world. Paranormal investigators use a variety of investigative techniques in their pursuit of proof of the existence of ghosts and, thus, of life after death.

Is this, however, a new phenomenon?

The truth is that humans have been trying to find scientific proof of the presence of ghosts for at least two centuries. As technology has advanced, so has our drive to find new, innovative methods to potentially communicate with the dead.

Electronic voice phenomena (EVP) and instrumental transcommunication (ITC) are considered to provide the most persuasive evidence of spirit contact. Researchers in the early days of EVP and ITC research attempted to interact with spirits using a variety of technical tools and technologies available at the time.

When Thomas Edison created the phonograph in 1877, his first recording was of himself reading the nursery rhyme

171

"Mary Had a Little Lamb." Forty years later, he disclosed plans for a bigger, more grand innovation. This was to be his most ambitious project to date. The little-known near-death experience of Thomas Edison shaped his belief that active living forms do not die; rather, their composition changes. This basic concept inspired him to imagine bigger.

Edison wanted to expand upon the phonograph by recording a different kind of voice: that of individuals who had passed away. Specifically, a "spirit phone" that could communicate with the dead. "I have been at work for some time creating an equipment to discover if it is feasible for people who have left this Earth to connect with us," he told the *American Magazine* in 1920. This, like all his others, was a scientific experiment. Edison was influenced by Albert Einstein's work, particularly his ideas regarding quantum entanglement and special relativity. He believed that if mass can be turned to energy, then perhaps the spirits of living people can be transformed to coherent units of energy once their bodies have stopped functioning. And if entangled particles can interact across great distances, as Einstein's quantum entanglement theory indicates, those energy bundles might have the ability to interact with our physical world.

Edison purportedly displayed a prototype of his spirit phone in late 1920. He invited mediums as well as scientists to witness a fascinating experiment. They observed a projector-like device on a workbench that projected a small beam of light onto a photoelectric cell. The illuminated cell was created to detect forces and things moving across the beam that were invisible to the naked eye. A meter linked to the photoelectric cell would alert them if a visitor from another world came to the gathering and passed through the light, according to Edison.

The famous American inventor Thomas Edison is known for many patents on technological devices. The telephone was not one of them (that was Alexander Graham Bell), but Edison did work on a "spirit phone" to communicate with the dead.

Visitors who expected scientific proof of ghosts were sorely disappointed. Because the meter needle remained stationary for hours, even the mediums there had to admit there was nothing supernatural going on. The inventor, on the other hand, remained unconcerned. Despite some dismissing Edison's forays into the paranormal as a hoax, a note in his own diary confirms his seriousness.

Edison died in 1931 with no proof of spirit communication, and his spirit phone, along with all his papers, have disappeared.

So, what about more modern efforts to communicate with spirits of the deceased? Great technological progress throughout the 1940s and 1950s led to greater interest among researchers to unlock the secret to spirit communication. Swedish film producer Friedrich Jürgenson began capturing bird noises in 1959. He didn't grasp what was going on until he heard his mother's voice say, "Friedrich, you are being watched" in German. "Can you hear me, Friedel, Friedel, Friedel, Friedel, Friedel, Friedel, Friedel, Friedel?" After that, he recorded hundreds of similar voices. As a consequence of his exceptional success in recording invisible voices, he was called "The Father of EVP." Jürgenson's study had piqued so much interest that he released two books about EVP, *Voices from the Universe* and *Radio Contact with the Dead*.

Konstantin Raudive, a Swedish psychology professor, was another EVP pioneer. In the 1960s, Raudive became aware of Jürgenson's work and he began his own tests in 1967, despite his initial skepticism. "Kostulit, here is your mother," Raudive recorded the voice of his departed mother. (His mother used to nickname him Kostulit when he was a kid.) According to Raudive, spirits may influence the white noise of radio static, which is formed when a tuner is placed between radio stations, to make speech communications that could be recorded on tape. Raudive coined the term "electronic voice phenomenon" (EVP) and wrote a book called *Breakthrough: An Amazing Experiment in Electronic Communication with the Dead* to describe it. Throughout his career, he captured thousands of EVP.

In the 1970s, Ernst Senkowski coined the term "instrumental trans-contact" (ITC) to describe communication between spirits and discarnate entities and the living using electronic equipment such as tape recorders, fax machines, television sets, or computers. His work was built upon that of Raudive and Jürgenson. An allegation made against his work occurred when he used ITC one day, and the image of EVP enthusiast Jürgenson (who was buried the same day) appeared on a television at a coworker's house that was tuned to an empty channel.

George Meek, a spiritual researcher, utilized radio oscillators to capture hundreds of hours of EVP recordings in the late 1970s and 1980s. George J. Mueller, an electrical engineer who died of a heart attack in 1967, is said to have had over 25 conversations with Meek, a director of the Meta-Science Foundation in Franklin, North Carolina. According to accounts, the late Mueller had told Meeks where he could receive his birth certificate and death certificate information. It was rumored that it had been checked out.

In the 1970s, Ernst Senkowski coined the term "instrumental trans-contact" (ITC) to describe communication between spirits and discarnate entities and the living using electronic equipment....

Moving forward to the 1980s, Sarah Estep founded the American Association of Electronic Voice Phenomena (AA-EVP) in 1982 in Severna Park, Maryland, to increase awareness of EVP and provide standardized procedures for collecting data. Estep claims to have recorded hundreds of messages from deceased friends, family, Beethoven, extraterrestrials, and an eighteenth-century Philadelphia lamplighter.

All these early innovators had set the stage for what was to become a literal paranormal revolution by one man. After being inspired by article in a 1995 edition of *Popular Mechanics*, "Are the Dead Attempting to Communicate with Us through Electronic Means?" Frank Sumption created the first "Ghost Box Hack" (also known as a "spirit box") in the 1990s. As a result, he began tinkering with the EVP–maker program. He made the first "Frank's Box" out of a rewired AM radio that had been salvaged from a junkyard automobile. His gadget was a simple way of "supplying raw" audio to spirits and other beings, in the hopes that they might utilize it to form replies (and potentially full sentences). Frank's early prototypes achieved this by employing a custom–designed circuit that allowed for frequency sweeping across AM, FM, and shortwave bands.

The concept is fairly straightforward: white noise is utilized to create unpredictability. The white noise is adjusted to provide a random voltage that fits the voltage tuning tolerance of the AM receiver. The output produces a split second of audio from a random frequency in the AM broadcast range of 535–1605 kHz. The audio is piped into a wooden echo-box for acoustic effect. Following early testing and investigation, Sumption realized that random frequencies were unnecessary and instead employed linear sweep tuning of the AM broadcast spectrum. Randomness has mostly been eliminated. The tuner started at a predefined frequency (535 kHz, for example) and gradually increased in frequency by 1 or 10 kHz until it reached a frequency higher than the starting frequency (1605 kHz).

Digital EVP recorders like this one are used by modern ghost hunters to this day.

Before passing away in 2014, Sumption created several iterations of his boxes (many of which he provided to this book's co-author Larry).

To this day, Sumption's design has inspired thousands of researchers to develop similar devices (and even apps that mimic the functionality). The fundamental design of the Frank's Box has allowed for cheaper and simpler designs. Although vintage Radio Shack $25 AM/FM radios are popular, several companies have created specialized spirit boxes based on Frank's original concept.

App designers have stepped up to the task with options ranging from free to a few bucks for people who don't want to invest in a real, physical spirit box. Since everyone appears to have a mobile phone, this provides quick and easy access to communicate with spirits.

For centuries, scholars and believers have debated the subject of spirit contact. Proponents of spirit communication believe they can communicate with the dead, angels, and other spirits. Skeptics of spirit communication argue that there is no scientific evidence that spirits exist or communicate with humans. While no definitive scientific proof has been presented, scholars have continued to investigate the concept of spirit communication in the hopes of solving one of humanity's greatest mysteries.

GHOSTBUSTING

The blockbuster movie *Ghostbusters* from 1984 focuses on a group of scientists who are rejected by the academic community because they believe that ghosts not only exist but can also be captured using state-of-the-art custom technologies. From proton packs to containment units, this movie provided a significant boost to would-be paranormal investigators worldwide. While this movie was not the first fictional story to portray the paranormal as a valid science, it is unquestionably the most famous and influential.

Because no tangible evidence of ghosts exists, they are considered to be in the domain of pseudoscience. As a result, it is difficult to establish—or deny—the existence of these entities. Nonetheless, throughout history, innovative scientists and technologists have attempted to devise methods of "detecting" and communicating with them. Ghost-hunting has become nearly a mass-participation sport as a result of the Hollywood phenomenon. A quick search of the internet reveals a vast range of ghost-hunting devices and gadgets ranging from ghost boxes and electromagnetic field–detecting teddy bears to Ouija boards and digital dowsing rods, among other things.

Let's take a look at some pieces of equipment that are widespread in the toolkits of most modern paranormal investigators.

EMF METERS

If you've ever watched a paranormal TV show, you've probably seen at least one of the actors wave around a small gadget. Electromagnetic field (EMF) readers are designed to detect electromagnetic energy waves, and paranormal researchers have begun to use these devices to detect spirits over the last 25–30 years, despite the fact that they are normally used to monitor hazardous quantities of EMF radiation from power lines or appliances.

A K-II meter is the most commonly used tool by paranormal investigators worldwide. This opulent-looking box has green and red LED lights that indicate the strength of a magnetic field.

But how did this device become famous for its ability to detect spirits? We haven't been able to figure out who first connected ghosts and electromagnetic energy, but it's worth noting that these sensors were originally designed to detect radiation leakage from early microwave ovens.

Today, numerous manufacturers sell EMF meters that are specifically marketed as ghost-hunting tools.

Why all the interest in this seemingly mundane piece of tech? Electrical and magnetic radiation occur naturally, but they can also be created and generated by electrical devices. Appliances such as refrigerators, ovens, microwaves, and even certain televisions and radios can release EMFs. EMFs are emitted by almost everything electrical. We are continually blasted with various quantities of EMF radiation in our daily lives. It is present, often at alarmingly high levels, in Wi-Fi, cellphones, radios, microwaves, VHF, and UHF.

Power company and telecommunication workers use EMF meters to monitor radiation from towers and other electromagnetic sources, but they can also used for ghost hunting.

Remember as a child when your mother told you to "sit away from the television" while watching it? She may not have realized it, but your exposure to high levels of EMFs had the potential to be hazardous. The radiation level in most modern television sets is around 20 mG, which is still significantly higher than ambient environmental levels.

Paranormal researchers believe that locations where paranormal activity has been actively documented often contain statistically higher electromagnetic radiation levels than the background average.

From a scientific perspective, it has been established that sources of high electromagnetic fields, such as those created by power lines or appliances, may be the source of many paranormal experiences due to the physiological and psychological impacts they have on humans.

High levels of electromagnetic radiation, according to research, activate parts of the brain capable of giving the impression of having had a supernatural experience. People who are hypersensitive to electromagnetic radiation may experience nausea, dizziness, skin irritation, headaches, paranoia, a sense of being watched, and even hallucinations as a result of radiation exposure. Not surprisingly, all of these symptoms have been described by individuals who claim to have a paranormal experience.

What is the significance of energy (particularly electromagnetic energy) in the afterlife? According to paranormal experts, the human soul is a type of energy that can manifest itself in a variety of ways. Paranormal researchers' use of EMF detectors is an attempt to define the soul, even if they are unaware of it. Even though the precise nature of the soul has never been determined, paranormal researchers and parapsychologists believe that soul energy can be found in the human body. According to popular belief, neurons, which are tiny cells in the brain, are the source of bio-electric energy.

The bottom line is that while this device is not designed to detect ghosts, the authors believe it may be used to reduce ambient variables such as high electromagnetic radiation that could be misinterpreted as something paranormal.

FLIR THERMAL CAMERA

Forward-looking infrared (FLIR) cameras and infrared thermometers are examples of thermal imaging devices that monitor temperature changes. Using FLIR sensors, real-time heat maps are generated. There are many paranormal investigators who claim that thermal imaging cameras (and infrared thermometers) may detect cold spots that prove the existence of ghosts and other supernatural beings.

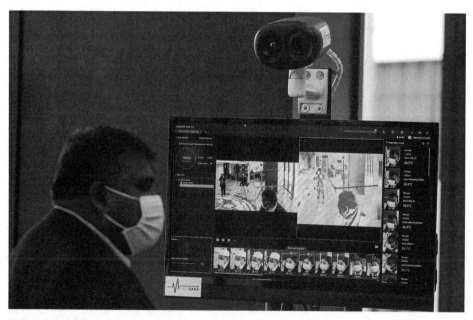

FLIR cameras like this one were recently in the news because they were being used to detect whether people entering a building might have a fever, indicating a possible COVID-19 carrier. Ghost hunters also use them to perceive things lurking behind smoke and vapor.

Contrary to popular belief, the FLIR thermal imaging camera is not the "Holy Grail" of ghost hunting but rather another tool in the paranormal investigator's arsenal. This strategy, according to the authors, works best when used to "debunk" hot or cold regions.

The appearance of ghosts on thermal imaging equipment is more of a theory than a proven fact. The appearance of visible figures and other anomalies in thermal imagers has been recorded, but these could be the result of unrelated events. While this does not rule out the possibility of ghosts appearing in thermal imagers, it does show that there is currently no convincing data to back up this claim.

The infrared portion of the electromagnetic spectrum, as opposed to visible light, is a component of the electromagnetic spectrum that extends beyond light to longer wavelengths. However, even though infrared (IR) is invisible to humans, it exhibits properties that are strikingly similar to those of visible light, including absorption, emission, reflection, refractive index, and diffraction. Recognizing that anomalous photos taken with thermal imagers can be created in the same manner as anomalous images captured with standard light cameras is crucial.

In most cases, a temperature reading should be collected from surfaces that are directly in the line of sight of the thermal imager, rather than from other surfaces. This is because they emit rather than reflect mid–far–IR. The fact that the image indicates temperature rather than light reflected off it means that there may be hot and cold patches that would not be seen in a traditional snapshot.

A surface that has been in contact with a hot or cold object that has subsequently been removed may also appear warm or cold depending on the temperature of the object. For example, when someone sits in a chair for a short period of time, a nice image of that person can be seen on the FLIR's display screen. Heat radiates rather slowly through solid objects and can linger on them for some time.

Why would a thermal imaging camera be used for paranormal investigation? When using a standard camera, the presence of air is frequently undetected. Thermal imagers are a useful tool for a variety of applications because they can "see through" smoke, mists, and sprays.

Using a traditional photographic camera, it is not possible to visualize temperature readings on diverse surfaces. Metals, for example, seem black to the naked eye yet reflect mid-to-far-infrared light when illuminated. Infrared radiation is reflected readily by a wide range of surfaces, including polished ceramics, glass, and natural stone. The "temperatures" or even pictures that appear on such surfaces are primarily visible only using thermal imagery equipment.

Thermal imagers are a useful tool for a variety of applications because they can "see through" smoke, mists, and sprays.

Because the mid–far–IR acts in a manner similar to light, the same kinds of anomalies that can be detected in conventional light images may also be seen in mid–far–IR photographs, in part because the mid–far–IR behaves in a manner similar to light.

It is possible that images captured by thermal imagers, like those captured by regular photographic cameras, will be out of focus. Furthermore, because mid–far–IR has a longer wavelength than light, photos captured with a thermal imaging camera will usually seem fuzzier when compared to ordinary light footage captured with a standard camera.

As a result, you shouldn't expect to notice a great deal of fine detail in infrared photographs of objects. Minor discrepancies are most likely visual results of the visualizing process, and they may be mistaken for such as a result of the visualizing process.

Because mid–far–IR ignores tiny particles in the air, thermal imaging cameras provide an unexpected benefit in that orbs (which are most likely airborne particulate matter, aka dust) will not appear in your thermal images because they are not visible in visible light.

AUDIO RECORDER

In the field of paranormal investigation, audio recorders have long been considered vital pieces of equipment. Paranormal investigators use both digital and analog recorders to record notes, interviews, and audio anomalies such as electronic voice phenomena (EVP) to better document their discoveries. Sound anomalies, disembodied voices, and footsteps are all common paranormal claims, and investigators employ audio recording equipment to try to document these occurrences during field investigations.

When sound recording equipment became more readily available in the early nineteenth century, mediums and psychics began to look into the possibility of utilizing this technology to establish a better connection with the dead. Photographer Attila von Szalay was one of the first to attempt to record what he believed to be the voices of the dead in order to enhance his studies of photographing ghosts.

Early recordings were done on 78–rpm records, while later sessions were recorded using a custom–built system consisting of an in–cabinet microphone coupled to an external recording device and speaker enclosed within a sound-proofed cabinet. Szalay mentioned in his report that he had discovered a number of noises on the tape that had not been heard on the speaker during the recording operation, many of which had been recorded while there was no one else present in the room. He had the impression that the sounds he was hearing were the sounds of deceased individuals.

In 1980, William O'Neil created the "Spiricom," an electronic audio instrument that could be used to communicate with the spirits of the deceased. It's worth noting that O'Neil was the first to do so. O'Neil stated that the device was created in accordance with specifications received psychically from deceased scientist George Mueller, and that it had undergone extensive testing before being released. After claiming that the Spiricom device allowed him to communicate with spirits, he decided to make the device's design specifications available for free to scientists who wanted to further their research into the subject.

For decades after O'Neil's pioneering work was first published, many other scientists and researchers tried in vain to duplicate it.

Does technology give conclusive evidence of the afterlife? Watching the popular TV shows, one might think so, though scientists are fairly clear on the subject. Some paranormal experiences can be explained by erroneous neuronal firings or abnormal brain activity, which can be traced back to the brain. It's been suggested that the phenomenon of sensing poltergeists is related to the inability to see objects moving, which in turn is linked to damage to the right hemisphere's visual processing areas. On the other hand, epilepsy sufferers may experience the unsettling sensation that someone is watching them, which is thought to be the source of reports of faceless "shadow people" lurking nearby.

James Randi offered a $1 million prize to anyone who could produce proof of the supernatural. Many people applied for Randi's challenge, but none were successful despite their best efforts. Randi noticed that they were all engaging in some form of deception. Other "challenges" throughout history have also failed to provide definitive proof of the afterlife.

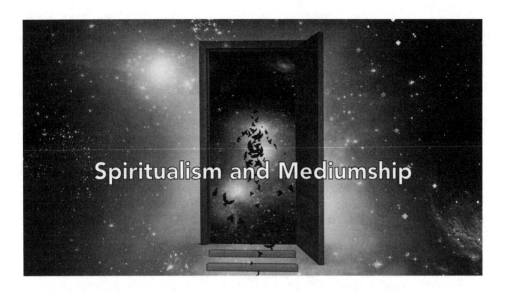

Spiritualism and Mediumship

When you are born, you cry, and the world rejoices. When you die, you rejoice, and the world cries.
—Buddhist saying

Die happily and look forward to taking up a new and better form. Like the sun, only when you set in the west can you rise in the east.
—Jalaluddin Rumi

For many people, the moment when a loved one dies a physical death doesn't necessarily mean that they cease to exist. They continue on, and within our minds the conversations continue. Even though they are no longer physically with us, their presence can be felt as we go about our daily lives. According to a study of widows and widowers published in the *British Medical Journal*, 39 percent said they felt the presence of their deceased loved one, 14 percent said they saw them, 13 percent said they heard their voice, 12 percent said they spoke to their spouse, and 3 percent said they felt their touch. On the most fundamental level, people want it to be possible to communicate with the dead in an attempt to maintain a sense of connectedness to their departed loved ones.

The attempt to communicate with "spirits" dates back millennia and is shared among many cultures, including Greece with the use of oracles; Egypt, where it was common

183

practice to attempt communication through the use of a board called a Senet, similar to a Ouija board, as well as letters to the dead; Mayan culture, where they held the belief that the dead communicated to them in dreams; Native American tribes, who used rituals and ceremonies; and in Central and West Africa, where Nkisis were used, along with a plethora of other cultures, each with their own distinct methods.

Communicating with the dead is often associated with Spiritualism, one of the major religious movements of the nineteenth century, a movement premised on the belief that the spirits of deceased souls can communicate and interact with the living.

Spiritualists created a modern religious movement based on communication with the dead. Spiritualism appeared first in the 1840s in the "burned–over district" of western New York, where other religious movements such as Mormonism and Millerism had emerged. This was the hotbed of the Second Great Awakening, a part of New York state where many people came to believe they could have direct communication with God, angelic beings, and spirits.

A broadsheet published in 1865 warns good Christians that Spiritualism is associated with witchcraft. Many Americans even blamed Spiritualism for causing the American Civil War.

The foundation of Spiritualism was the belief that the spirits of the dead not only existed but also could be communicated with. They were sentient ghosts, not imprints or loops that have no awareness of their observers. Spiritualists believed these dead beings could impart great wisdom from the other side, even predict events, and tell us all about God and the afterlife. Growth exploded in the movement from the 1840s to 1897 when there were more than eight million Spiritualists in the United States and Europe. There were no formal organizations, but in the late 1880s, Spiritualists suffered from accusations of hoaxing and fraud from the many mediums trying to make money, and more formal organizations appeared as a result. Spiritualism peaked in the 1920s but still has many adherents today in the United States, Canada, and the UK. The Spiritualist National Union was founded in 1901, and there was the creation of the National Spiritualist Association of Churches, as well as formal Spiritualist education organizations in the 1920s such as the William T. Stead Center in Chicago, Illinois, and the Morris Pratt Institute in Wisconsin.

Much of the foundation in their belief in communicating with what they called "discarnate spirits" came from the writings of Emanuel Swedenborg (1688–1772) and Franz Mesmer (1734–1815). Swedenborg claimed he could communicate with spirits while he was awake although he warned people to not try to contact spirits themselves. He was an inventor and scientist who studied anatomy and physiology and then began, in 1714, having visions and claiming he was called by God to reform Christianity by introducing a new church.

Mesmer was not into the religious aspects of Spiritualism and was instead focused on his form of hypnosis, later called mesmerism, as a technique that could induce a trance state and allow for subjects to contact supernatural entities. His mesmerizing hypnosis was often the topic of lectures, and those who taught it would entertain their audiences by demonstrating how hypnosis could be used to talk to the dead and the divine.

Many Spiritualists will point to 1848 as the foundational year for Spiritualism. That year, in March, the Fox sisters of Hydesville, New York, came on the scene, reporting they had contacted the spirit of a murdered peddler whose body was found in their house, even though no record of the peddler was located during their lifetimes. Kate and Maggie Fox told of how the spirit communicated via rapping noises that anyone could hear and soon became the first "celebrity mediums" when they began holding public séances.

FOXY SHENANIGANS

On a cold March day in 1848, Margaretta "Maggie" Fox, 14, and Catherine "Kate," her 11–year-old sister, approached a neighbor to describe some frightening events that occurred at night around bedtime. They claimed they heard a series of raps on the walls and furnishings that seemed to have some otherworldly intelligence. They purportedly determined the identity of the ghost over the course of several months–Charles B. Rosna, a peddler who had been killed in their house and buried in the cellar.

The Fox sisters (left to right) were Margaretta Fox, Catharine Fox, and Leah Fish.

The girl's next-door neighbor came to see for herself, and she joined the girls and their parents in their little room. Maggie and Kate were nestled up on their bed when their mother, Margaret, began the demonstration.

"Now count to five," she commanded, and the room shook as five loud thuds reverberated across the space.

"Count to fifteen," she murmured, and the unknown presence followed her instructions. She then asked it to give her the next-door neighbor's age, which resulted in 33 different raps.

She said, "If you are an aggrieved spirit, manifest it through three raps."

Three raps were heard all of a sudden, and a revitalized concentration on interacting with departed spirits was born.

The Foxes' outlandish allegations prompted a frenzy of attention in the United States and Europe. Many individuals joined Spiritualist churches to learn more about this new religion, believing it could help them communicate with their departed loved ones. The trouble, though, was that according to tests conducted in 1851, the knockings were made entirely by the girls themselves, without the assistance of any supernatural forces. Surprisingly, the sisters' reputation was not tarnished, and Spiritualism's expansion was not slowed as a result of their exposure.

Later, in 1888, the Fox girls confessed that the whole thing was a hoax. Margaretta Fox said, "There is no such thing as a spirit manifestation. That I have been mainly instrumental in perpetrating the fraud of spiritualism upon a too-confiding public many of you already know. It is the greatest sorrow of my life. . . . When I began this deception, I was too young to know right from wrong." Additionally, the peddler's bones were eventually discovered in the decaying walls of the Foxes' house in 1904, many years after the Fox sisters had passed away.

Before the hoax had been revealed, the Fox sisters were even invited to perform a séance in the White House by First

Lady Jane Pierce, the wife of President Franklin Pierce. Prior to the inauguration, the Pierces had suffered the tragic loss of their 11-year-old son, Bernie, in a horrific train accident while the family was traveling in Massachusetts, and she had vowed to reconnect with him in order to express the depth of her love while also pleading for his forgiveness for withholding the fullest capacity she was capable of while he was still alive.

Jane Pierce was not the only First Lady to bring Spiritualism inside the White House during her tenure. Several well-known Spiritualists, including Cranston Laurie and Nettie Colburn Maynard, were contacted by Mary Todd Lincoln, the wife of President Abraham Lincoln. The Lincolns had lost two sons: Eddie died from consumption shortly before his fourth birthday and 11-year old Willie died of typhoid fever. Mary invited the Spiritualists to perform what she referred to as "calls to the dead" in the Red Room of the White House in an attempt to contact her sons. In a letter to her sister Emilie, Mary wrote of Willie, "He comes to me every night and stands at the foot of my bed with the same, sweet, adorable smile he has always had; he does not always come alone. Little Eddie is sometimes with him." The assassination of her husband drove Mary even deeper into Spiritualism as she searched for comfort. In a letter to a friend, she wrote, "A very slight veil separates us from 'the loved and lost,' though unseen by us, they are very near."

During the Civil War, a woman named Cora L. V. Scott became a popular trance medium. She was a young beauty, which helped her cause of getting audiences to accept her spiritual stage shows. At the height of her popularity, she went by the name Cora Hatch. She was followed by a number of famous Spiritualists, many of whom were also involved in women's rights and the abolitionist movement.

Because many of the Spiritualists who were also mediums needed a way to make money, fraud was rampant at many of the mediumship gatherings and séances. These séances became more like entertaining stage performances, and because it was important to put on a good show, "evidence" of spirits ramped up to satisfy the audiences, who often fell for it easily. Independent commissions were established to investigate these séances, such as the Seybert Commission in 1887, yet despite widespread fakery and fraud, the Spiritualist appeal and promise of a connection to the dead stayed strong. In fact, during World War I, Spiritualism membership skyrocketed because of the mass casualties on the battlefield.

Still, many of the scientists who set out to find fraud ended up believers, such as chemist and physicist William Crookes, evolutionary biologist Alfred Russel Wallace, and Nobel laureate Pierre Curie. Physician/author Sir Arthur Conan Doyle was also a believer and member of the famous Ghost Club founded in London in 1862 to scientifically investigate paranormal phenomena. Other famous Ghost Club members included Charles Dickens, Harry Price, and Sir William F. Barrett. Marie Curie once attended a Paris séance by the group but remained a skeptic.

There were also many who opposed the practices of Spiritualism, such as biologist Thomas Henry Huxley. Huxley was so adamant in his opposition to Spiritualism that, when invited to serve on a committee to investigate and report claims of Spiritualism, he responded, "I regret that I am unable to accept the invitation of the Committee of the Dialectical Society to co-operate with a committee for the investigation of 'Spiritualism'; and for two reasons. In the first place, I have not time for such an inquiry, which would involve much trouble and (unless it were unlike all inquiries of that kind I have known) much annoyance. In the second place, I take no interest in the subject. The only case of 'Spiritualism' I have had the opportunity of examining into for myself, was as gross an imposture as ever came under my notice. But supposing the phenomena to be genuine–they do not interest me. If anybody would endow me with the faculty of listening to the chatter of old women and curates in the nearest cathedral town, I should decline the privilege, having better things to do. And if the folk in the spiritual world do not talk more wisely and sensibly than their friends report them to do, I put them in the same category. The only good that I can see in the demonstration of the truth of 'Spiritualism' is to furnish an additional argument against suicide. Better live a crossing–sweeper than die and be made to talk twaddle by a 'medium' hired at a guinea a séance."

Author Charles Dickens was one of several famous people who belonged to the Ghost Club.

Spiritualism continued to flourish, and the skeptics continued to investigate for fraud. In one especially strange incident, in February 1921, Thomas Lynn Bradford tried an experiment to prove or disprove the existence of an afterlife. He blew out the pilot light in his apartment and committed suicide by turning on the gas. Afterwards, there was no further communication with Bradford by any of his associates.

Some of Spiritualism's key tenets made it sound like the perfect American religion, attracting those who believed in taking personal responsibility for one's actions, spiritual growth, and religious freedom. This helped to spread the popularity, along with psychic mediums and mentalists, who put on more séances and demonstrations, often to large crowds to raise money. Spiritualist churches of today offer services that don't differ much from a nondenominational church, with the exception of an on–site spiritual or psychic medium who will do readings for service attendees.

MEDIUMSHIP

The main communication method of Spiritualists is mediumship. This is the practice of serving as a "mediator" between the world of the living and the world of the dead and can be done in a variety of ways. Mediums were thought to possess this skill, although some people believe it is a dormant skill we all have; like singing, though, it is a skill not all are equally talented at.

During the nighteenth century, mediums became the celebrated "rock stars" as the Spiritualist movement spread, often putting on public shows to display their gifts and help others connect with a deceased loved one. They usually charged money or raised money for their particular church or group. Some were later revealed as frauds for using some of the same techniques stage magicians used to distract and fool their audiences.

There are both physical and "mental" mediums. Physical mediums have a knack for assisting spirits to materialize via physical effects such as knocks, raps, moving objects, and apporting, which is the ability to make an object appear or disappear. Other physical manifestations might include apparitions and ectoplasm that often show up during a séance. Mental mediums focus more on tuning into the spirit world to get messages by listening, finding symbols, intuiting, and sensing the presence of spirits. They are adept at things like

Spiritual mediums can use many different techniques to connect us with the spirit world, including cards, potions, charms, herbology, and hypnotism.

channeling, telepathy, and hearing (clairaudience), seeing (clairvoyance), and sensing (clairsentience) spirits and using their own voices to pass along messages.

Direct voice communication might occur when a medium successfully connects to the other side and allows a spirit to speak in their own voice. Strangely, in the past, trumpets were used to assist the medium in amplifying the signal to let the spirit voice come through.

Mediums get into a trance state or an altered state of consciousness to tap into the spirit world, which is often described as another reality that is parallel to our own but invisible to the naked and unskilled eye. Some mediums go so far as to allow a spirit to take over their minds and their voices and "talk through" them to family and friends seeking a message from a dead loved one. This is possession, but of a positive sort and meant more to communicate words of comfort and information than take over in a destructive sense. Once in this possessed state, the best mediums could manipulate energy itself and help a spirit make a physical appearance.

Trances were popular methods of mediumship in the 1860s and 1870s. Later, Edgar Cayce popularized this form of prophesizing and mediumship when he would go into a sleep state to access information and knowledge. Trance states bypass the analytical, reasoning part of the brain and open the mind up to serve as a channel through which information can be passed. Shamans get into a trance state before they go on their journeys through other realities or worlds to access healing and information.

Modern mediums are also often called psychic mediums, but psychics are not necessarily mediums themselves. Psychics do not contact the dead or spirit world but are able to look into the future and use things like tarot cards and divination methods to access information for someone. Mediums do not usually do this or use divination, as their focus is basically serving as a spokesperson for the afterlife. Many mediums do possess a sixth sense or psychic abilities in addition to their skills at communicating with spirits.

Communicating with spirits is not new, as religious texts including the Bible feature stories of raising the spirits of deceased prophets or speaking to the spirits. Ancient Greeks consulted with oracles, and the Assyrians and Romans practiced divination to access wisdom and teachings from the gods. Indigenous traditions and metaphysical teachings often involve the belief in spirit guides–animal, human, or divine. Village witch doctors, shamans, and healers would go into trance states to converse with spirits and assist those who sought healing and comfort.

The New Testament of the Bible includes many stories of Jesus appearing to his disciples and to Mary Magdalene after his death, but the fourth-century Council of Nicaea ended the use and acceptance of mediums and stated that only the Holy Spirit could offer divine guidance from that point on, and only to those in the priesthood to boot. Normal people were told it was a sin to communicate with spirits and to leave that to the wiser elders of the church. Later, as we know from history, anyone who did claim to be able to talk to the dead or channel spirits was labeled a heretic or witch and tortured and killed.

Fraudulent mediums hurt the Spiritualist movement when stage magic tactics used by physical mediums, including the Fox sisters, spread and tainted the entire practice for a while and gave skeptics plenty of fodder to denounce the entire movement as fake. But the practice regained its footing and saw a modern revolution with the metaphysical/New Age movement of the 1970s–1990s, and by the early 2000s, there was an abundance of mediums with their own reality television shows, bringing Spiritualism more mainstream in society compared to the fringe corners of society it had occupied in the past. Every year, more than 20,000 people travel to the Lily Dale Assembly in New York, which is the country's oldest and largest Spiritualist organization, to benefit from the psychic abilities of the dozen or so regular local mediums at the Assembly.

Fraudulent mediums hurt the Spiritualist movement when stage magic tactics used by physical mediums, including the Fox sisters, spread and tainted the entire practice....

TECHNIQUES OF THE TRADE

There are several ways to communicate with spirits.

Automatic Writing–This involves getting into a trance state and then free writing whatever messages or words come through the person doing the reading. Also called "direct writing" or "spirit writing," the key is to not control or censor what is coming through and onto the page. Famous automatic writing mediums include Geraldine Cummins and James Padgett. This is something anyone can try by getting into a trance state and writing freely. Many mediums are not aware they are even writing until the session ends and they come out of the trance to read back what came through.

Automatic art is a form of the above where the medium gets into a trance or altered state of consciousness and then draws or paints images and symbols they receive from the spirit world. Sometimes a person's spirit guide is drawn during a reading.

Channeling–A person becomes the channel through which a spirit or disembodied entity speaks, like a vessel or conduit. This can be a deceased person, an angel, a divine being or ascended master, or a spirit guide. The channel might allow themselves to be used vocally, where the spirit speaks through them, or via writing, as above. Some channels enter what is called a cataleptic state, and many will adapt the behavioral characteristics and voices of the entity they claim to be channeling, while others maintain their own personalities during the process. They may channel with their eyes opened or closed.

Some famous channelers include J. Z. Knight, who channels the spirit Ramtha, said to be a Lemurian warrior who existed some 35,000 years ago and fought with the Altanteans; Esther Hicks, who channels Abraham, a group of nonphysical entities using that name to communicate with; and Jane Roberts, who channeled a 30,000–year-old man named Seth until her death in 1984. These channelers created thriving businesses writing books, doing speaking events, and holding seminars during which they have channelled their respective entities and have done cold readings for people in the audience. The entities they channel are discarnate beings that represent infinite intelligences that speak of

Channeling—often conducted at seances—is when a medium is able to have a spirit speak through them as a conduit.

life beyond the fixed, physical, mortal world, and in the case of Abraham, they teach millions of people how to use the law of attraction, that people do not die, and that the death of the physical body is not the end.

Roberts, who channeled Seth, wrote a seminal book, *Seth Speaks: The Eternal Validity of the Soul*, that features a plethora of references to life after death from her sessions during the 1960s and 1970s. The book continues to provide comfort to those seeking evidence of the beyond with Seth's own words, especially Chapter 9, which covers "The 'Death' Experience."

> A belief in Hell fires can cause you to hallucinate Hades' conditions. A belief in a stereotypical Heaven can result in a hallucination of Heavenly conditions. You always form your own reality according to your ideas and expectations. This is the nature of consciousness in whatever reality it finds itself.... There are teachers to explain the conditions and circumstances. You are not left alone, therefore, lost in mazes of hallucinations. You may or may not realize immediately that you are dead in physical terms.

You might meet with deceased loved ones, as described:

> Now, you may or may not be greeted by friends or relatives immediately following death. This is a personal matter, as always. Overall, you may be far more interested in people that you have known in past lives than those close to you in the present one, for example. Your true feeling toward relatives who are also dead will be known to you and to them.

On recalling a past life and choosing the next one:

> When you realize the significance and meaning of the life you have just left, then you are ready for conscious knowledge of your other existences. You become aware, then, of an expanded awareness. What you are begins to include what you have been in other lives, and you begin to make plans for your next physical existence, if you decide upon one. You can instead enter another level of reality and then return to a physical existence if you choose.

These channeled nuggets of knowledge and wisdom often match the messages received by those who have experienced NDEs and spoken with entities and beings before being sent back to their current life, where they feel a new-found sense of joy and the dissipation of fear of death.

Although there has been ongoing debate as to whether these and other popular channelers are truly gifted at accessing infinite, intelligent beings from some other realm, or just plain folks using their own higher wisdom, the truth is they have helped millions of people experience greater love, abundance, and hope. As always, people need to trust their own discernment and intuition when working with a channeler.

OTHER METHODS

Cold and Hot Readings–A cold reading involves reading for someone the medium knows absolutely nothing about. A hot reading involves having some knowledge of the person the reading is done for. Sadly, many stage shows and demonstrations involve the psychic medium having access to key information before the readings they gleaned in preshow interviews or other means. This happens often on television shows with psychic mediums who claim to pick someone at random from the audience but actually pick someone who has been prescreened. Not all mediums engage in this fraud, of course, but the quest to make mediumship entertaining television has created a ripe scenario for not–so–gifted mediums to become celebrities.

Sadly, many stage shows and demonstrations involve the psychic medium having access to key information before the readings they gleaned in preshow interviews or other means.

Cold readings are frequently a series of hit–or–miss conversations between the medium and the person being read, with vague questions that often lead to more specifics that the medium can then use to lead to more questions, all to get a "hit" for the person being read. It's unclear whether the medium is receiving information from a spirit or a deceased loved one, or if they're making it up as they go and leading the person with pointedly vague questions. "Do you know anyone whose name starts with the letter M?" is an example of a leading question. The person may then reveal information about a dear Uncle Mike who recently died, allowing the medium to claim to have received a message from Uncle Mike.

Modern mediums can use anything that helps them get into the right state of mind and consciousness to open themselves to messages and signs they can then pass onto the person they are reading, but the key is to remain open and not block, censor, or analyze what is coming through. They might not have the insight to correctly interpret the information and leave that to the person they are reading for; they are simply there to serve as messengers and conduits, not ministers and counselors. The most skilled mediums are those who can give information to the clients they could not possibly have known other than by communicating with the dead loved one or some spirit guide or entity. Often this information is a beloved phrase or image, such as a blue and yellow butterfly that the medium might "see" and tell the client, to find out that the deceased grandmother they are channeling loved blue and yellow butterflies and that no one knew this but the grandmother and the client.

A medium might get a message in the form of words, a song, or a phrase that the client will recognize as something only the dead person knew about, such as a private nickname or line from a poem. It's important to use discernment when seeking out a medium to work with, and to get references from others who have had successful readings, to avoid getting taken for a ride by those who take advantage of our inherent desire to connect with our lost loved ones for monetary gain.

SÉANCES AND OUIJA BOARDS

The Spiritualism movement uses séances to do most of their readings, private and public. The word "séance" comes from the French word for "session" and the Old French *seoir*, meaning "to sit." Séances involve people sitting around a table with the medium in order to receive messages and manifestations from the spirit world. Many a modern teenager has engaged in a séance or two, and they have become popular fodder for horror movies.

Some séances would make use of special cabinets in which the medium would be bound by ropes to prevent them from committing fraud. Spirit tables or séance tables were often very light in weight and had rotating centers that the medium could easily manipulate and make levitate when a spirit was present. Because séances were usually held in dim or dark rooms, it would be simple to fake a rising or turning table, and no doubt many mediums imprisoned knew how to free themselves from rope shackles. Spirit trumpets, which were horn or trumpet–shaped tubes that magnified whispered voices of the spirits so they could be heard more easily, were also a common tool.

Historically, séances have involved everything from sitting around a table holding hands while a medium goes into a trance and channels a spirit, to using a spirit board or Ouija board. Those involved would use the board and planchette to point to letters and numbers to spell out a specific message as they asked questions of the spirit. One or more séance participants would put their finger or fingers on the planchette and allow it to move around of its own volition, spelling out a word or phrase, often a name.

A séance being conducted by John Beattie in 1872 is shown in this photo from Bristol, England.

Ouija boards have been and continue to be all the rage despite a clear, scientific explanation for how they work. It's called the ideomotor effect and is nothing more than the body's own involuntary and unconscious movements that move the planchette across the board. The ideomotor effect is so subtle, you might not see a person, even yourself, move the planchette, but many scientific experiments have shown this effect in action. Skeptics argue that if a spirit or ghost wishes to communicate, they shouldn't need a wooden or plastic board to do so, and as several experiments revealed, when subjects were blindfolded and asked to use the boards, they ended up spelling out gibberish, which you can try yourself at home or with friends. Clearly, being able to see the board was important to the ideomotor effect, as the subconscious mind used the minute and imperceptible movements to spell out a name or words that were not random and incoherent.

Psychologist and psychic researcher Stanley LeFevre Krebs exposed the popular Bangs Sisters as frauds during a séance where he used a hidden mirror to catch them tam-

Ouija boards are still very popular today. Place your fingers gently on the planchette, and a spirit will spell out an answer to your questions.

pering with a letter in an envelope and then writing out a reply under the table. They of course claimed the letter was written by a spirit. In another fraud case in 1874, a British medium named Rosina Mary Showers, who was known for materializing spirits, was caught during a séance with Edward William Cox, who grabbed a spirit that manifested in a cabinet. The headdress the spirit wore fell off, revealing it to be Showers.

Yet another exposed fraud occurred at a séance at the home of John Snaith Rymer in July 1855 when a sitter named Frederick Merrifield noted that a spirit hand was a false limb attached on the end of the medium's arm! The medium, Daniel Dunglas Home, was also exposed as a fraud during a séance with poet Robert Browning and his wife, Elizabeth Barrett Browning, in 1855. Home claimed to have materialized the face of the son of Browning who had died as an infant, but Browning discovered it was Home's bare foot. To make matters even more embarrassing, Browning admitted never having lost an infant son in the first place.

Hundreds, if not thousands, of mediums have existed throughout history, and the vast majority do not set out to

The Scole Experiment

Between 1993 and 1998, the most important and scrutinized physical mediumship séances took place in the home of Robin and Sandra Foy at Street Farmhouse in the village of Scole, Norfolk, in the UK. The sixteenth-century farmhouse had a cellar that was perfect for séances, which often lasted almost three hours depending on what experiments were conducted. The goal of these experiments was to prove conclusively that death does not occur and that there is a higher-dimensional existence that is hidden from our normal limited five senses and current capabilities of detection by scientific instruments.

Over the course of five years, the experiments produced tangible objects from the spirit realm from lights, sounds, tastes, smells, touches, manifestation, and messages imprinted onto photographic film, audio tape, and videotape. A team of spirit communicators, consisting of what they claimed were thousands of minds working in unison to prove the existence of the afterlife, made their presence known to the investigators. They were called the Scole Group, and they opened their work to scientific scrutiny. All experiments were done in the presence of the scientific researchers, including Arthur Ellison, David Fontana, and Montague Keen. The results of the Scole Experiment were thought to be a huge step toward proving that there is no death and that the scientific evidence would one day have great implications.

be frauds or forgeries. Unfortunately, bad characters make it more difficult for the legitimate ones to maintain credibility and respect, but many modern mediums go out of their way to be transparent about how they do what they do, and with the rise of reviews and social media, those who engage in fraud are much easier to expose and warn others about.

Today's mediums frequently have their own television shows or books to their credit, and they now perform séances or readings on massive stages in front of thousands of people. People like John Edward, the late Sylvia Browne, self-proclaimed medium Theresa Caputo (aka the Long Island Medium), and James van Praagh are well-known. Other noted mediums of the past and present include:

- George Anderson–Called America's greatest medium for his over 50 years of work bridging the worlds of the living and the dead performing over 35,000 sessions for the bereaved.

- Albert Best–He is revered as one of the most important Spiritualist mediums of the twentieth century.

- Rosemary Isabel Brown–She was a pianist and medium who began in 1964 transcribing original compositions she claimed were dictated to her great musicians of the past.

- Gordon Higginson–He was a charismatic medium and speaker known as "Mr. Mediumship."

- Leonora Piper–America's most renowned medium in the late nineteenth century and early twentieth century.

- Florence Cook–She claimed to hear the voices of angels as a child.

- The Campbell Brothers (Alan and Charles)–They were known for their spirit typewriting, slate writing, and spirit portraits and paintings.

- Gordon Smith–A psychic medium known as the "Psychic Barber" who authored the best-selling classic *The Unbelievable Truth*.

- Estelle Roberts–One of the most versatile mediums, who encountered spirits as a child.

- Helen Duncan–One of the last mediums to be convicted under the Witchcraft Act of 1735.

- The Davenport Brothers (Ira and William)–They were American magicians in the late nineteenth century who reported similar occurrences to the Fox sisters after they were publicized. They were known for their "cabinet illusion" where they were tied inside a cabinet containing instruments. When the cabinet closed, the instruments would play, but when opened, the brothers would still be tied up. Despite numerous accusations of fraud, they remain two of the greatest mediums of their type.

- Harry Edwards–A medium and healer who established the Harry Edwards Healing Sanctuary.

- Leslie Flint–The best-known direct voice medium whose sessions were captured on audio tape.

- William Stainton Moses–Called the most remarkable medium of the nineteenth century.

An 1897 illustration shows the Davenport brothers inside their spirit cabinet. The brothers would be tied up, the doors closed, and the instruments would mysteriously play.

- Coral Polge–A world-renowned British psychic and spirit artist who appeared on radio, television, and in the media and worked in countries around the world with grieving people.

Despite the number of people who claim to talk to the dead, there is not a lot of scientific research on how they manage to do so. One organization, the Windbridge Research Center, hopes to change that by using the scientific method to appropriately study the accuracy of mediums' statements and assess their characteristics and experiences. The Center looks at several aspects of mediumship, including:

- Accuracy levels using controlled, double-blind experiments with 20 mediums.

- Brain activity using EEG findings from prescreened mediums.

- Psychological characteristics of mediums and any mental illnesses or disorders.

- Demographics looking at membership in organized religions, gender, right and left handedness, and so on.

- Disease burden, which includes physical ailments mediums may suffer from more than nonmediums.

- Experiences and whether they were in an altered state of consciousness, specific bodily sensations, emotional components, and other aspects during their readings.

If more scientists and researchers were willing to collaborate with channels, mediums, and those who communicate with the dead, we might get a better understanding of the mechanisms they use to make contact and serve as conduits, as well as whether the information they gleaned is evidence of an afterlife.

If the dead do wish to talk to us, then any one of us should be able to cultivate our skills at communicating with them, using whatever technique works best for us. Skilled mediums can provide positive and beneficial services for those of us who don't feel we possess such skills and help us to connect to lost loved ones, spirit guides that can help us fulfill our goals and purposes, and beings and entities that have messages, information, and knowledge from another realm, one we cannot access at the snap of a finger.

However, skepticism must be maintained in this area because not every medium or psychic is correct in their readings, and a misreading can sometimes cause great emotional harm to the families of deceased loved ones. Sylvia Browne, a regular on *The Montel Williams Show* at the time, informed the parents of a missing child named Shawn Hornbeck in 2002 that their son had died. Browne claimed that his body would be found in a forested area, hidden between two large stones, and that he had been kidnapped by a tall, "dark-skinned guy" with dreadlocks. Hornbeck and another child were indeed kidnapped but were later found alive at the home of Michael Devlin, a nondreadlocked Caucasian from Missouri.

While Spiritualists and mediums work to communicate with the dead in their own ways, others who specifically focus on hunting proof of ghosts have their own ideas and tools for trying to prove that life beyond death is real. The end goal always goes back to answering the same question—does the afterlife exist?

Immortality: Who Wants to Live Forever?

Surely God would not have created such a being as man, with an ability to grasp the infinite, to exist only for a day! No, no, man was made for immortality.
—Abraham Lincoln

Immortality is the negation of death. We do not usually speak about 'innatality'—about having not yet been born—yet this is something we would have to regard as the other aspect of the human soul. We are just as unborn as we are immortal.
—Rudolf Steiner

What does immortality mean to me? That we all want more time; and we want it to be quality time.
—Joan D. Vinge

If we become immortal, there will be no afterlife. Immortality would eliminate the fear of dying and being reduced as ash to ash, dust to dust. Living without the fear of death would present many philosophical challenges, such as a world in which everyone does whatever they want, good, bad, or ugly, without fear of being punished in Hell (or the promise of Heaven). Rules would no longer apply because you could abuse someone in any way you wanted while never being charged with murder. Laws based on the threat of future spiritual punishment, as well as many religious traditions based on those laws, would be abolished. Who needs

203

God when you're already God? Eternal. Invincible. Immortal. Like a superhero.

If given the choice between being immortal and never dying or living longer but still dying, what would you choose? Some argue that death is a natural transition and that we don't know or understand how there might be another level of existence that, without dying, we could never achieve. It may be a state of consciousness or becoming one with everything that, because we chose to keep on living, we will never rise to. It's a dilemma. Live forever here on Earth, or die and see where that leads?

The idea of living forever sounds appealing "on paper," but it is fraught with difficulties. Every human being has the desire to live and continue to live so that we can see our children grow and thrive, and our grandchildren grow and thrive, and the planet heal. We want to stay aboveground for a variety of reasons, the most important of which is undoubtedly fear of death because we don't know whether we will survive in some form or not. We eventually tire or become bored and want to move on to the next experience. Not to mention the environmental disaster that would result from having too many people born and no one dying.

Regardless of our wishes, we, like all living things, age and die. We may die as a result of old age, a disease, or an accident. Thankfully, we no longer must fear the predators that once shortened our ancestors' lives. We've greatly improved sanitation and medical knowledge enough to extend our good years past middle age, depending on where we live. We've mastered plastic surgery, stretching what sags and lifting what droops enough to take ten years off our natural age.

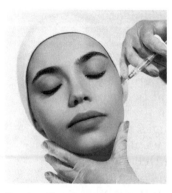

People will go to extremes to try to maintain youth, such as getting Botox injections to remove wrinkles, because looking old reminds them of their impending death.

But the Grim Reaper shows up at our door eventually. Until then, we spend billions of dollars every year trying to fend off aging and death, to no avail because when our number is called, we cannot switch numbers with someone else like we can behind the deli counter waiting to order salami or cheese. We go when we are called.

Healthy habits such as diet, exercise, sleep, meditation, and stress-relief techniques can help us live longer lives. Even the healthiest people die, and sometimes at a young age. Children are killed. There is frequently no rhyme or reason.

If there is an afterlife, immortality is irrelevant. We would only want to remain on Earth to be with our loved ones. But, if there is an afterlife, wouldn't we meet them again on the other side? Immortality is less about the body or mind and more about the ego's desire to never find out. After decades of moving us around, our bodies become tired, sick, and infirm. Minds become exhausted, confused, and muddled when confronted with decades of memories and experiences. Even so, when faced with the prospect of death, we will kill in order to survive.

WHERE THE OLD FOLKS ARE

According to Guinness World Records, the five oldest verifiable people ever to live are:

- Jeanna Calment, died in 1997 at the age of 122

- Shigechiyo Izumi, died in 1986 at the age of 120

- Sarah DeRemer Knauss, died in 1999 at the age of 119

- Lucy Terrell Hannah, died in 1993 at the age of 117

- Marie-Louise Fébronie Meilleur, died in 1998 at the age of 117

The *New York Post* ran a story in December 2021 about a woman named Alimihan Seyiti who allegedly lived for 135 years. The supercentenarian, from Xinjiang in Western China, was born on June 25, 1886, during the imperial Qing dynasty. In 2013, she was officially recognized as China's oldest living person by the China Association of Gerontology and Geriatrics. Her age at death was not able to be verified yet by Guinness World Records or any other source. She is one of a handful of other people said to have lived into their late 120s and early 130s, but none have been verified to date.

BLUE ZONES

Blue Zones are areas of the world where people live longer lives than the average. There are only five major Blue Zones on the planet. Dan Buettner, a National Geographic Fellow and author, has studied Blue Zones and the people who live in them and has written about them in his books, including *The Blue Zones*. He discovered that people in these zones generally lead active lives and are surrounded by friends and family. They are more spiritual or religious, eat a lot of plant foods, and have specific cultural and geographical components that allow them to live longer.

The five Blue Zones are:

- *Sardinia, Italy*–The longest–living men live on this island, mainly shepherds who eat a variation of the Mediterranean diet high in beans, sourdough bread, and flavonoid–rich wine called *Cannonau* made from local grapes. In the mountain province of Nuoro, the traditional diet includes fresh, seasonal foods, whole grains, and little meat, and the people walk daily. Older people in Sardinia are celebrated, not cast off as seen in most Western countries. Sardinians may have a genetic edge with the M26 genetic marker associated with longer life. There are almost ten times more centenarians per capita here than in the United States.

- *Okinawa, Japan*–Despite an aging population of millions of people living alone, which had led to an epidemic of loneliness in Japan, the island chain of Okinawa is much different. Tight-knit communities have helped residents live to 100 more commonly

Porto Servo, a seaside town, is an idyllic town on the island of Sardinia, Italy, one of the world's five Blue Zones, where people tend to live longer lives.

than any other place on Earth. The traditional social groups called *moai*, which are formed in childhood and extend into adulthood, mean that people get together often and share support, a sense of purpose called *ikigai*, and community. Lifelong friendships are important for living longer and thriving, as well as growing their own fruits and vegetables. They also follow the mantra *hara hachi bu*, which means eat until you are 80 percent full. The islands are home to the world's longest-living women.

- *Nicoya, Costa Rica*–The lowest rate of middle-aged mortality in the world is found on Costa Rica's Nicoya peninsula–where more people live to the age of ninety and beyond. Nicoyans consume a diet mainly of corn tortillas, black beans, squash, and tropical fruits. It's a sustainable diet for the land available and does not involve depleted soil or animal raising. The trio of beans, squash, and corn is called *las tres hermanas* (the three sisters), because these crops grow in harmony and balance carbs, fiber, and protein. These people also have a strong sense of purpose and optimism, known as *plan de vida*, and a rich family life. They also get a lot of exercise, plenty of healthy sunshine, and clean, clear water.

- *Loma Linda, California*– With the increased obesity rates and highly processed diets of most Americans, it's stunning to find Loma Linda on the Blue Zones map. That's because the residents are Seventh-day Adventists who have an incredibly healthy, Bible-based diet that is all about plants, seeds, and fruits and vegetables. They have strong community ties, don't smoke or drink, and have strong religious traditions. They live on average ten years longer than other Americans.

- *Ikaria, Greece*–People live on average eight years longer than most Americans, with a third living into their 90s. They stay sharp (dementia is practically nonexistent) from a healthy Mediterranean diet and a lot of herbal teas made with oregano, rosemary, and sage. Their plant-heavy diet includes about 120 types of greens that are ordinarily called weeds in the United States. These greens have ten times the antioxidants found in wine. They are a self-sufficient people with strong social bonds and rarely, if ever, consume refined sugars. Their pace of life is slow and relaxed.

Key Blue Zone factors include whole and healthy foods, less meat and more vegetables and fruits, lack of sugar and processed foods, exercise, strong social networks, spirituality and religion, and a positive attitude. This increased longevity can fortunately be achieved anywhere on Earth with some change of habits and lifestyle.

THE SCIENCE OF IMMORTALITY

Living forever may be beyond our scientific comprehension, but increasing longevity is not. According to a 2021 study published in the journal *Nature Communications*, the average human lifespan before illness or injury would be between 120 and 150 years. Furthermore, cellular damage would prevent continued life, necessitating new research into preserving and extending cellular lifespans.

Even at the cellular level, immortality would be impossible without some major intervention from cutting-edge medical advances or the merging of technology with biology. Without some serious medical, divine, or technological intervention, the quest for immortality becomes more a quest for adding extra years on. Not just living longer, though. Thriving longer. It's pointless to extend human lives if we are riddled with cancers, suffering stroke after stroke, or have dementia to the point of not even knowing who we are. Quality of life is important, and most people might rethink living to 150, even forever, if the quality of their existence was diminished each year.

It's one thing to live a long time, but it is quite another if that extra time is spent with a high quality of living. If you could live 50 more years but were confined to a bed, would you want those extra years?

For the time being, scientific research into extending human life is focusing on fasting and caloric restriction, diet changes, lifestyle, exercise, stress reduction, genetic health, cell regeneration, and the importance of social and spiritual support as tools that the average person can use right now.

The human body as it currently exists may not be strong enough to withstand the effects of climate change or changes in food production that may place a strain on our digestive systems. Not to mention the increased stress caused by a difficult economy, geopolitical strife, a lack of clean water, droughts, rising homelessness, finding decent jobs, and caring for an aging population.

That's a lot of stress on an already stressed body, mind, and spirit.

The term "senescence," derived from the Latin *senescere*, "to grow old," refers to the process of how living things decay over time. It also describes the biological process by which we age and suffer damage to macromolecules, cells, tissues, and organs, as well as telomere shortening and excessive DNA damage. *Senescence* is a term used in botany to describe the process by which fruit ripens to the point of withering, drying out, and eventually dying. Cells stop dividing and eventually die at the cellular level. It also refers to the same process in an organism (when a living thing is no longer able to respond adequately to external stressors) or to specific organs or tissues (like leaves dying in the fall).

There are a few species that escape the aging process completely. One of them is the jellyfish, *Turritopsis dohrnii*, considered biologically immortal. These small, transparent oceanic creatures have the uncanny ability to revert back to earlier stages of their life cycles when faced with environmental stressors such as starvation or injury, similar to a frog turning back into a tadpole. This allows them to turn back the clock on a cellular level for healing and longevity.

Turritopsis dohrnii can still be consumed by predators or killed by other means. However, their ability to switch back and forth between life stages means that, in theory, without such stressors in their environment, they could live forever.

Another such critter is the hydra, a simple animal similar to the polyp stage of a jellyfish that lives in freshwater ponds and rivers and stings with their tentacles at passing prey. Hydras do not experience senescence but instead have the ability of infinite stem cell renewal thanks to their FoxO genes, found in everything from worms to humans. These genes regulate how long a cell will live. Hydras have an abundance of such genes, which offer them an endless life unless they are eaten by another predator. It seems there is no way to completely stop that part of life, and death, from happening.

Lobsters can live for a long time because they have an infinite supply of telomerase, the enzyme that works to keep regenerating telomeres, but they are not immortal. They repeatedly outgrow their shells and must grow a new exoskeleton each time, which consumes so much energy that the poor lobster succumbs to disease, shell collapse, or predation. Other animals, such as the naked mole rat and the ocean-dwelling quahog, Ming, who died accidentally after 500 years, live hundreds of years and appear to never age. Desert tortoises can easily live to be 120 years old. Trees outlive humans, with the oldest living redwood trees estimated to be between 2,000 and 2,200 years old and one colony of quaking aspens estimated to be approximately 80,000 years old.

Then there are creatures like the fruit fly or hummingbird with incredibly short life spans. Humans seem to be nicely placed somewhere in the middle, for now.

OF TELOMERES AND TIME

Aging and longevity may come down to caps, namely the protective caps at the end of our eukaryotic chromosomes. These are DNA–protein structures that safeguard and prevent chromosome degradation and maintain genomic integrity. The length of our telomeres is crucial to the health of our DNA, and multiple studies with mice have shown that improving telomere length leads to longer life. One such study, from 2014, appearing in *Current Vascular Pharmacology*, titled "Telomeres and Their Role in Aging and Longevity," by Irene P. Tzanetakou, Rosine Nzietchueng, et al., stated, "Accelerated telomere loss has been associated with many chronic diseases of aging. Premature aging or cellular senescence, seen in early life, through increased oxidative stress and DNA damage to telomeric ends may be initiators of processes related to these diseases. During the recent decade, research around telomere biology has rapidly expanded due to its dynamic involvement in aging and longevity. However, longevity is not necessarily an indication of disability–free aging. There is substantial scientific disagreement and controversial results, regarding even the basic nature of aging and the path to longevity."

Another study, "Telomerase Reverses Ageing Process," published in *Nature* on November 28, 2010, found that protecting these chromosome tips not only prevents but also reverses aging. The study was conducted on mice, but more research into the role of telomeres and telomerase, the enzyme in the caps, is indicating that this is also applicable to humans. By reactivating telomerase in cells where it is no longer working, increasing telomerase activity may be able to prevent or reverse illnesses and diseases, as well as the effects of premature aging. However, some researchers believe that increasing telomerase in humans may promote tumor growth.

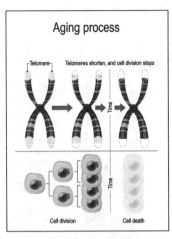

Scientists have discovered that parts of our DNA called telomeres break down slowly over time with repeated cell division. This is related to the aging process, so the key to slowing or possibly stopping aging is to keep telomeres from degrading.

Telomerase, which was discovered in the 1980s, is considered a potential fountain of youth, spurring additional research. The *Nature* study states, "Some studies have uncovered an association between short telomeres and early death, whereas others have failed to back up this link. People with rare diseases characterized by shortened telomeres or telomerase mutations seem to age prematurely, although some tissues are more affected than others."

Though the outlook for potential telomerase therapies appears promising, it is only one of many options for increasing cellular longevity. On a larger scale, attention must be paid to the rest of the body, with improvements in diet, movement, and inflammatory responses to stress.

Is it ethical to live forever? Would we run out of resources on a planet with a population of nearly eight billion people? Food? Water? Room? How would we manage all those people? Where would the population explosion end if no one died and every new baby born lived forever? We would have to consider the issue of overpopulation at some point, which leads to the moral question of how to deal with overpopulation. Depopulate? If so, how?

This is reminiscent of eugenics, the belief that certain groups of people are more deserving of life and resources than others. Would we become a science fiction novel, allowing citizens of the world to only live to a certain age before they are killed off to make room for the next round?

Who gets to decide who is "depopulated" and who isn't? The elderly and infirm, the disabled and mentally challenged, the poor and homeless (both of whom would in-

News of a Fountain of Youth

Dr. Shinya Yamanaka is a Nobel Prize laureate and stem cell researcher from Japan.

In February 2022, StudyFinds.com posted an article about a study from scientists at San Diego's Salk Institute for Biological Studies involving a new therapy that claimed to reverse the aging process by partially resetting cells that impact skin, eyesight, muscles, and the brain. The technique was called safe and effective and could extend the cell's life span, as well as help people become more resistant to stress, injury, and disease.

The team cautioned that the treatment, which involved adding four reprogrammed molecules known as "the Yamanaka factors," after Nobel laureate Dr. Shinya Yamanaka, not yet a fountain of youth for humans, having only been tested on mice. "Animals at the late stage of their lives treated with cellular rejuvenation therapy started to show signs of getting younger after just seven months. New tests are now underway to determine whether the treatment only 'pauses' or reverses aging. In the study, the researchers note that all cells carry a molecular clock that records the passage of time. By adding a mixture of four reprogramming molecules known as the Yamanaka factors, the cells will reset the clock to their original patterns." The scientists tested three groups of mice at ages equivalent to humans of 35, 50, and 80 years old (12 months, 15 months, and 25 months in mice).

After seven to 10 months, the mice resembled younger animals in both appearance and ability, and their skin healed with less permanent scars. Metabolism remained stable, showing no aging. No cancers were reported. "At the end of the day, we want to bring resilience and function back to older cells so that they are more resistant to stress, injury and disease," says co–first author Dr. Pradeep Reddy of the Salk Institute in a university release.

crease in number on an already overcrowded planet), and the sick would most likely be first on the list. Eugenicists believe that the unimportant bottom feeders should be exterminated to make more room and resources available for the more desirable people, usually the wealthy and powerful elite. Those in power would undoubtedly turn off the lives of those they despise as long as they kept enough around to create a stable workforce.

Tech in Asia featured an article in its March 15, 2016, weekly column, *Disconnect*, by Charlie Custer, "The Age of Immortality Is Coming, and It's Going to Suck," that said living forever won't be for everyone, especially the poor. Custer said it might be made available to the middle class once the technology is advanced enough that it can be scaled on that level in an economically feasible way. Until then, it will be "insanely expensive, both because it'll be extremely advanced technology and because people will be willing to pay it."

"In fact, there's a fair chance that immortality technology will widen the gap between rich and poor. Most people would pay *any* sum to prevent their own death or the death of a loved one, even if it meant going into tremendous debt and essentially becoming a debt slave. And if people *will* pay the money, what incentive do you think immortality companies will have to lower prices? Until the technology is cheap enough to be truly universal, prices will stay high, shareholders will stay happy, and the rest of us will scrimp and struggle to keep ourselves and our families alive," Custer wrote.

Death is a great equalizer and a balancer.
It keeps the population levels sustainable
without human intervention.

Those with money and power would decide who lives and who dies for the entire planet, as if they were the new gods. This may not be the world we want for our children or their children, who, due to their youth, will not be cut down unless their numbers exceed sustainable levels with sky-high birth rates.

Death is a great equalizer and a balancer. It keeps the population levels sustainable without human intervention.

It is required to avoid uncontrollable population growth. Removing death from the equation would be both cruel and counterproductive to the evolution of the species, because there would always be too many people of all ages competing for limited resources on a planet that is already struggling to keep up.

TRANSHUMANISM: SAVIOR OF HUMANITY OR THE END OF HUMANITY?

Transhumanism claims to solve the problem of aging and dying by merging technology and biology, and the proponents dream of a time when humans are more like computers or machines and less like the frail physical bodies we have been born with. The goal of transhumanism, a social and intellectual movement, is to create a better human by researching and developing human enhancement technologies that will help the body heal itself, live longer, learn more, and integrate technology into the body directly.

Julian Huxley, a British biologist and philosopher, coined the term "transhumanism" in a 1957 essay. His essay, which focused on changing humanity's future through social and cultural change, was adopted by transhumanists, with technology replacing social and cultural change. Ray Kurzweil, a computer scientist and futurist, introduced the concepts of the future in his 2006 book *The Singularity Is Near: When Humans Transcend Biology*, which describes the coming age of man and machine merging with knowledge and skills literally embedded in our brains to turn us into the ultimate supercomputers.

This is something the tech world has long been heralding, but there are many opponents of such an outcome for humanity, as it opens the door for all kinds of problems. Who inputs the information? Who controls the human machines? What happens when parts break down? How does this affect our spiritual nature? Are we playing with fire by playing God?

Transhumanism is already being used every time someone gets a pacemaker or prosthetic limb, as we find ways to improve and enhance the human body. But the real followers of this movement are envisioning a time when we will be greater-than-human machines with intelligence far beyond what we have now. They also speak of altering the genetic makeup of humans, creating a totally different species by tweaking our DNA. Can we one day even control consciousness with a chip in the brain that allows us to access other levels of consciousness? Will we be able to biologically enhance the brain itself and control our minds with specially implanted chips? Will we gradually create a human that is more artificial intelligence than human? These are valid questions that must be addressed as we hurtle toward that brave new world of human and artificial intelligence interfacing.

These ideas have gained a lot of traction in recent years, thanks to the rise of tech behemoths like Tesla, which stands to benefit the most financially, and the World Economic Forum's launch of the Great Reset Initiative in 2020, a plan to achieve a sustainable future that some have interpreted as a quest for control over every aspect of human life. At the helm is the Forum's founder and chairman, Klaus Schwab, who writes about humanity's future and how transhumanism will play a significant role in it.

That there is even a question over who should have the right to decide if they want to be fully human or half-human/half-cyborg is concerning. According to some conspiracy theories, Schwab and his supporters, who are the rich, the powerful, and the elite all over the world, have been

People often think of humanity as being at the height of evolution, but the truth is we are still evolving, and a growing number of people believe the next step will be "transhumans" who will be advanced by genetic engineering, nanotechnology, and artificial intelligence.

pushing for a New World Order of sorts that will see every-one owning nothing and being happy about it. That is the motto of the Great Reset. Through their push for trans-humanism, that will no doubt include their ownership of our own bodies, and they will make this choice for us. Once we are enhanced with chips and computer-altered DNA and technology, who will really control us? Will we be the prop-erties of the powerful behind the Great Reset, such as Schwab? Is that any way to live life, under the control of others who see us as nothing but tools for their means?

The *Guardian* published a piece in 2018 titled "No Death and an Enhanced Life: Is the Future Transhumanism" by science editor Robin McKie, which included the following quote: "The concept of technologically enhancing our bodies is not a novel one. However, the extent to which trans-humanists take the concept is debatable. We used to make things like wooden legs, hearing aids, spectacles, and false teeth. In the future, we may use implants to augment our senses so that we can detect infrared or ultraviolet radiation directly, or we may connect ourselves to memory chips to boost our cognitive processes. Science will eventually pro-duce humans with vastly increased intelligence, strength, and lifespans by fusing man and machine; a near embodi-ment of gods."

The article goes on to document the many technologi-cal advances in human health, but it also suggests that we are still a long way from the types of technology that would eliminate death. Many transhumanists, including Ray Kurzweil and his followers, believe that this shift will occur around 2030, "when biotechnology will enable a union be-tween humans and genuinely intelligent computers and AI systems." The resulting human–machine mind will be free to roam its own universe, uploading itself on demand onto a suitably powerful computational substrate. We'll become gods, or, more likely, "star children" like the one at the end of *2001: A Space Odyssey*.

The new deities that may bring about this immortality are the leaders in Silicon Valley, who treat this as a new re-ligion and are behind the push to upgrade humans within the next 30 years or so. Yuval Noah Harari, author, historian, and Hebrew University of Jerusalem history professor, stated in an interview with Sarah Knapton for the May 25, 2015, *Telegraph*, "The most interesting place in the world from a religious perspective is not the Middle East, it's Silicon Valley where they are developing a techno-religion. They believe even death is just a technological problem to be solved." He says that only the wealthiest will be able to afford this "cyborg" technology, increasing the gap between rich and poor. Sounds like something right out of a science fiction novel.

Only time will tell.

> *If only the elite, the wealthy, and the powerful can afford to do this, it does not bode well for the 99 percent of the rest of us....*

If we achieve immortality through transhumanism and the body never dies, we will require space for the bodies unless we plan to transplant our brains into new bodies. If only the elite, the wealthy, and the powerful can afford to do this, it does not bode well for the 99 percent of the rest of us, who will be at the mercy of their decisions about our worth, alive or dead. But this raises the question of what happens to the soul, if one exists. Is it worth living as a half-human?

Technology has the potential to do many wonderful and amazing things, but perhaps we should reconsider giving up our humanity and the mystery of life and death as we embrace more of it.

IMMORTALITY IN POP CULTURE

I don't want to achieve immortality through my work. I want to achieve it through not dying.
—Woody Allen

Personally, I would not care for immortality in the least. There is nothing better than oblivion, since in oblivion there is no wish unfulfilled. We had it before we were born yet did not complain. Shall we whine because we know it will return? It is Elysium enough for me, at any rate.
—H. P. Lovecraft

If we cannot find a way to live forever in a physical sense, we can achieve immortality through the memories we leave behind and the work we have shared with the world.

The Afterlife Book

Because we can't take it with us, whatever we leave behind becomes our legacy. Since our primitive ancestors sat around a fire and told of deities and beings with powers beyond those of mortal men, novels, books, movies, television shows, podcasts, and merchandising have celebrated the immortal in their own right, instilling stories of eternal life into the collective consciousness of humanity.

Our pop culture has long envisioned life that does not end as a storytelling trope or device, usually in fantasy, science fiction, and horror. It allows the mere mortal to vicariously live on through these characters and figures and also get a glimpse of the pros and cons of living forever.

The quest for immortality has driven many a story's plot, with some finding success in an elixir or spell, and others failing to live out their numbered days, perhaps with a new understanding of the importance of the present and living in the now.

GILGAMESH

"I will proclaim to the world the deeds of Gilgamesh. This was the man to whom all things were known; this was the king who knew the countries of the world. He was wise, he saw mysteries and knew secret things, he brought us a tale of the days before the flood.

"He went on a long journey, was weary, worn-out with labour, returning he rested, he engraved on a stone the whole story."

**–The Epic of Gilgamesh, translated by N. K. Sandars
(Harmondsworth, England: Penguin Books, 1972)**

The Epic of Gilgamesh is believed to be the oldest written story on Earth and one of the most beloved stories of ancient Mesopotamia. It is also the oldest known tale of immortality, originating from Ancient Sumeria and written on 12 clay tablets in cuneiform script around 750 B.C.E., which were discovered in the ruins of Ashurbanipal's library in Nineveh by Assyrian archaeologist Hormuzd Rassam in 1853. Scholars have since then discovered additional texts and fragments of texts that place the origins of the Gilgamesh stories in the Sumerian city–states. According to a list of kings, there was a ruler of Uruk named Gilgamesh around 2600 B.C.E.

The epic poem recounts the exploits of a historical king of Uruk who reigned between 2750 and 2500 B.C.E. Gil–

gamesh is a handsome and athletic young king in Uruk whose mother is the goddess Ninsun and his father a priest–king named Lugalbanda. As a result, Gilgamesh is semi-divine and driven, but also cruel and arrogant, constantly challenging his peers to physical contests, including combat, and demanding the right to have sex with any new bride he chooses.

This narcissistic behavior angers the citizens of Uruk and they beg the God of Heaven, Anu, for help. Anu sends a wild man who lived with animals named Enkindu to challenge Gilgamesh. A temple priestess, Shamhat, seduces Enkindu and teaches him how to eat like a human, somewhat civilizing him. Then he sets off for Uruk where he meets Gilgamesh and engages in a fight. Gilgamesh wins and the two become fast friends, and their adventures make up the first half of the epic poem/story. They slay the monster Humbada together. Gilgamesh rebuffs the seductive ways of Ishtar/Inanna. She asks the god Enlil for the Bull of Heaven, to attack Gilgamesh with.

The Epic of Gilgamesh tablets were stolen from Iraq in 1991, purchased by Hobby Lobby, and put on display at the Museum of the Bible in Washington, D.C., before being seized by the U.S. government and returned to Iraq in 2019.

Gilgamesh and Enkidu kill the Bull, angering the gods, who punish Gilgamesh by killing Enkidu.

In the second half of the epic, Gilgamesh deeply mourns Enkidu's death and worries about his own life, which is the start of his quest for immortality. He searches for Utnapishtim, an immortal man who survived the Great Flood (and a precursor to the Bible's Noah). Gilgamesh finds Utnapishtim, who tells him he must accept his mortality. Gilgamesh returns to Uruk and becomes a good king and rules for 126 years.

Gilgamesh was both an epic hero and a historical king, as evidenced by inscriptions discovered in archaeological records. His story is one of human mortality and semidivinity, with powerful themes of friendship, immortality, sexual relations, civilization versus nature, and human–deity relationships. It also depicts the transformation of Gilgamesh's personality from arrogant and selfish to humbled and selfless.

As for finding immortality, to make a long story, or epic poem, short, Gilgamesh is given a magic plant from Utna–

pishtim that confers eternal youth, something that only Utnapishtim and his wife possess, but on his travels home he loses the magic plant, and Utnapishtim tells him that an immortal life is not in store for him. He did find immortality, just not for himself. It is his quest for eternal life triggered by the grief of losing his friend, though, that makes the story most memorable and a fixture of academic studies into literature, epic poetry, and Mesopotamian history.

Qin Shi Huang, China's first emperor, who reigned from 259 to 210 B.C.E., sought immortality because he feared death, and he sent out hundreds of people to seek the legendary elixir of life. He was obsessed with obtaining immortality and was duped by many who offered him alleged elixirs. He went to Zhifu Island three times in the hopes of discovering the secret to immortality. He allegedly died of mercury poisoning after taking mercury pills prescribed by his court doctors, who told him they would make him immortal. He was said to be so afraid of death that he ordered the construction of tunnels and passageways to each of his over 200 palaces, believing that traveling unseen would keep him safe from evil spirits. Clearly, it didn't protect him from his own doctors.

Mahavatar Babaji, born in 203 B.C.E., was an Indian Kriya Yoga guru believed to have first appeared over 5,000 years ago in India. He is alleged to still be alive as himself in his current physical body somewhere in India or the Himalaya mountains.

Olumba, born in 1918, was a Nigerian religious leader who founded the Brotherhood of the Cross and Star, which was more of a cult than religious group. He claimed he was the Abrahamic God in human form, and his followers believed he was immortal. He allegedly died in 2003, after resigning from his position as leader in 1999.

Immortality is a common theme in fiction, video games, movies, and television shows. Whether it's superheroes with the ability to live forever or video game characters who can never die, these figures take on the roles of pop culture deities, interacting with mere mortals and ordinary people. We get to live vicariously through these larger-

China's first emperor, Qin Shi Huang, tried a variety of elixirs to make himself immortal until one of them, containing mercury, ironically poisoned him to death.

Immortality Tropes in Pop Culture

In the film *Indiana Jones and the Last Crusade*, the title character searches for the Holy Grail, which can grant immortality to those who drink from it.

In pop culture, tropes are everywhere. They are significant or recurring motifs and themes found in movies, novels, and the like, and can be archetypal, such as the damsel in distress, the girl next door, or the chosen one. Some of the most widely used tropes are metaphor, irony, euphemism, and allegory in literature and storytelling. When it comes to immortality, tropes include:

- Complete immortality: The character cannot ever die. Ever. No matter what.

- Retroactive immortality: The character is capable of dying, but won't stay dead, and is either born again or resurrected.

- Biological immortality: The character is unaffected by time but still can be mortally injured.

There are also ageless characters, those who can shift from one physical body to another (body snatchers), and those who can only die after completing a specific purpose or quest.

cont'd on next page

cont'd from previous page

How do they achieve such immortality? More tropes abound, such as drinking from a fountain of youth, finding an elixir of life or Holy Grail object, hiding their soul away until a danger passes, going to a particular place that imparts immortality, being granted immortality by a god or demon or other person, and absorbing the life force of someone else to keep on keeping on. These can lead to challenges, though, such as the ageless immortal who falls for a mortal who does age or being the undead like a zombie and never being able to awaken fully to life, or maybe coming back from the dead minus a few body parts. A character might sell his or her soul for immortality, only to find they want out of the deal.

Some people seek fame as their method of immortality, or a legacy, both of which live on long after the character dies.

than-life characters, even if they're villains and bad guys, or tragically flawed in other ways. Our heroes can fly, see through walls, and shape–shift into wolves in the world of make-believe and made–up stories, but the most valuable and sought–after skill is eternal life.

Then there are those who possess eternal life until they are killed in one particular manner, such as the vampire or werewolf who lives for thousands of years until a wooden spike is driven through the heart or a silver bullet nips eternity in the bud. Zombies, or the undead, can eat brains indefinitely until someone blows out their brains and kills them. So there appear to be levels to eternal life, and true eternal existence appears to be the domain of only certain special entities such as angels, aliens, and demons, supernatural beings who defy the known laws of nature to begin with.

In June 2019, Ranker conducted a poll titled "The Greatest Immortal Characters in Fiction" and asked readers to vote. Finally, the top characters who will live forever ranged from movies to comic books to video games.

Doctor Who is a long–running BBC television show. Since the show's inception in 1963, thirteen different actors have played the lead character, a centuries–old alien known as a

Time Lord from the planet Gallifrey. He or she, along with companions, can travel through space/time in the TARDIS. Each new character is explained by the device of "re-generation," a Time Lord biological function that allows changes to occur in his/her cellular structure and appearance to heal and recover after an otherwise fatal injury.

The hugely popular *X-Men* series offers a mutant named Logan, who has sharp animal senses, enhanced physical abilities, regenerative healing ability, and three retractable claws in each hand. Otherwise known as Wolverine, this superhero seems invincible.

Actress Jodie Whittaker plays the thirteenth incarnation of Doctor Who, an immortal Time Lord on the hugely popular BBC sci-fi television series.

Marvel Comics character Loki, created by Stan Lee, is based on a Norse deity, the Asgardian God of Mischief, Loki. He is the adopted brother and enemy of Thor, another deity, and has often been depicted as an androgynous antihero. His abilities in various films run the gamut from magic to healing, telepathy, clairvoyance, and shapeshifting.

Deadpool is a fictional Marvel Comics hero who began as a supervillain before evolving into an antihero. He is disfigured and mentally unstable, but he possesses superhuman healing and immortality abilities, as well as teleportation and incredible strength.

Legolas is a Sindarin Elf of the Woodland Realm and one of nine members of the Fellowship of the Ring from J. R. R. Tolkien's legendary novels. Elves were immortals of great power and importance. Another immortal character from the Tolkien universe is Galadriel, a royal elf of both the Noldor and the Teleri with the power of telepathy.

Count Dracula is the title character of Bram Stoker's 1897 gothic horror novel *Dracula*, inspired in part by the fifteenth-century Wallachian Prince Vlad the Impaler. Flight, magic, shapeshifting, superhuman strength, telepathy, and immortality were among the vampire's abilities, unless he was killed in a specific way by a specific weapon. He disliked garlic as well.

Back to the comic book world with the Hulk, of Marvel Comics fame, created by Stan Lee and Jack Kirby. *The Incredible*

Hulk is a huge and muscular green humanoid version of his alter ego, Bruce Banner. Bruce is a reserved physicist who transforms into the Hulk when under great stress or danger. He can heal, live forever, warp reality, and shape-shift, and he possesses superhuman speed as well as brute strength, but only in his Hulk form.

The *Underworld* film series features a heroine named Selene, who has been portrayed in flashback scenes by Kate Beckinsale and her daughter, Lily Mo Sheen, and possesses superhuman strength.

Other noted fictional characters who don't die include Doctor Doom, Hellboy (who ages in reverse dog years), Hercules, Galactus the demigod, and the octopus/dragon/human Cthulhu of H. P. Lovecraft fame.

MYTH AND RELIGION

In myth and religion, we most commonly speak of people who achieved immortality through religious means, such as Jesus Christ, who died, was resurrected, and now resides eternally in Heaven for those of Christian faith, or Parashurama of Hindu mythology. Then there are the deities and gods, like those on Mount Olympus or the Taoist Eight Immortals on Mount Penglai. Gods and goddesses were above mortal humans and thus often possessed traits of immortality or even the ability to return after death, as was one of the legends surrounding King Arthur, who died and was believed to return after a period of death in a manner similar to the story of Christ.

To make deities and holy figures mortal would make them no more inspiring or larger than life than humans, so it's no wonder the "immortal trope" has been assigned to the realms of myth and religious belief.

Endymion was a shepherd in Mount Latmus in Asia Minor. Selene fell in love with him at first sight, but Endymion was mortal, complicating things. Selene asked Zeus to grant Endymion eternal life, but the price was a long sleep. Endymion kept his beautiful, smiling face through his sleep, and Selene was so moved by his beauty, she would watch him sleep. Tithonus, from Greek mythology, was granted eternal life but not youth, and was eventually turned into a grasshopper.

The most common immortal figure in Hindu myths is Ashwathama, a Kauravan warrior who was cursed by Krishna to an eternal life of roaming the Earth without love, respect, or social acceptance.

> *The Wandering Jew was a Jewish shoemaker who who ... taunted Jesus on the way to his crucifixion. Jesus cursed him to "go on forever till I return."*

The Wandering Jew was a Jewish shoemaker who, according to legend, taunted Jesus on the way to his crucifixion. Jesus cursed him to "go on forever till I return." The aptly named Wandering Jew will live until the second coming of Christ.

The Three Nephites (c. 34 or 35 C.E.) were given immortality in the Book of Mormon to minister among men until the return of Christ.

Sir Galahad (c. 2nd–6th century) was one of three knights of King Arthur's court to find the Holy Grail but the only one to achieve immortality. Merlin,, the famous magician of Arthurian legend, was in some accounts enchanted by Nimue. One account has Merlin dying, and another has him trapped under the enchantment in a tomb, mist, or cave.

RESURRECTING THE DEAD

Some people ask if zombies are immortal, but in most storylines, they can be killed off with a good blow to the head (allegedly, their own brains are the only thing that keeps their rotting bodies moving). The concept of the walking dead raises another intriguing aspect of immortality: resurrection or raising the dead. This is not the most accurate definition of immortality, but it does defy the typical death of mortals.

"Zombie" comes from the Haitian French *zombi* or Haitian Creole *zonbi*, an undead entity created when a human corpse is reanimated. This can be done, according to the usual horror and fantasy genres, by a plague or virus, a drug or herb, a mad doctor procedure as in many horror movies, or, as indicated by Haitian folklore, magic or voodoo/hoodoo. Zombies, now a pop culture staple, are not the only humans who can be reanimated or resurrected.

In his 1997 book *The Serpent and the Rainbow: A Harvard Scientist's Astonishing Journey into the Secret Societies of Haitian Voodoo, Zombis, and Magic*, author and ethnobotanist Wade Davis documents his time in 1982 in Haiti studying Haitian *voudoun* and *zombis*. These were people who reappeared in Haiti years after being officially declared dead. He researched the use of zombification as part of the traditions and history of the African origins of the Haitian beliefs.

Director and filmmaker John Carpenter made the story into the feature film *The Serpent and the Rainbow* in 1988.

Resurrection, also known as anastasis, is the process of bringing someone back to life after they have been officially pronounced dead. In religion and myth, it is usually a deity or god/goddess who dies and then returns to life after a certain period of time. It is the concept of the "dying and rising god" in myth. This is not the same as reincarnation, in which a soul incarnates into a new body, but rather the actual person returning as themselves. The Abrahamic religions believe in the resurrection of the dead, but this concept is divided into two parts: the ongoing resurrection of souls and the final resurrection of the dead that occurs in the Last Days.

The word "resurrection" comes from the Latin noun *resurrectionis* and from the verb *rego*, "to make straight, rule," and can be loosely translated as "a straightening from under again." The most famous resurrection is that of Jesus Christ, who was crucified and after three days in the burial tomb rose from the dead and walked again, but there is debate over whether he resurrected in spirit or into a material body. Regardless, he ascended to Heaven eventually, so it was a short return trip.

Becoming a zombie is one way of defeating death, although certainly not a pleasant method of resurrection and existence!

Other religious traditions, including some extant Egyptian and Canaanite writings alluding to dying gods like Osiris and Baal, mention resurrection as well. Many deities in ancient Greece were thought to be physically immortal through resurrection: Asclepius, who was killed by Zeus and resurrected in the form of a major god; Achilles, who was killed and removed from the funeral pyre by his goddess mother, Thetis, and resurrected into immortality; Memnon, who was also killed by Achilles and resurrected; and Castor, Heracles, and Melicertes, who all found immortality through resurrection. Many of the Trojan and Theban warriors, including Menelaus, were said to have become immortal without first dying. True immortality, according to the ancient Greeks, was the eternal union of the body and the soul.

One story that mirrors that of Christ is Alcestis, a Greek princess and daughter of King Pelias, who was resurrected after three days when she was rescued from the Underworld by Heracles, but she did not become immortal in that form.

As part of his healing missions, Jesus was known to raise the dead. In the New Testament, Jesus raised the deceased daughter of Jairus, a young man in the middle of his own funeral procession, and Lazarus of Bethany four days

Jesus' raising of Lazarus from the dead is likely the most famous such act in the Bible, although a couple of His apostles performed similar miracles.

after his burial. Jesus also charged his twelve apostles with the same task of raising the dead.

In the Acts of the Apostles, we learn of their deeds when Peter raised a woman named Dorcas (Tabitha), and Paul raised a man named Eutychus, who fell from a window to his death. The Gospel of Matthew recounts how, after Jesus's resurrection, many dead rose from their tombs and were witnessed in Jerusalem.

Saints were also said to be able to resurrect the dead, but it was Jesus's resurrection, as well as his ability to perform miracles, that served as one of the central tenets of Christianity and the promise of life after death mentioned throughout the New Testament.

Resurrection in Judaism focuses on three main examples in the Hebrew Bible:

- The prophet Elijah prays, and God raises a young boy from death (1 Kings 17:17–24)

- Elisha raises the son of the Woman of Shunem (2 Kings 4:32–37), whose birth he previously foretold (2 Kings 4:8–16)

- A dead man's body that was thrown into the dead Elisha's tomb is resurrected when the body touches Elisha's bones (2 Kings 13:21)

The early Israelites believed the graves of their family or tribe were a part of Sheol, a common grave. Sheol was defined in the Tanakh, the canonical Hebrew scriptures, including the Torah, the Nevi'im, and the Ketuvim, as an underworld where the souls of the dead went after physical death. The Babylonians had a similar underworld called Aralu, and the ancient Greeks had Hades. Sheol also appears in the Bible as Abaddon ("ruin"); Bor ("pit"); and Shakhat ("corruption").

The resurrection of the physical body in 2 Maccabees stated it as more of a re-creation of the flesh than the raising of the dead body. Resurrection also appears in the extra-canonical Book of Enoch, 2 Baruch, and 2 Esdras.

According to the great historian Josephus, the Sadducees did not believe in an afterlife. The New Testament claims the Pharisees believed in the resurrection, but it is not specific as to whether this is only of the flesh. Josephus wrote that his fellow Pharisees believed the soul was immortal and the souls of good people will "pass into other bodies," while "the souls of the wicked will suffer eternal punishment." The Book of Jubilees refers to the resurrection of the soul only, or an immortal soul that does not include the physical body.

Islamic belief in the Day of Resurrection is an essential component of Muslim traditions. At that time, which God has predetermined, the trials and tribulations described in the Quran that occur before and during this day will result in physical resurrection, ushered in by the Lord of the Resurrection, chosen from the progeny of Muhammad and his Imams to symbolize the purpose and pinnacle of creation. This person will bring the world out of darkness and ignorance and into the light, where they will be rewarded by God. First, God will hold everyone accountable for their sins and transgressions and sentence them accordingly. Those who have been wronged by others and have never received justice will have their rights restored on the Day of Resurrection.

> *Those who have been wronged by others and have never received justice will have their rights restored on the Day of Resurrection.*

From Islamreligion.com, we read of the timeline to the Day of Resurrection:

- Quran 20:55: The soul will then begin its journey up to the Heavens; for a believer permission would be sought for the gates of Heaven to be opened and the gates would be opened till it reaches the seventh Heaven, whereby God says: "Thereof (the earth) We created you, and into it We shall return you, and from it We shall bring you out once again."

- Quran 7:40: It would then be returned to the body. As for the non-believer, permission would be sought for the gates of the lowest Heaven to be opened, but the angels refuse and it will be cast back to earth. God, Almighty, tells us: "Verily, those who belie Our Signs and treat them with arrogance, for them the gates of Heaven will not be opened, and they will not enter Paradise until the camel goes through the eye of the needle. Thus, do We recompense the criminal sinners."

- Quran 39:68: Thereafter, one will remain in either continuous bliss or punishment in the grave until the Final Hour is established. Nearing the end of time, the trumpet will be blown and creation will cease to exist. God, Almighty, says: "And the Trumpet will be blown, and all who are in the Heavens and all who are on the earth will swoon away, except him whom God wills."

- Quran 36:51: It will be blown a second blowing, and all creation from the beginning of time till the end of time will be resurrected. "And the Trumpet will be blown (i.e., the second blowing) and behold! From the graves they will come out quickly to their Lord."

Eastern traditions focus more on reincarnation and karma, but there are stories of resurrection in Buddhism, namely in the Chan or Zen traditions, such as the legend of Bodhidharma, an Indian master who brought the Ekayana school of India to China, where it became known as Chan Buddhism. The legend goes as follows: Three years after Bodhidharma's death, Ambassador Song Yun of northern Wei claims to have seen him walking while holding a shoe at the Pamir Mountains. Song asked Bodhidharma where he was going, to which Bodhidharma replied, "I am going home."

When asked why he was holding his shoe, Bodhidharma answered, "You will know when you reach Shaolin monastery. Don't mention that you saw me or you will meet with disaster." After arriving at the palace, Song told the emperor that he met Bodhidharma on the way. The emperor said Bodhidharma was already dead and buried and had Song arrested for lying. At Shaolin Monastery, the monks informed them that Bodhidharma was dead and had been buried in a hill behind the temple. The grave was exhumed and was found to contain a single shoe. The monks then said, "Master has gone back home" and prostrated three times: "For nine years he had remained and nobody knew him; carrying a shoe in hand he went home quietly, without ceremony."

Another Buddhist story of resurrection involves the Chinese Chan master Puhua as recounted in the Record of

Linji. Here is the account from Irmgard Schloegl's *The Zen Teaching of Rinzai*.

One story of resurrection from Chinese legend involves the Chan master Puhua, who rose from his coffin into the clouds and rang a bell that alerted his followers to his presence.

> One day at the street market Fuke was begging all and sundry to give him a robe. Everybody offered him one, but he did not want any of them. The master [Linji] made the superior buy a coffin, and when Fuke returned, said to him: "There, I had this robe made for you." Fuke shouldered the coffin, and went back to the street market, calling loudly: "Rinzai had this robe made for me! I am off to the East Gate to enter transformation" (to die).
>
> The people of the market crowded after him, eager to look. Fuke said: "No, not today. Tomorrow, I shall go to the South Gate to enter transformation." And so, for three days. Nobody believed it any longer. On the fourth day, and now without any spectators, Fuke went alone outside the city walls, and laid himself into the coffin. He asked a traveler who chanced by to nail down the lid. The news spread at once, and the people of the market rushed there. On opening the coffin, they found that the body had vanished, but from high up in the sky they heard the ring of his hand bell.

Hinduism has its own folklore and mentions resurrection in sacred texts. The folklore of Savitri, who saved her husband's life; the Ramayana Sanskrit epic of Ravana being slain by Rama in a great battle; and Mahavatar Babaji and Lahiri Mahasaya, who allegedly performed their own self-resurrections, are all important.

Hinduism does not see resurrection in a positive light. In "The Concept of Resurrection in Hinduism" by Jayaram V for Hinduwebsite.com, we learn that "in Hinduism, all living beings possess souls. It also draws a clear distinction between the soul and the body. They represent the Self and the Not-self realities of the objective world, which are very different, without any correlation between the two except in the objective, predicate relationship as the subject and object.

"In its purest state, the soul has no attributes, name, or form. Hence, it is more appropriately called the Self (atma), which is indescribable, incomprehensible, formless, and beyond the mind and senses. In its impure state, the Self acquires a body and becomes embodied as a being. In that state, it remains bound to the cycle of births and deaths and experiences duality and delusion. Therefore, from the perspective of Hinduism, the physical resurrection of an embodied Self does not elevate the Self. Rather, it degrades it and keeps it bound to the mortal world."

THE NEW TECHNO-RESURRECTED

In one particularly amusing episode of the brilliant comedy series *The Golden Girls*, the four ladies agree to have their heads removed and frozen upon death so that they can always be together. Only Sophia, the wisecracking one, refuses, preferring to keep her entire body. Cryonics is the freezing of a human corpse or severed head at a low temperature (usually 196°C or 320.8°F) in the hope that resurrection will be possible in the future. The mainstream scientific community regards cryonics as a pseudoscience.

Roboticist Hans Moravec proposed in his book Mind Children *that a future supercomputer may have the ability to resurrect long-dead minds from the information that has survived.*

There has been a persistent rumor that movie mogul Walt Disney had himself frozen and buried in a vault underneath a popular attraction at his main theme park in California after his death in 1966, but family members have persisted in shooting down the rumor. The concept of cryonic preservation started getting noticed in the 1950s and 1960s with a major boost to its popularity arriving with Robert Ettinger's book *The Prospect of Immortality* (1964), which could have had something to do with the Disney rumor's timing.

Roboticist Hans Moravec proposed in his book *Mind Children* that a future supercomputer may have the ability to resurrect long-dead minds from the information that has survived. This would leave people with half the memories they had when they were alive, which doesn't sound like a very appealing prospect, but the concept has become popular fodder for science fiction films and novels.

In the science fiction novel *The Light of Other Days* by Sir Arthur Clarke and Stephen Baxter, the authors write of a future where we can resurrect the dead by going back to the past through micro wormholes and nanorobots to download snapshots of brain states and memories.

In 1985, the film *Re-Animator*, an American horror film loosely based on the 1922 H. P. Lovecraft novelette series "Herbert West–Reanimator," told the story of a medical student who invents a reagent that can re-animate deceased bodies and whose experiments with his girlfriend don't quite go as planned. *The Crow*, a classic 1994 film adapted from the graphic novel of the same name, starred a charismatic Brandon Lee as a musician named Eric Draven who, along with his fiancée, is brutally murdered the night before his wedding. On their one-year anniversary, he rises from the dead to exact revenge on their killers.

The films *Flatliners* (1990) and *The Lazarus Effect* (2015) focused on college students or adult researchers secretly toying in the lab with near-death experiments and dying while hooked up to a number of horrifyingly haywire gadgets, proving that we should not play God with the forces of life and death.

Perhaps the most disturbing pop culture reference to resurrection comes from horror master Stephen King, who wrote the 1983 novel *Pet Sematary*, which was later adapted into two films, about a sinister ancient Indian burial ground where kids bury their beloved pets, resulting in some rather gruesome reanimations. The lesson here: never bury Fluffy or Rover in an Indian burial ground.

DIGITAL AFTERLIFE

Would you have your brain scanned in detail to create a mental duplicate, or have this done to a loved one who has passed away? Imagine your mother or father dying and having their brains scanned into a video-game reality where you can interact with them indefinitely. These digital parents may even act, think, and behave in the same way that your biological parents did in perpetuity.

The idea of living on forever digitally is explored in a July 2016 *Atlantic Monthly* article, "Why You Should Believe in the Digital Afterlife," written by Michael Graziano, a pro-

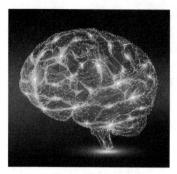

What if science could recreate your brain digitally and then transfer all your memories and personality into this electronic brain? Would the result be you living an immortal life or just a copy?

fessor of psychology and neuroscience at Princeton University. Graziano first asks the basic question: is it possible to duplicate yourself in a computer program? His answer is probably, but not for a while. It would come down to simulating neural networks on a microchip with extraordinary computing capabilities to create "an organized intelligence when compounded over enough neurons connected in enough complexity."

Graziano wonders if technology can be scaled up enough to preserve or copy someone's consciousness. There are start-up companies and organizations in Europe, such as the Human Brain Project, that are asking the same questions and working toward the ultimate goal of digital immortality, or at least some kind of digital afterlife. "No existing scanner can measure the pattern of connectivity among your neurons, or the connectome, as it's called. MRI machines scan at about a millimeter resolution, whereas synapses are only a few microns across." Graziano discusses the difficulties in scaling the technology to the point where it could one day capture the connectome of a human brain.

One of the biggest challenges is capturing the quirks and complexities of an individual human mind, and not just copying the mind and ending up with a sort of "Frankensteinian, ruined, crippled mind you would create." Again, merely simulating a brain does not necessarily encompass consciousness and might just be a "computer crunching numbers in imitation of your behavior." There are many theories about consciousness, one of which is the Global Workspace Theory. It holds that the fusion and sharing of information among the many areas of the brain is what causes awareness. According to integrated information theory, awareness is a byproduct of information, hence any computing equipment with enough information would be referred to as conscious.

Michael Shermer, *Skeptic* magazine's publisher and a Presidential Fellow at Chapman University, wrote "Who Are You?" for the July 2017 issue of *Scientific American*, arguing that the "you" in the afterlife would not be the same as the "you" now. He cited *The Discovery*, a 2017 Netflix film starring Robert Redford as a scientist who develops a machine that measures brain wavelengths on a subatomic level after death. There are parallels to quantum consciousness theory, but Shermer notes that it is presumptuous to assume our memories store our identities. Memories are believed to be permanently recorded in the brain, so if memories could be copied and pasted into a computer or a resurrected body, we would be reanimated or restored exactly as we are at the time of our deaths.

"But that is not how memory works," says Shermer. "Memory is not like a DVR that can play back the past on a screen in your mind. Memory is a continually edited and fluid process that utterly depends on the neurons in your brain being functional." He also states that copying the brain's connectome, which he describes as the diagram of its neural connections, would re-create yourself as you are now. But a copy of your memories, mind, or soul is not you, just a copy or replica of you. Then he points out that point of view (POV) has so much to do with who we are and how we view the world from our own eyes. "A POV depends entirely on the continuity of self from one moment to the next, even if that continuity is broken by sleep or anesthesia." Death would be more like a permanent break in that continuity, and POV cannot be moved or copied over to another medium.

Until we truly understand what consciousness is, attempting to duplicate it in a way that doesn't smack of a dull-eyed, drooling clone is far into the future, and maybe should stay there. Having Mom and Dad around for a longer amount of time is one thing, but not if they aren't really Mom and Dad, but rather some reasonable (or unreasonable, as the case may be) facsimile of them.

A NOT-SO-SIMPLE CHOICE

There are advantages and disadvantages to living forever, whether through immortality, reincarnation, or resurrection. While it may sound fantastic to live forever in your current body and life, imagine what it would be like after another hundred years of the same. Two hundred people? There may be enough time for continued personal development, even changing up your appearance from time to time, but at some point, one wonders if the same life will feel more like a death sentence, a Groundhog Day movie that never, ever, ever ends.

The Philosopher's Stone

For centuries, alchemists endeavored to find the "philosopher's stone," a mystical gem that could turn ordinary metals to gold and also be used to create an elixir of life (*The Alchemist in Search of the Philosopher's Stone* by Joseph Wright of Derby, 1771).

The philosopher's stone is a mythical alchemical substance that transforms base metals into gold. It is also called the elixir of life because of its powers of immortality. The stone is created through an alchemical process called the magnum opus, or the Great Work, and involves a series of color changes or chemical processes. When expressed in colors, the work progresses through nigredo, albedo, citrinitas, and rubedo phases. As a chemical process, it happens in seven or twelve stages that culminate in multiplication and projection.

The earliest known mention of the stone comes from the *Cheirokmeta* by Zosimos of Panopolis (fl. c. 300 C.E.). Some writers such as Elias Ashmole and the anonymous author of *Gloria Mundi* (1620) claim that its history goes back to Adam, who acquired the knowledge of the stone directly from God. Knowledge of the stone was passed down through patriarchs who achieved longevity, such as Methuselah.

The starter ingredient for the stone is said to be first matter, or "prima materia," which is associated with chaos and is the first matter of all existence.

Legend has it that thirteenth-century scientist and philosopher Albertus Magnus discovered the philosopher's stone and claimed to witness the transmutation of base metal into gold. Sixteenth-century Swiss alchemist Paracelsus believed in the existence of *alkahest*, the undiscovered element from which all other elements were derived. Paracelsus believed that this element was the philosopher's stone.

The equivalent of the philosopher's stone in Tibetan Buddhism is the Chintamani, sometimes depicted as a luminous pearl. In Hindu mythology it is the Syamantaka Mani, a brilliant ruby with the

cont'd on next page

cont'd from previous page

power to stop droughts, floods, and other natural disasters from affecting its owner.

The stone has powerful healing and immortality properties and is a perpetual source of fuel. It can turn simple crystals into diamonds and revive dead plants. One of its most bizarre properties is its uncanny ability to create a clone or homunculus—a miniature, fully formed tiny human produced artificially without a natural mother.

According to various alchemical texts, the stone comes in white for making silver and red for making gold.

The most famous pop culture reference to the philosopher's stone is from the Harry Potter book *Harry Potter and the Philosopher's Stone*, the first novel of the series, published in 1997, by J. K. Rowling, which introduced the world to an 11-year-old boy who discovers his magical heritage after he receives an acceptance letter to Hogwarts School of Witchcraft and Wizardry.

If you are reincarnated, you may like the idea of getting out of Dodge and into a different body and life entirely, but just as you cannot choose your family or neighbors, you cannot choose your family or neighbors in the new incarnation–unless you believe that you plan everything in advance for the advancement of your soul. But what if you don't have a choice? Can you accept the possibility that the next incarnation will be even worse than this one? Or will you eventually tire of living different lives and want to die of exhaustion?

The question of resurrection begs the question, "Will you have the same body you had at death?" If you were old and sick when you died, that might not be preferable to death. Can you choose the age you want to resurrect into? What happened to your youthful body? If you return to the same body but others do not, what kind of future will you have, watching loved ones die while you continue on? Will you perish in the end?

We would all prefer to live longer lives so that we could devote more time to ourselves, our dreams and goals, and the people we care about. But for how long? Even if we don't, that might get old after a while.

The question of resurrection begs the question, "Will you have the same body you had at death?"

Would you remember everything that happened to you if you lived forever? You won't, because memory decays exponentially over time, so while you might remember everything that happened today, it drops to about 10 percent for most people after a few days. One month from now, you would have a difficult time recalling more than 1 percent of today's events, and after a year, that drops to one-tenth of 1 percent.

The brain normally forgets a lot of the past to make room for the present, so you can remember where you left your keys or what you need at the grocery store when you forgot the list at home. You simply must accept living forever and forgetting your distant past on a regular basis, in effect being born anew with no memories of loved ones who have passed on or the life you once led unless they are constantly right in front of your face as new memories. This doesn't even address the issue of brain aging, but perhaps that's what artificial intelligence and transhumanism are for.

There are so many questions that arise when we consider life and death to be anything other than what they are, which is why these topics are widely and continuously debated in the halls of academia, science, religion, and psychology.

Instead, you could always read a novel or watch a movie to get your fix of immortality and never growing old in pop culture.

Conclusion

The Ivy on the Wall

*Life is eternal, and love is immortal, and death is only a horizon, and
a horizon is nothing save the limit of our sight.*
—R. W. Raymond

*Our brain is but a sleep and a forgetting. The Soul that rises with us,
our life's Star, Hath had elsewhere its setting. And cometh from afar.*
—William Wordsworth

A Happy Man

*When these graven lines you see,
Traveller, do not pity me;
Though I be among the dead,
Let no mournful word be said.
Children that I leave behind,
And their children, all were kind;
Near to them and to my wife,
I was happy all my life.
My three sons I married right,
And their sons I rocked at night;
Death nor sorrow never brought
Cause for one unhappy thought.
Now, and with no need of tears,
Here they leave me, full of years,—
Leave me to my quiet rest
In the region of the blest.*

—Edwin Arlington Robinson

239

We should take heart from Edwin Arlington Robinson's poem "A Happy Man," in which he declares that he has lived a full life and never had an unhappy thought. Now, when he dies, he knows he is going to the land of the "blest," and there will be no need for those he leaves behind to cry. Death frightens us, but perhaps not fully living the one life we have been given frightens us more. Death is also what makes life so precious and sweet, because without the threat of death, we would have little appreciation for each passing day.

Nonetheless, the promise of life after death is equally compelling. It is sufficient to keep people from causing harm to others and to keep those who are suffering and in pain from giving up. It gives us hope that we will survive in some form and that the lives we've lived on this planet weren't just blips on a cosmic radar screen or a parenthesis in a long sentence of time.

We want to know that we mattered and will continue to matter after our bodies decompose into ash and dust, that we loved, and that our purpose and love were not only temporary but would outlast our physical bodies and be felt on some level by future generations. We are driven to find a way to make ourselves immortal in some way, because the thought of coming to a complete halt one day is too much for us to bear. All this life, and we just come to an end?

The afterlife is more than just a destination we wish to visit; it is an inspiration for both the individual and collective human struggle. Death is a constant threat, but if there is an afterlife, that fear–the one that most grips us and refuses to let go as the days, weeks, and months pass–would dissipate and lose its power over us.

Some argue that proof of an afterlife would cause us to be more careless with our lives and take advantage of the present, causing us to be less acutely aware of the value of each moment. Others believe the exact opposite. Being free of the existential dread that underpins so much of our on-going misery and pain, suffering, and doubt would allow us to savor every moment with joyful abandon. It would be completely liberating. There may still be the prospect of pun-ishment or reward in a Hell or Heaven to drive our morals and behaviors, if they are not already inherent in our per-sonality, but we would do so many things outside of our comfort zone if we were not afraid of death. We would allow ourselves to explore and embark on adventures that we had previously deemed too dangerous. We'd take chances in life and in love.

We may also have such a low regard for life that we would easily take it away from anyone who irritated or hurt us. We might treat each life with a lot less importance or value if we knew life was eternal.

But here's the thing: whether death is final or just another rest stop on the long journey of the soul, shouldn't we be treating every moment as a gift? This life will come to an end. Whether we continue or not, the moments we have right now with family and friends will end. Because the promise of another life beyond this one will not change that fact, it is incumbent upon us to be fully present in the current experience, the lives at hand, and to be present for the good, the bad, and the ugly, because it is all beautiful, all a part of being human and the experience of being alive.

We use words like "life" and "death" as if they are polar opposites, which they are in our limited perception and perspective. Nonetheless, we are aware of all the possible ways in which we may be lacking information from which to form those perceptions and perspectives. We cannot see or hear every part of the light spectrum or every range of sound. Perhaps there are many levels of life going on all around us that we are unaware of, or perhaps our cats notice when they stare at something we cannot see. We have no idea what is going on in the universe or at the subatomic level, where particles are waves and waves are particles, and some things defy logic while remaining real and observable.

When perception and perspective are altered, it can appear as if we have been introduced to a completely new reality.

During the writing of this book, co-author Marie had a revelation. Her desk faces a wall of ivy with tiny berries that, during spring and summer, is lush and green and filled with birds and critters, often distracting her from her work. During the fall, the leaves turn beautiful colors and drop off onto the ground. In the winter, the wall is dead. There

Whether or not there is a life after this one, we should never forget to enjoy and appreciate the life we have right now.

The Afterlife Book

is not a touch of green, of life, just a big wall of grey, dead branches that appear to have no possibility of future life within them. Even on closer inspection, there is no discernable way for life to be hiding in those dead branches.

But it is.

In the spring, the smallest buds emerge, and within a few weeks, the huge green leaves and tiny berries are in full bloom. The birds and animals have returned. The rebirth is now complete. This cycle will continue indefinitely unless someone deliberately kills the entire wall of ivy or acid rain falls to poison it at the root. Life, death, and rebirth. Rinse and repeat.

If there is an ivy wall within this cycle, what makes us humans think we are immune? But we do, and we make all kinds of excuses for why and how. The dead ivy wall doesn't care about our excuses. It does what nature does, transforming something devoid of life into something brimming with it. Perhaps we don't notice the minutiae that occur below our level of sight and perception. We don't see the seed of life within the dead branches where new leaves and berries will sprout in a few months. We can't see it, so it doesn't exist until we see it.

The afterlife, or the continuous existence of the nonphysical part of us, may be a matter of perception, with its roots and mechanisms hidden but inherent within our nature, much like that ivy wall. An even more difficult problem in proving the existence of the afterlife is that we still have so much to learn about life itself: how it works, what gives it, the intricacies and complexities of every aspect of it, where it came from, and if it has a greater purpose. Biology, physiology, anatomy, and other disciplines that study the inner workings of our cells, organs, tissues, brains, and bones and how each system works to keep us alive, as well as how the bodily systems all work in tandem, are still rife with unanswered questions and undiscovered truths. This complicates our quest to comprehend death and what might come after.

We've been taught and told to assume death since we were children, trying to understand why someone we loved was there one minute, gone the next, and never returned. We continue to make assumptions because we don't yet understand the bigger picture or the broader perspective. Those who have crossed the border between this life and the next have returned with stories to tell and proof of an afterlife experience. We choose whether to believe it or not based on how it fits into our current perceptions of death, whether taught to us by our parents, teachers, religious leaders, or our own imaginations.

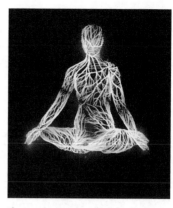

What survives? Energy. Perhaps the soul, or consciousness. The body returns to the earth as energy once more. As a result, we continue to exist, albeit in different forms, manifesting as various types of energy. But where are we going? What happens to the part of us that is animated and interacts with our surroundings? Why does a chair or a hammer last forever, but we living and dy-

If we are just energy and energy cannot be destroyed, then mustn't we, in some manner, survive the demise of our physical bodies?

namic beings have such a short shelf-life, if life is so precious? It seems strange to us that an artist or sculptor, for example, would use their energy to create a beautiful painting or statue that would last long after they died. The energy remains in the form of the creation, but the creator, at least in the form he or she once was, has vanished.

Why are we even here in the first place? If there is a strong spiritual reason for our existence, wouldn't it include the evolution of our soul or consciousness and not be a one-time event? We wouldn't be able to learn from our mistakes and get another chance to level up and do better if it were. It would be as if life is just a blip on the radar screen, meaningful only in terms of how we affect and influence the blips around us. Perhaps it is our human egos that refuse to accept that we are not important enough to continue, or that there are some mysteries that we are never meant to solve, no matter how smart, advanced, or special we believe we are in the grand scheme of things.

Writing a book about the afterlife is difficult because it forces you to confront your own mortality, as well as all the unanswered and possibly unanswerable questions that arise from the realization that one day you and those you love and who love you will turn off and cease to exist in this life. Even if doing so doesn't really answer any questions, facing these things is frightening but liberating. The stories of others who claim to have been on the other side and say it does not end, well, that is where the hope lies, and where a little faith may be required to navigate life and death.

Here's the deal. Only death will satisfy our insatiable curiosity, and by then, it won't matter because we'll be on the other side. Those left behind will react differently, mourning and grieving until they, too, make the same transition and discover for themselves. Until then, we live on in the memories and stories that the living enjoy telling, or in the things we made, created, and invented. We will be remembered for the love we shared and the hope we inspired. We live on through the DNA of our children and their children.

This book will outlive its authors, publisher, printer, editors, and readers. It's an odd sensation to have created something that will exist long after we've all died physically. Perhaps it is not too far-fetched to believe that something as valuable as a human life, or any living, breathing being, will do the same.

Death Is Nothing at All
Henry Scott Holland

Death is nothing at all.

It does not count.

I have only slipped away into the next room.

Nothing has happened.

Everything remains exactly as it was.

I am I, and you are you,

and the old life that we lived so fondly together is
    untouched, unchanged.

Whatever we were to each other, that we are still.

Call me by the old familiar name.

Speak of me in the easy way which you always used.

Put no difference into your tone.

Wear no forced air of solemnity or sorrow.

Laugh as we always laughed at the little jokes that
    we enjoyed together.

Play, smile, think of me, pray for me.

Let my name be ever the household word that it
    always was.

Let it be spoken without an effort, without the
    ghost of a shadow upon it.

Life means all that it ever meant.

It is the same as it ever was.

There is absolute and unbroken continuity.

What is this death but a negligible accident?

Why should I be out of mind because I am out of
sight?

I am but waiting for you, for an interval,

somewhere very near,

just round the corner.

All is well.

Nothing is hurt; nothing is lost.

One brief moment and all will be as it was before.

How we shall laugh at the trouble of parting when
we meet again!

This poem is often read at funerals. The author, Henry Scott Holland (1847–1918), was a priest at St. Paul's Cathedral of London. He originally delivered it as part of a sermon in 1910. The sermon, titled "The King of Terrors," was given while the body of King Edward VII was lying in state at Westminster.

APPENDIX: PERSONAL STORIES OF DEATH AND THE AFTERLIFE

Talking to the Dead: It Isn't Like the Movies

Denise A. Agnew
Agnewcreativemedium.com

Sometimes it isn't easy to explain the esoteric. At least it isn't for me. After all, I was in touch with the spirit world my whole life but didn't understand that until I was 56 years old. I've always been a late bloomer.

Originally, I called this "Working with Spirits: Common Misconceptions." Then I realized the title didn't convey what I meant. Because working with spirits might sound like I'm building a house or renovating a kitchen. Then I realized I just needed to state the truth about *my* mediumship.

Once I understood that what I'd been experiencing since childhood was sometimes mediumship and not just the extremely over-the-top imagination of a fiction writer, I started thinking I needed to find the perfect way to be a medium. To do it … drum roll … *Right. Correctly.*

In mediumship classes, there is sometimes a lot of meditation and ceremony to get in the proper frame of mind to bring forth spirit for a client. When that didn't quite do it for me, I started to think that meant … another drum roll … that I *wasn't* a medium and all of it had been one big delusion. Until I ran into a medium who explained that it isn't the same for everyone. The spirit world isn't reserved only for people who meditate or prepare a ceremony. A medium must find the door that works for them and open it.

It means spirit communicates with me the way spirit knows I'll understand. Spirits come to me because they know I can see them in a way that makes sense for the client.

I'll use movies and television as examples because I write screenplays and television pilots.

Many people have watched television series and movies with psychic and/or medium characters. One of the shows I found most realistic for me was *Medium*, not for the full body apparitions or dreams but rather for the way the clues worked for the fictional character Allison DuBois. For me it isn't as if the dead person always walks right up and says, "This is what happened to me, and this is where you can find me." Or, "This is how I committed suicide, and this is how I did it." Sometimes the clues aren't that clear, just as they aren't for the fictional Allison.

Sometimes the clue I'm given (most often a visual) is vague, and it isn't until I tell the client what I see that the client then recognizes the clue. During one reading, I felt as if I was in someone else's body, and I was walking down stone stairs into a semi-dark cellar. I was compelled to hold my hands up to my neck. I didn't have a clue what that meant, but the client reported that I was describing the basement of her husband's grandmother's house and the grandmother had hung herself in the basement. Hence, my hands up to my own neck.

The TV series *Profiler*, which wasn't about mediumship or psychic abilities, resonated with me a lot. The main character seemed to understand things about people and places that many others didn't. I related to her character because I've been that way all my life.

I swear that the person who wrote the *X-Files* episode "Clyde Bruckman's Final Repose" really hit it on the head for me. Agent Fox Mulder asks Bruckman how he knows where they should look for a particular deceased person. Bruckman just says, with a hint of annoyance, "I don't know." That's how psychic stuff is for me most of the time. I don't know how I know. I just do.

Every medium is asked, at one time or the other, "How do you connect with spirits?"

I recall the first time someone asked me that question, and I also recall the mini panic it started inside me. How did I do it? Somewhat like the Bruckman character from the *X-Files* episode, I wanted to shout, "I don't know! Ya know???"

Earlier I mentioned that I'm a late bloomer and didn't even know I was a medium until I was 56. Not because the signs weren't all there, but like a lot of people, I thought mediumship looked and felt like something other than what I was experiencing. It's ironic that over the last 10 to 15 years, as I embraced the understanding that I am an empath and a psychic, that I would say out loud to people, "But I'm not a medium or anything."

I look back at that sometimes and think, "Wow. I could've been working on this mediumship ability a long time ago." Regrets, in other words. But here I am, and I'm embracing it all now.

A few years back, my dear friend Arlene (who has since passed into spirit) asked me, "Did you ever think that some of the information from some of the books you've written, especially the historical, was channeled?" She asked me this way before I discovered my mediumship abilities. I was floored. It didn't seem likely to me, but now that I know what I know about channeling, I think she's right! Some of that information was my writer imagination. Some of it wasn't.

So how does this ability come to me in my unique way?

When doing a photo reading, I write out what I see, hear, sense, feel, and the like. The client receives this "info dump" of everything that is coming to me about the person who is in spirit. I'm not cleaning it up on the way, I'm just giving the client everything that comes to me. I want the client to see everything I see because the clues could be important. If I pretty it up or try to "make sense" with it, I may accidentally hold something back that the client recognizes and understands as evidential.

Let me give you an example. I'm not telling any identifying information, so I think it's safe to use this case. I was doing a photo reading and the spirit said to me, "Ask her about the yada, yada." I'm calling it "yada, yada" because what he was saying was something vastly intimate and personal between the spirit and the client. I hesitated. Should I tell her what he said? I mean, that could be really embarrassing and if I tell her he said that, and it makes no sense, that could be mortifying. I got over myself and told her that he'd asked me to ask about the yada, yada. She laughed and confirmed that, yes, the detail he mentioned was only something between them that no one else on earth knew about. Evidential!

When I do any reading, I prefer if the client doesn't tell me who they are hoping to contact. I close my eyes and visualize my crown chakra opening like a lotus to universal energy (much as I do for Reiki sessions) and allow this white light to flow down through my entire body and to spread out and flow into the room and as far as I can visualize.

After this, I immediately visualize a real place. It's called Crescent Moon Picnic Site in Sedona, Arizona. I've visited there two times over the years and loved it more than I can say. (You should visit!) A creek runs through the site, and at one time there were benches where people could sit and listen to the beautiful sounds of the creek. The benches were concrete, but in my mind during a reading, they are lovely wood with supportive backs. My bench even leans up against a tree on the left side, so I can touch the tree and feel its energy.

Once I am settled, I wait and see which spirit(s) arrive and sit on the bench to my right. This is where I can see and hear them. Most of the time they show me images of what they want me to know and convey to the client.

At this point in my mediumship journey, I know this isn't the end of my development. I'll continue to learn and grow as a medium.

The truth for me has been finding my own way through mediumship and psychic abilities–understanding how it works for me so that I better understand how I can help others contact the spirits of those who have passed on.

Denise A. Agnew is the award-winning author of over 69 novels and several optioned and produced screenplays. Denise is also a paranormal investigator (SOS Paranormal Investigations), Reiki master, certified creativity coach, and evidential medium. Denise lives in Arizona with her husband. You can finder her at agnewcreativemedium.com and deniseagnew.com.

Phone Calls

J. M. Ree

When my father's mom, whom we called Nana, died, me, my sister and my father all got phone calls at 11:07 P.M. PST. This was back in the day when landlines were a thing, so the call came over our landlines. The phone rang a few times and when we each answered, there was no one on the other end of the line. We had no idea we had all gotten these calls until my father's wife contacted us to tell us Nana had died–at 11:07 P.M. on that same night. It was later at the funeral that I brought up the eerie phone call, and my sister and father both got really excited, saying they, too, had received the same call. None of us had caller ID, and we didn't think of contacting the phone company to see what number was calling. It didn't really matter because we knew it was her. I know this is not proof of the afterlife, but we all truly believed that Nana was letting us know it was time to move on.

(Author's note: Phone calls from the deceased at the time of death are incredibly common and reported on forums such as Reddit and Quora. This includes calls from the cell phones of the deceased that can be traced back to their real cell phone numbers with the call time upon death or shortly afterwards.)

Deathbed Appearance
C. Whittaker

My parents were away on a cruise and my father had not been well, but when they left everything seemed OK. One night, I woke up to see my father standing at the foot of my bed. He was not solid, but I could tell it was him. He was just looking at me; he didn't say anything. After what must have been just one minute–but could have been shorter or longer because I had no sense of time then–he vanished into thin air. I sat there shaking and wasn't sure if I had really seen him or been half asleep, but a few hours later, my mom called to tell us that my dad had died on the cruise of a heart attack around the same time he appeared at the foot of my bed. He had come, I believe, to say a final goodbye to me.

The Psychology of Ghost Hunting
Brandon Alvis

Death is an inevitable part of life. Reminders of our own mortality surround us every day. Any time we read a newspaper, turn on the news, or consume media we are shown heartbreaking stories of a tragic loss of life. As the old saying goes, "If it bleeds, it leads." At some point throughout our lifetime, we will experience the loss of a loved one, a friend, an acquaintance. With each passing, we are faced with a question: What happens when we die? I was first faced with that question on September 8, 1995, when my oldest brother Eric passed away from cancer at the age of 24.

Learning about Death

I was only eight years old at the time of my brother's passing. The concept of death was a lot for a third grader to take in, let alone understand.

It confused me.

Much of my childhood was spent at the cemetery where my brother was laid to rest. The more time I spent surrounded by tombstones, the more I started to comprehend what death was and how we would all meet the same end. As my mother would visit my brother and grieve, I did what any eight-year-old kid would do: explore. I'd walk around the cemetery. I'd read the grave markers, the names, the dates of birth and death. I'd speak with the groundskeepers and ask them questions about their job. What was it like working in the death industry? I watched as they would prepare the ground for upcoming burials and funerals taking place close to my brother's gravesite. I would listen to the eulogies and observe how others handled grief. This is macabre, but it helped me begin my own grieving process. As the years passed and I grew older, thinking of our ultimate end became easier for me. In 2002 my grandmother passed away, peacefully in her home at the age of 73. She was ill in the later years of her life. During our final conversation before her passing, I knew her time on earth was coming to an end; and while I fought to cherish the little time she had left, I was prepared to grieve for her once she took her last breath. However tragic death was, I readied myself for this anguish.

I was confident I could properly grieve for my grandmother. Death wouldn't catch me off guard. But in 2004, my brother Gary took his life. I couldn't see it through the rage I felt at that time, but my way of thinking about our final end would change forever.

"That is not dead which can eternal lie, / And with strange aeons even death may die."

–Howard Phillips Lovecraft, *The Nameless City*

Paranormal Investigation as Grief Therapy

There are many reasons why people get involved in the search for ghosts and hauntings. Some are looking for an adrenaline rush, some for notoriety. One common reason is the passing of a loved one. In my 17 years of research, I have met hundreds of individuals who are willing to journey into the dark for answers about the afterlife, just as I was after the death of my two brothers. Many paranormal investigators have found a sense of peace in trying to communicate with those who have come before us. After hearing countless stories from those in the field, I realized that the act of paranormal investigation was a form of grief therapy. I only ever made that connection when I read a book titled *Corpses, Coffins and Crypts: A History of Burial* by Penny Colman, which showed up on my radar for a research project I conducted many years ago. In chapter two of Colman's book, she cites a study performed by psychologist Maria Nagy in 1948:

"The children, who nicknamed Nagy 'Auntie Death,' had discussions with Nagy and drew pictures. In addition, the older children followed Nagy's request to 'write down everything that comes to your mind about death.' Nagy studied their responses and concluded that some children go through three stages in understanding death. The youngest children aged three to about five tend to be curious about death and ask matter-of-fact questions about funerals, coffins, and cemeteries. To them, death is a continuation of life but at a lower level: dead people can't see and hear as well as living people, they aren't quite as hungry, and they don't do very much. And they might return.

"Younger children appear to think that death is at best not much fun and boring and at the worst lonely and scary. Beginning at about the age of five or six, children tend to realize that death is final and move into what Nagy named Stage 2. Although at this stage, many children realized that death was final, some of them thought that they could escape death if they were clever, careful, or lucky. Christy Ottaviano remembers thinking like that when she was in elementary school. 'I had to walk past a cemetery to get to school,' she recalls. 'I thought that I wouldn't die if I held my breath the whole way. So, I did until I was about nine or ten years old.' Christy may have stopped because she moved into what

Nagy identified as Stage 3 in understanding death. This is when children tend to realize that in addition to being final, death is also inevitable. Everyone dies, even clever, careful, and lucky people. Or people who hold their breath when they walk past a cemetery. 'Death is destiny,' wrote one ten-year-old child. Another ten-year-old wrote, 'Everyone has to die.' According to Nagy, Stage 3, which starts at about age nine or ten, continues throughout life" (Colman, 29, 30, 31).

Death and the Final Frontier

Reading Maria Nagy's "The Child's Theories Concerning Death" completely transformed my thought process. Having basically grown up in a cemetery and losing someone so close to me at such a young age, I made the jump from Nagy's proclaimed stage 2 to stage 3 in a more advanced timeframe. Other studies have shown that "children who experienced a parent's death, who are dying themselves, or who have witnessed violent, traumatic death will perceive death in an adultlike manner at much earlier ages than children who have not had such experiences" ("Death: The Development of a Concept of Death"). These experiences of the human condition led me early on in a lifelong pursuit of finding answers about the possibility of retaining consciousness after the brain dies. Like many others in the study of ghosts and hauntings, I have found comfort in journeying into the dark, and I carry this into every investigation I conduct, into every bit of research I perform, and the hours upon hours of footage I review. And I will continue to do so, until I meet my own ultimate end.

The Light Before Life
A Pre-Life Experience
Scott Westmoreland

I was born into this world on December 23, 1964. The following is a vivid flow of memories and sensations that never left my consciousness from the moment I experienced them. It wasn't until adulthood (when I heard the eerily similar accounts of near-death experiencers) that I had the realization I was in a prebirth state, nearly returned to the Spirit realm, before being instructed to go back and experience the incarnation I now call "my life."

I have a sudden awareness of being in the womb. I have just been elsewhere, but now my mind is placed in an environment that is warm, dark, safe; and I seem to be reclined back, feet up, like an astronaut ready to launch. I can hear muffled sounds, and I sense dim light at times, but mostly darkness. It is a new sensation, but one of purpose, safety, comfort. I am not afraid. I am in and out of this space–perhaps I never really leave, but dream, and then awaken again? I am here for an unknown amount of time. Occasionally I feel the jostling and movement of my host, my mother. Again, it seems I can sleep and then wake again–a shift in consciousness–but always feeling totally safe and comfortable. And then there is a break in the continuity of this existence: I am in complete, inky blackness, much darker than the dimly lit belly of my mother. I am not afraid. I begin to swim, dog-paddle really, until I instinctively reach for a wall with my hand. I feel a soft, smooth, velvety texture. I remember liking the touch very much. And then I sense a presence to my left, a guide of sorts, who beckons me to follow. I travel along until I reach a gray, foggy area. I see shadows of beings criss-crossing in front of me. Lots of activity, energy. I again hear faint, muted voices. I reach out my "ethereal" hands and arms, but only to get my bearings. This doesn't last long before I am once again in darkness–about to enter a huge tunnel, still following the guide as the pathway curves to my left at the entrance. Seems as though it is slightly inclined. I notice a pinpoint of light in the distance.

Next thing I experience is that of being cradled like an infant in a tight, warm embrace. I am suddenly rocketing at great speed towards the light, all the while feeling warmth, safety, total love. Now I am instantaneously "placed" in front of an all-encompassing light–brighter than a thousand suns–that surrounds me, loves me ... *is* me! My instinct is to continue into it, but a powerful male voice goes directly into my head. "No," it lovingly commands. "You must not go any further. You must go back!" I recall my guide to my right, quietly nodding? The voice tells me, "You will love these parents, this family. This life will be a 'good one,' you will be glad to live it." I sensed the previous life was much more harrowing. I can sense a smile from this Godly presence, even humor if that's possible? And with that, I am whisked away quickly, back to where I came from–descending faster than the speed of light. New vantage point: I am looking down from about 12–15 feet above a pair of glass doors. The hospital entrance. I see my father burst through from the interior, hurriedly. He is wearing khaki slacks and a cardigan sweater. (Was it light blue? Maybe burgundy? My human mind can't decide in retrospect.) In a rush, he has left the car in an unsafe spot in the middle of the lot and must move it to a designated space. These details were absolutely confirmed by my parents!

Next, I am back to the darkness of the womb, being birthed. It is very constricting, uncomfortable. I feel squeezed, unbearably tight, and my head is being grabbed and pulled. There is commotion, loud voices, upset, and strain. I am concerned for a moment, until I am finally free! I feel extreme cold, and wet–like when you get out of a hot tub on a winter's night. Uncomfortably bright light hurts my eyes (not like the light in my NDE, which was much, much brighter, but soothing). I made it, I'm here, I tell myself. I know I am in a new state of being, new surroundings, and yet my consciousness doesn't feel like I am starting at point "A," but rather, awareness extends backwards as far as forwards. Again, I'm not afraid. I scream and cry because I can. It is wonderful and natural to express yourself as a material being. There are cuts and pokes that give me reason to wail, but I know this is where I belong now. After the initial protocol, and things are calm, I decide to close my eyes until the brightness and blurriness are gone. I decide to sleep. I do remember the moment I was awakened and could finally see clearly, with no light sensitivity. I am ready to begin my earthly journey.

As it relates to my experience, I was too young–prebirth actually–to have had a life review, but I *have* had stunning past–life recall of lives during the American Civil War and as an Ancient Egyptian Royal (perhaps I can share the experiences at a later time). I also carried with me into this life a heightened creative ability (as both a performer and artist). I have always had psychic and spontaneous mediumship gifts and even the awareness of past lives shared with some of those I encounter this time around. I do not know what caused me to suddenly leave the safety of a healthy body and try to return to a spirit state before I was born. This part is understandably concerning to my parents when I tell them about my experience. I do know I was anemic and quite sickly as an infant and even a toddler–conditions I thankfully outgrew! And I have gone on to fulfill the destiny of that "good life" that God promised. I would even say it has been tremendous!

In conclusion, I have had, and continue to have, countless experiences and validations that confirm my claims. Not only is our current "life" a brief book or movie that seems real, but it is also merely a sidebar for our soul, a tangent to the greater reality. I wish each of you peace, love, and the assurance that we live eternally without judgment, condemnation, or the inability to create our own existence. That is God's loving gift to each of us, forever....

Scott Westmoreland is an internationally acclaimed artist and art instructor. He has been a performer and writer. He can be reached at Scottfineart@sbcglobal.net.

The Making of a Medium
Karen McAfee

It was back in January of 2001, and I was on the last plane out of Atlanta, on my way home to Ohio, where my mother was in a hospital room, close to death after surgery and a week on a respirator. I remember just sitting there in the darkened cabin of the airplane, alone, with nothing (and no desire) to read, constantly checking my watch. The last time I looked it was 10:50 P.M.

I closed my eyes and felt myself drifting into a daydreamy state of consciousness. I became aware of a scene taking shape in my mind's eye and saw my mother emerging out of a mist, wearing a pale blue nightgown, walking across what appeared to be a theater stage. The words "Now I can rest" popped into my head, and I felt what I thought felt like a kiss on my forehead. An incredible sense of peace washed over me, and in that one moment, I knew that my mother took away any fear I had of mortal death and allowed me to feel what she was feeling as she transitioned from her physical body back to the world of Spirit. I opened my eyes and realized that I had been weeping. I brushed my tears aside and looked at my watch and was startled to see that 20 minutes had passed in what seemed seconds. But in those 20 minutes, I knew my life had unmistakably changed forever.

When I arrived at the hospital, my younger sister, Joey, came to escort me to my mother's room. Just before getting on the escalator, she stopped me, and gently placing her hand upon my arm, quietly said that she had "something" to tell me. I told her that I already knew.

I asked her if Mom had passed at 10:50 pm, and she said no. "Was it 11:10?" I asked.

She looked at me a little sideways, so I began to tell her what had happened to me on the plane. I could see the color draining from her face as I spoke, realizing that what I had experienced on the plane with Mom must have been real. Joey told me they were all gathered around Mom's bedside, telling her that it was "okay to go" and that she should try to find me, and my older sister, Kathie, who lived in Texas. Kath had just been diagnosed with leukemia and could not travel. Joey said that she remembered looking at Dad's watch just as Mom was drawing what turned out to be her last breath and that the time on his watch was 11:08 P.M.

A month or so later, I began to notice little things that could have only been interpreted as signs from my mom. Eventually, I would demand them from her. And not just any old sign. I wanted specific things like monarch butterflies or pairs of dolphins at the beaches or for hummingbirds to come to my feeder within two minutes. And she always came through. I bet I have at least 100 sand dollars on my bookshelves by now.

Discovering You're a Medium on Your Very First Ghost Hunt

My husband had taken a keen interest in the paranormal ever since shows like *Ghost Hunters* and *Ghost Adventures* hit the airwaves back around 2006. I actually decided to join his group mostly because I was tired of spending Saturday nights alone. Being raised in a conservative Catholic home, I had never really given the idea of an afterlife much thought, and so I was a real skeptic back then. As far as I knew, when you died you stayed buried until Jesus came to tell you if your soul was going to Heaven or Hell.

So, this investigation was at a restaurant where a lot of paranormal activity like ghost sightings, chairs being oddly stacked on tables, salt and pepper shakers being moved around, and the like was being reported regularly by the staff. I like photography, so I brought my camera that night. As I was reviewing my first shots, I noticed that I had captured what looked like three or four huge soap bubbles, and they were getting closer and closer to me with each photo I took. I will admit it was weirdly unnerving at the time, but I didn't know anything about orbs back then.

After setting up the equipment, we did an electronic voice phenomenon (EVP) session and then the men left to investigate another area of the property while the women stayed with the equipment in the upstairs dining room. I was sitting across the room by myself when the Trifield meter began to whine, alerting us to a new energy being present. I went over to join the others, and when I stood near the meter, it started to whine louder. I felt a chill run up my spine. When the meter stopped, so did the chills. The meter went off a second time. The chills were back, but this time they crawled all the way up my spine and into my scalp before receding, and the meter went silent. The women asked questions of the entity, and the video recorder recorded it all.

My friend, Nadine, was sitting at a table beside me (where she had witnessed a chair moving on its own a short time earlier) when the Trifield's meter needle swung all the way to the top of the scale and the chills not only ran up my spine, but they also whipped around to my belly button and straight up to my throat.

Again, I was startled, but oddly, not afraid. As I stood there, my eyes gently closed and I began to weep just a little. Although I could not explain it at the time, I had a sense that "someone else" had somehow entered my body and that this person was lost and did not know why or how she became lost. I opened my eyes and tried to speak, but all I could manage was to hesitatingly squeak, "This … isss … nottttt … meeee.…"

Everyone looked at me like deer caught in headlights. I'll never forget that moment. I was me, but at the same time, I was not "just me." A few moments later, my shoulders dropped, I exhaled heavily, and the meter went silent. Someone ran out of the room to get the men. I could feel Nadine rubbing my arm, which she later told me felt ice cold. The others quickly came back to the room to make sure we were okay after what happened. When we reviewed the videotape, we discovered that an EVP of a woman's voice was captured answering "yes" to one of our questions, and to our collective amazement, we saw one of the "soap" bubbles I had captured earlier with my camera exiting my arm at the very moment my shoulders dropped and I exhaled.

That's when I knew *for sure* that my life would never be the same. And it hasn't been.

It's better now.

It took me many years to rebuild my spiritual foundation so that I could accept and surrender to the abilities that came to me as a result of my awakening. I am a light trance medium (allowing the recently departed to use my physical body and senses to communicate, speak, see, breathe) and light trance energy healer (channeling healers who use my hands to do energetic healing). I am deeply drawn to the indigenous all over the world and learning about shamanism. I enjoy gardening, hiking, and making handcrafted walking sticks. I love changing a person's perspective from conventional to one that makes them say, "Hmmm, I never thought of it that way."

Deathbed Visions
Alexandrea Weis

Ask any nurse, and they will tell you about that one patient who, right before passing, carried on a conversation with a dead relative, reached out, and seemed so at peace. This is a deathbed vision (DBV). They can occur immediately prior to death or sometimes weeks ahead of time. Nurses most often witness them since so many patients die in hospitals, nursing homes, or hospices. For many of us, deathbed visions are a crucial indicator your patient is getting ready to depart.

Many in the medical community would love to chalk up these instances to the last gasps of a dying brain. Still, many of the deathbed visions I have witnessed were with lucid patients who knew they were dying and were aware that the relative in the room with them had already passed on. It is troubling as a health care provider to see such an event, but it is also comforting.

Anecdotes of deathbed visions have appeared in literature and biographies throughout the ages, but it wasn't until the twentieth century that the subject received scientific study. Dr. Karlis Osis of the American Society for Psychical Research conducted the most extensive studies. Osis interviewed over one thousand doctors, nurses, and health care providers to the dying. He believed they had the most objective approach to describing this phenomenon.

The spirit encountered is usually someone to whom the dying was closest. The most common sightings are family members who the patient reports have already passed on.

Mothers are the most common, followed by grandparents and aunts or uncles. But sometimes young children will see someone hanging around they have never met before, such as grandparents or, in some instances, great–grandparents. These are the most intriguing events for many health care providers since these children describe the visitor at their bedside, often shocking parents and relatives with their accuracy. One child I tended gave a thorough description of an older woman who smelled of vanilla. The young girl's mother broke down, claiming her grandmother often smelled of vanilla.

The second most frequently appearing figures are angels, religious icons, and even mythical figures. There are many times I've heard patients speak of Jesus coming to get them. The one that stuck with me the most was when I tended a dying child. She expressed surprise that the angel at her bedside had no wings and asked me why that was. This one instance convinced me that deathbed visions are not hallucinations. A child would have described an angel with wings as depicted in art and literature. This child insisted her angel didn't have any and that her angel told her she didn't need wings in her world.

One of my patients was in her last hours and claimed that a dear friend had come to visit. The family reported the friend was still alive and well, casting doubt on the patient's mental status. It wasn't until after the man died that I discovered the friend he'd seen at his bedside had been killed hours before his passing in a car accident.

A few patients don't see people in their visions but rather beloved pets. A man with not much time left found great comfort in seeing his favorite childhood dog sitting on his bed. He'd even stroke it, moving his hand back and forth, and spoke of the adventures he'd shared with the beloved Labrador.

For some, there are only auditory experiences. Patients often speak of hearing the most beautiful music coming into their room. Or they describe a comforting humming, like the sound of a mother rocking a child to sleep. With a few, there were stories of bright lights, colorful displays of rainbows, and one woman talked about the thunderstorm that played out on her hospital room ceiling, complete with a lightning show and beautiful silky gray clouds.

There are also nonverbal cues that the patient is having a deathbed vision. Some will stare into a corner or laugh out loud without a prompt. You may see them move their eyes about a room as if following something or someone we can't see. They may speak or mouth words, reach out with open arms, or smile, seemingly at peace. It gives you profound reassurance as a health care provider to know they are comfortable in the end.

Many of the experiences I have witnessed had a calming effect on me. Usually, the end of life in a hospital is a chaotic affair where code carts are pulled into rooms, and everyone is fighting to save the patient's life. But when patients in hospice or labeled "do not resuscitate" speak about others in the room who have moved on before them, it brings peace to you.

Over the years, I have seen the dying express great happiness. No patient I encountered ever showed signs of distress at seeing loved ones in their room. The dying also seemed quite willing to go with these apparitions. Their mood lifted, and their faces changed after having a deathbed vision. The darkness lifted from their features if they were depressed or consumed by pain. The people having these experiences are not hallucinating or in an altered state of consciousness. Many are aware of their surroundings. Whether or not they believed in where they were going, my patients' reactions remained the same.

Every dying patient I tended changed my preconceived notions of death. When you witness such events, your fear of what may come recedes. You believe there is more after we die because you have seen it in the tranquil smiles of those you have stood by as they take their last breath.

Deathbed visions are unique to every dying patient and can't be explained away by science. If you have been around the dying, you understand that there is more than a physical explanation for these experiences. They are profound and life-altering for the living. For the dying, they are a comforting transition filled with understanding and peace. If all the visions I have had the privilege to behold have taught me one thing, it is that death is never the end. It's a new beginning that begins in love.

Alexandrea Weis, RN-CS, Ph.D., is a multi-award-winning, international bestselling author, screenwriter, and advanced practice registered nurse who was born and raised in the French Quarter of New Orleans. Having grown up in the motion picture industry as the daughter of a director, she learned to tell stories from a different perspective. A member of the Horror Writers Association and International Thriller Writers, Weis is also a permitted wildlife rehabber with the Louisiana Department of Wildlife and Fisheries.

Elvis Has Left the Building

For my first wedding anniversary, my husband gave me a black and white kitten. I hated cats, but we lived in a small apartment in Los Angeles and couldn't have a dog. He loved cats and wanted to "break me in." I fell madly in love with Elvis immediately, and he took to me as well. We became fast friends.

Elvis didn't meow when he was a kitten. He instead made a sound like, "Meh, meh." It was something he continued to do all his life when he was being pet or was content and happy. "Meh, meh." When he was 12, we had moved to San Diego and gotten a townhome. We had a second cat at that time, who we named Jerry Lee, but Elvis was the king of the house. He started to get sick and it progressed pretty quickly, to the point where he was put into an animal hospital with metastatic cancer.

We spent thousands of dollars on surgery and blood transfusions to keep Elvis alive. He was my buddy, and my heart was breaking. But the cancer only continued to spread. Then I found out that I was pregnant, something that was a total surprise because I was 38 years old and not trying to have kids!

We moved into a house so that I wouldn't have to go up three flights of stairs. Three months before I gave birth to my son, we had to finally put Elvis to sleep. He was just too sick, and it was only causing him pain. I was devastated. Through our tears, my husband and I joked about how Elvis had finally left the building. But he wasn't completely gone.

Then my son was born. The first sounds he made? "Meh, meh." He did that throughout his infancy, and it sounded just like Elvis. During that same time, I would often wake up at night from the sensation of something jumping on the bed and there would be an indentation on the exact spot on the bed Elvis would sleep on. This went on for about two years and then stopped, and my son stopped saying, "Meh, meh." It was the strangest thing, but I am convinced my cat's spirit somehow went into my son or at least was around him, influencing him. I miss Elvis, but imagine he finally let go and moved onto a much better cat heaven.

Why do ghosts stop visiting after a while? Do they decide to finally pass on into the light after comforting those they left behind or after comforting themselves by taking a final peek at the living? If ghosts have the power to communicate with the living, it seems we hear more about reports of this happening in the initial months and years after a death. Ten years down the road, those visitations may have stopped altogether.

Maybe it's about letting the living get on with life. If the dead keep coming back to make us feel better, we might keep expecting them to and never face the loss and grief in a healthy way so we can move on to a new life. It's impossible to say whether the dead want to hang on longer or the living do, but at some point, it does appear that these visits slow down or end for good.

The Eternal Bond with Our Beloved Pets

Kitty Janusz

I believe we all have that one special pet that changes our lives forever. It may be our childhood pet, or a beloved dog that comforted us in our darkest hour, showing us that love conquers all. Sharing your life with an animal teaches us compassion, discipline, patience, and to live in the moment, for that is where joy resides. The bond that we share with this one, special animal truly makes us a better human.

When we bring a pet into our home, we become both parent and best friend. We try our best to teach them good manners and skills to successfully cohabitate in a human's world. We fuss and groom and exercise and purchase endless toys and fluffy beds. I can honestly say my pets have always eaten better than I do. And in return, our pets give us uncompromising devotion and steady us when we may find this world a scary place. They love without judgment. To look into our pet's eyes is to know all is right in the world.

They are with us for what seems such a short time, yet they touch our hearts more than the people in our lives. I've been blessed to have a few special pets in my lifetime. Scout was one of them. Scout was close to 22 years old when he passed. He had lived a long. full life.

He wasn't just a cat; he was something much nobler.

Maybe it was his Bobcat lineage. Pixie Bobs are descended from a Bobcat–Tabby pairing.

Scout owned the ground on which he stood. Even in his prime, he only weighed 7 pounds yet he was the alpha in a house that had an 80–pound pit bull.

Smarter than any cat I ever knew, home became his domain and he was sheriff. (Hence the nickel star collar he often wore.)

He stayed with me as I lost two dogs, my brother, and my husband. He was one of the last reasons that where I lived I called home.

Cats are arrogant. Especially Scout. I say this with immense love. A cat's vanity and sense of dignity are what we love about them. It makes them unique in the animal kingdom to possess such an air of superiority over us mere humans. But their ego and dignity are a double–edged sword.

As a cat's time on earth draws to a close, they cling to that dignity with all their might. They finally turn to us to make the right decisions for them and a lifetime of vulnerability spills in our arms. But he has returned to Heaven now. He was my shadow, my book companion, my precious little boy. I still don't know how I find a way to use the computer key–board without his intrusion.

Scout made life here on Earth so joyful. But as with any soul that has lived a long, full life, he was ready to continue his journey. His job here was over, and Scout is content in the afterlife.

I believe dogs have a much more Zen approach to life and what lies beyond the physical realm. I think dogs view death as just relaxing at the end of a happy, carefree life. Their humility and joie de vivre carry them over easily into the end of days.

Like Scout, I have had one other animal to touch me so very deeply. I shared 13 wonderful years with my big chestnut boy here on Earth. Reggie was my one, most special horse, and our bond did not break when he left this world. Reggie is still with me.

I had been showing the family's backyard mare at local shows for a few years and felt ready to step up my game and get my first, really good purebred horse to exhibit at the big regional and national specialty horse shows.

Enter Reggie, or known by his registered name, Regency Larkspur. I wanted a Morgan horse because I admired their beauty and versatility. Historically used for working in the fields, they were bred to be flashy and snappy enough to pull the carriage to church on Sunday. Morgans are shown with full, flowing manes and tails and are known for their beautiful gait. Purchased as a barely broke-to-ride, gangly two-year-old, Reggie was all legs, squishy with baby fat, and had yet to grow into his long, goofy head. Reggie was green as grass but he came from a good bloodline, and when I tried him out under saddle, his stride was smooth as silk.

Reggie and I learned together. I pored over books and magazines on young horse training. We worked with long lines and had him move around me as I watched his stride and walked with him in the center of the circle.

Our hard work started paying off. As our partnership grew, the wins in the show ring grew. This great-grandson of the legendary UVM Promise started turning his blueblood into tricolor championship ribbons.

One thing about winning in a large horse show. After all the placements have been handed out and the other entrants have exited the ring, the winner, with his blue ribbon flowing from his bridle, gets to strut his stuff with a victory lap, complete with organ fanfare and crowd applause. Reggie. Loved. Victory. Laps. He *knew* when he'd won a class and couldn't wait to glide around the ring, having it all to himself, as the crowd cheered him on. Yes, Reggie was a horse with a big dose of ham.

Reggie became champion of a three-state region as a four-year-old. We were the envy of professional stables with ribbon after ribbon being awarded. His versatility shined as we could enter a class under Western tack, showing in the required slow-rolling pace and win the blue. Dashing out with only a ten-minute tack change, I'd run into the bathroom and change into my English riding garb while friends frantically switched Reggie into English saddle and bridle. Gliding into the ring ten minutes later, Reggie instinctively extended his gait and moved like a king. Another blue ribbon and applause. Reggie was the best and he knew it too well.

I showed Reggie in Western, English, and over fences. He enjoyed every minute of it. At the end of the day as I drove home, Reggie without fail would trot outside and whinny to me as I drove away. Those were the happiest memories I have of my boy.

At thirteen, Reggie broke a small bone in his leg during a routine workout. It didn't bother him much at first but after a couple years of therapy and countless vet visits, the options became limited. The discomfort for him was becoming too great, and I had to make the hardest decision I have ever had to make.

With his best interest in mind and a broken heart, I had Reggie euthanized so he could run free forever.

And run he did. For years as I drove my car, I could see Reggie running alongside, jumping fences and shaking his flaxen mane. I would call out his name and I would swear I could hear his high-pitched whinny. I enjoyed having the visions of my boy happy again, even if it was all in my head. I assumed it was all in my head at least, that is, until other people started asking me about the ghost horse.

I was working nights at the time. It must have been about three AM and I just had my head down. Working and letting my mind wander. Around this time, I had been a paranormal investigator for a few years and had been trying to embrace any psychic abilities I might have. Since we were all working in the middle of the night, my coworkers and I had our share of ghosts popping in and out and to be honest, it wasn't unusual to say, "Hey, did you see that shadow dart over there?"

I actually was a bit surprised when a coworker called out, "Kitty, who's the horse running around you?" Startled, I looked up from my work. Indeed, I could make out an almost hologram image of a horse galloping and head tossing in my area. Smiling, I answered, "Oh, that's just Reggie."

It seemed Reggie remained my companion in spirit. But was it real? I wanted an expert opinion. I attended a lecture by a well-known psychic. After his talk, he started a Q & A session. I nervously took the microphone. I asked, "I see my horse's spirit. Others see him too. But are we really seeing what is a spirit, or by thinking about him and revisiting memories of him, am I simply manifesting moving memories of him? Are these visions current or just past moments?" He pondered. "It doesn't matter." I was puzzled. He explained. "By you calling his name, you are indeed manifesting him, but his spirit comes to you at that moment. It's a bit of both."

Reggie continued to visit me and dance around, and I was pleased to know he was free from pain. His presence could be so strong that if I stood against a white wall, folks could make out his tall gold aura on my right side, where he always walked beside me in life. Reggie was so strong even in spirit form that he could physically shove a living person if they came on my right side! His soul was amazing and so protective.

But as I continued to work in the paranormal, spirits both light and dark became attracted to Reggie's bright light. Things took a dark, dangerous turn.

As I said before, Reggie would come to me and stay on my right side. Spirits approaching us could only approach from the left, as Reggie pinned his ears and gnashed his teeth if they came too close. I believe darker entities were attracted to Reggie's bright light and his innocence. This took a scary turn one late night at work.

A couple coworkers had seen what appeared as a young girl spirit walking around. She asked if she could "feed the horsey an apple." I just had a really bad feeling about this. I just knew this was not some poor child spirit looking to feed an apple. My heart and my gut told me everything about this ghost girl was evil. She wanted to poison my Reggie; I just knew it. My blood ran cold.

The more we investigate the afterlife, the more we learn how little we know. Was it indeed possible a negative entity had tried to harm the innocent spirit of a horse? How could this be?

I was in a panic. Reggie was staying because he loved me and felt he needed to protect me, even from beyond the grave. But dark, horrible things exist on both sides of the veil. Who would protect my Reggie? How could I keep my boy safe from the other side?

I so enjoyed having my boy with me. I feel blessed knowing our bond was so strong that Reggie recognized my soul and stayed with his mom. But a mom needs to protect their children, and I had to find a way to protect Reggie from the dark that lurks in his realm.

I am not a religious person. I work with angels in a nonreligious context and although angels predate Christianity, I call upon them by their Christian given names.

I called upon Archangel Michael. I called upon the angels to surround my Reggie and keep him safe. Yes, I had asked for protection before, but I had one more task for Archangel Michael. I needed the angels to take Reggie where he needed to be, where he should be. He needed to be kept safe and I tearfully knew he might not be safe if he continued to try to be my protector. He was just too innocent. I told Reggie I would love him forever, but he needed to go with the angels. He would always protect me in my heart. I saw an image of Archangel Michael drape a golden saddle over Reggie and take him home.

Love hurts, but it is so worth the moments we keep in our hearts.

Kitty Janusz is an award-winning author and paranormal investigator, with over 30 years' experience in the paranormal field. She is featured on Ghost Adventures *and* Haunted Hospitals. *To learn more about Kitty Janusz and her work, visit her website at kittyjanusz.com.*

Unexpected End-of-Life Visitors
Dr. Rita Louise

It was June 10, 2013. My husband, Wayne, and I had just left an imaging center where they did a CT scan of his chest. He had been complaining for about six months of difficulty breathing and a chronic coughing. He had been to several doctors and each time they diagnosed him with pneumonia and simply sent him home with new medications to take.

We found ourselves back at the doctor's office when Wayne started to cough up blood. The CT scan was scheduled "stat."

Imaging complete, we left the medical center with the test results in hand. We were to give them to the pulmonologist the next day so that he could present the findings. Yes, the big reveal. I don't know what they were thinking. I started reading the results as soon as we pulled out of the parking lot. The scan exposed masses in his liver, in his chest cavity, and on his pancreas. Wayne asked me, as I worked my way through the report, what it said. I looked at him and said, "You're screwed." Okay, I did not use exactly those words. I speak fluent French.

We both had backgrounds in medicine and health care. We knew exactly what the test uncovered. It was the Big C. It seemed evident that the tumors had metastasized and were throughout his body. We both knew deep down it was just a matter of time. Just how much time was the big question.

Over the next few weeks, Wayne had some additional testing done: a full body MRI and a lung biopsy. Then we were off to the oncologist for our next step. The oncologist gave him a 1 percent chance of survival, three to six months without treatment, or eight to twelve months after chemo and radiation. To us, the decision was a no-brainer.

Wayne refused the chemo. He knew the ravishing effects that chemotherapy places on the body and did not want to spend his last days dealing with the side effects of the treatment. He did opt to have some targeted radiation on several of the tumors in his chest that had closed off air flow to his left lung. He believed that it would improve the quality of his life. I agreed.

His radiation treatments started just after the Fourth of July. When they brought him out of the treatment room in a wheelchair, weak and struggling cognitively at the close of his seventh treatment, I had had enough. Thankfully, his left lung had opened back up and his breathing was easier. He had achieved his goal, and I insisted that he stop his radiation. The trajectory of the side effects was hard to watch, and I felt like they were killing him, and maybe they were.

The lifesaving efforts we pursued, one concluded, opened the door to hospice care. Working with hospice was a breath of fresh air. They had our backs. They immediately brought over an oxygen concentrator to help support his breathing and what seemed like miles of tubing, which allowed him to navigate the two-story townhouse we lived in. They put him on palliative medications to help with the pain and nausea he was experiencing. Whatever we needed, they were there for us.

This quasi-okay, but weakened, state lasted for about two weeks. Instead of getting stronger, he got weaker.

A hospital bed was brought in and set up in the living room to eliminate the need to walk upstairs. Day by day, things kept deteriorating. By week's end, I had a nurse staying at the house full time to care for him. Hospice only provides full-time care like that when they believe the person is in the twilight of life. For me it was an unwanted blessing. Wayne was a big man. I was afraid that I would be unable to do simple tasks like help navigate him to the restroom, change the sheets, or reposition him in the bed. But the full-time appearance of the hospice worker also meant that my time with him was short, even shorter than I could have imagined.

This is when things started to get interesting. There was the hospice worker and there was his home healthcare nurse. The nurse came for a routine visit, stopping by a couple of times a week. Wayne started making comments that a light in the room was glowing red. I suggested to the nurse that he might be hallucinating. The nurse, a bit concerned, wanted me to tell him right away if he started "seeing people." I laughed on the inside and thought, well, I hope he starts seeing people. To me, that would only be natural and appropriate for this stage of life as the veil between this world and the next begins to thin.

In my work as a medical intuitive and energy healer, I have helped people move on to their next plane of existence. Many times, an individual will hang on to life because they are scared afraid to let go. In these situations, I have asked deceased loved ones, a parent, a grandparent, or, in one situation, a beloved dog to come forward to offer a friendly smile or a warm embrace. Often this alleviates their fears, and they can let go and move on. I prayed that as time got closer, deceased friends and family members would gather around Wayne to support him as well.

When I think of this process, it reminds me of the closing scene from the movie *Ghost*. Patrick Swayze, having saved Demi Moore from a near-death situation, is freed from his obligation to protect her and can now leave the earth plane. Small figures begin to appear as Patrick moves into the bright illumination that shines before him. They embrace him and surround him with love. If for some reason you have not seen the movie, to me, this ending scene seemed like a very realistic representation of what will occur when we die.

With Wayne, however, I wasn't sure how this would play out. His parents, who he had a challenging relationship with, were still alive. His brother, who was deceased—well, to be honest, I was just not feeling it. After that, I was unsure who, if anyone, would show up for him.

I don't mean to talk about my dog here, but she played a critical role in what happened next. Bitsy, the famous *Poodle in a Tinfoil Hat*, was, well, not the sharpest stick in the box. Poodles are in general a very smart breed; however, Bitsy, although a super sweet dog, must have been at the end of the line when they were giving out smarts. Additionally, if someone came to the door, many times they would be inside the house long before she would wake up and begin to bark.

Wayne's health took an even further turn for the worse. Phone calls were made to friends and family members. If they wanted to say goodbye, the time was now.

It was during this time that for some reason Bitsy got up off the sofa, walked over the front door, and started barking. The doorbell never rang, and no one knocked, yet she was inconsolable. I tried playing with her, and I told her there wasn't anyone there, but her barking would not stop. Finally, I opened the door and said, "See, no one is there," and closed the door. She would immediately calm back down and go back to her spot on the sofa.

When it happened the first time, it was weird. When it happened the second time, it was even weirder. When it happened, the third time—all within the course of a few days—instead of getting mad at the ruckus she was creating, I got curious. What was she barking at? I opened the door and looked outside. There were a group of people—invisible dead people—standing outside my front door. I opened the screen door and shouted, "Come on in!"

This caused me to stop and look around the room. I was flabbergasted. My living room, dining room, and kitchen were packed with these imperceptible, ethereal beings. I could only assume that many were family members who had come to greet him on the other side. What astonished me the most was that many of the individuals wore military uniforms.

Wayne had been a medic and managed airlift support at a hospital in Germany during the Vietnam War. In a moment of intuitive insight, I realized that many of the solders, who came to be with him, were young men who he helped make their transition from this world to the next. They were returning the favor for the love he showed them in their final hours.

The experience brought me to tears. It also let me know that he was in good hands. Wayne took his last breath on August 19, 2013, at 3:15 P.M.

When we die, we often think that we are going alone, that we are traveling down a road to some unknown destination by ourselves. It is frightening—no, downright scary to most. But that is not the case. It is my belief that when we move from this life to the next, we will be supported by those we love, by those who have gone before us. They will be there to help us navigate these unseen waters. So, if you find yourself with someone who is on death's door, don't be afraid for them. Instead, say to them what I said to Wayne as he took his last breath. "Go into the light, Wayne, go into the light."

Bestselling author Dr. Rita Louise is the founder of the Institute of Applied Energetics and former host of Just Energy Radio. *She is the author of the books* The Dysfunctional Dance of the Empath and Narcissist; Stepping out of Eden; E.T. Chronicles: What Myths And Legends Tell Us about Human Origins; Avoiding the Cosmic 2x4; Dark Angels: An Insider's Guide to Ghosts, Spirits & Attached Entities; *and* The Power Within: A Psychic Healing Primer; *as well as hundreds of articles that have been published worldwide. She is also the producer of a number of full-length and feature videos. Dr. Rita has appeared on film, radio, and television and has spoken at conferences around the world covering topics such as health and healing, relationships, ghosts, intuition, ancient mysteries, and the paranormal. Her website is: https://soulhealer.com.*

Something in the Darkness
Jason Roberts

Technology has helped the paranormal field come a long way since the day's investigators used dowsing rods and snap photography. Since taking over Road Trip Paranormal in 2014, I have seen our team grow—not just with team members but also with all the new technology of today in the paranormal field. Dan Galleher has been on a quest to find the answers to the afterlife for most of his own life. When he was young, he would go out to cemeteries with a flashlight and an old cassette tape recorder in hopes of recording a voice or seeing something in the darkness. Dan has been with the team since the end of 2017 and has truly upped his stock of equipment, always buying new gear for investigating. What he never thought about is how the equipment would help enhance the communication with spirits to the point of physical contact.

In late 2018, the team had an opportunity to investigate the old Fort Dodge Hospital, which has been closed and abandoned since the 1980s. The hospital is located just outside of Dodge City, Kansas, and has no running water or electricity inside, which always gives us a slight challenge at times, but we make do with our gear.

As we got started investigating with hopes that something or someone was still inside, Dan decided to put on his "spectacles," which is a head gear device that allows you to see in night-vision mode, amplifies the audio around you, and records everything you encounter. Wearing the device, Dan began walking down the hallway, while Jake Frisbie and Roth Christopherson followed him with the SLS camera on to map out any figures in the darkness that might come out to join them. Dan started hearing voices and what sounded like shuffling of feet at the other end of the hall, so he paused, took off his head gear, and said, "I'm going to use the Spirit Box and hopefully whoever is down at the other end talks to me." Dan turned on the SB7 Box and speaker and started asking questions to whoever was down at the far end of the hallway. Asking questions like "Who is down here with us?" and "Can you give us your name?" led to Dan asking, "Can you tell me what my name is?" At this moment, came a response that shocked Dan, Jake, and Roth—yet also made them laugh: "White trash!" Dan stopped walking and tilted his head saying, "Oh, well, that's not fair!" At this moment, Jake watched the SLS camera and saw an orb floating fast down the hallway towards Dan, who was about ten feet in front of Jake and Roth. Just as they were telling Dan that an orb was coming at him, it struck Dan right in the chest as Dan hollered out, "Oh my god, I just got hit in the chest," as he stopped walking and bent over to catch his breath. "I have never had that happen before, getting hit in the chest like that from a spirit. I think I saw it coming too!" The rest of the night was very interesting.

For Dan, the Fort Dodge Hospital was the beginning of trying new tactics in communications with the deceased. This led us back to Wichita, Kansas, at an old warehouse that has had a lot of activity from voices, objects thrown, shadow figures, and full-body apparitions. We have been inside the warehouse on multiple occasions to help the owners figure out what or who was haunting the location. When we went in this night, it was Dan, Roth, Jake, Leo, and me. We brought a lot of our gear, but we wanted to test out the SLS camera to find out if it was truly legit with what it captures. Now the warehouse dates to the early 1900s when the railroad went past it to drop off cotton, and we have encountered a lot of activity inside that seems to be intelligent.

Dan and Jake got the SLS setup, and we all started our way through the warehouse, hearing noises along the way. Leo Fernandez was in front of us and saw ahead of us a shadow figure moving around in the darkness, almost pacing back and forth. I saw what he was talking about and wondered if we should go after it or try and communicate with it. Dan then said, "I see it on the SLS. It's moving towards the side of the room." As he said this, we were all watching the camera and could see that the figure was now climbed up onto the forklift that was to the side of the warehouse. Dan handed off the SLS to Jake and said, "Okay, I am heading down there to it." Dan walked slowly, so as to not spook the shadow figure away, while we could see the figure sitting on top of the forklift swinging its feet like a child or teenager. Dan reached the forklift and turned so his back leaned up against it and was directly underneath the figure we all saw on the SLS camera. I thought to myself that it would be awesome if it reached down at Dan while Leo hollered out, "Hey, since you're right there with Dan, can you reach down and touch him?" As we watched the SLS, we saw the figure reach down and make a motion as if it was patting Dan on the head, as Dan yelled out, "Oh my god, it is patting me on the head! I can feel a hand patting my bald head!"

It was a moment for us that helped determine that the equipment validates our experiences, because Dan had no way of knowing that we were seeing this figure reach down to touch his head right after Leo asked it to do so if it could. The technology of the equipment we have today helps on so many levels of investigating as long it is recorded, which we do every time. To this day, we are still encountering and communicating to the figures in the darkness at the old warehouse.

The Traveling Soldiers

It continues to amaze me every time I meet up with my team for a case and see all the new equipment they have bought and are ready to use, because I can't seem to keep up with the technology in the paranormal field. Take my friend and teammate Jake Frisbie, who has spent a good chunk of the last few years since joining the team with me gathering an enormous collection of gear–at a rather high cost, I might add. Jake has been diving into the paranormal for many years, going to haunted locations such as the infamous Sallie House as well as the Wolf Hotel where he caught one of the best "class A" photos of a spirit I have ever seen. Now what is funny though is that out of all the gear he has, it is a simple SB7 Spirit Box that has changed how we conduct the endings of our cases. For those who do not know what a Spirit Box is, it is just a modified radio to change stations very quickly so that all we hear is white noise across every station it scans. The theory is, if a voice or statement or even a full sentence comes through, then it's most likely a true spirit speaking to us because of the radio changing stations at such a high speed.

Jake and I went out to El Dorado, Kansas, for a case one night, meeting up with two more teammates, Andi and Roth. The family lived in a pretty good size home out in the country and was having issues with seeing an adult male and what they can only describe as the lower half of a young boy wearing what appeared as swimming trunks. The sightings of these two spirits made the family nervous, so we went out to help.

When I arrived, Andi and Roth were waiting for Jake and me outside; Jake was on his way. Jake was a little skeptical about coming to work this case. (Jake is our biggest skeptic when it comes to hearing claims of a haunting somewhere. Too often we are misled by folks desperately wanting their home to be haunted, leaving us discouraged because we just spent time driving there and setting up our gear only to have our time wasted by false claims.)

Jake arrived and Roth went out to help him unload all his gear as I spoke with the owner. As Roth was out there helping, he saw a shadow figure dart from the tree in the front yard and go behind the house. Excited, as Roth always is, he hurried in the house with the gear and told us all what he just saw. Jake came up and asked me, "So, what do you think? You have a game plan?" I replied that I did, and we started unpacking gear and setting up cameras and every other random gear we brought. After setup, we toured the house, and then the four of us stepped outside to discuss what could be here and looked around at the land. While out by the field and tree line talking, Jake turned to look at the house and screamed out, "Oh, no way! I just saw a shadow figure peek around that tree like he's watching us out here!" This excited all of us, and we headed in to conduct the investigation.

We spent the next few hours investigating along with the wife of the home, whose husband is in the Army and was out of town that weekend. As we walked the house and heard some noises here and there, we couldn't get anything to happen with the adult male or the small child they had seen. So, we decided to sit down and do a "Frank's Box Session," which involves the Spirit Box and a pair of noise canceling headphones. I had started to believe that Jake was a master at doing this type of session where we try to speak with whoever was there and have a conversation. It's a little bit like an EVP session but different. During the investigation, the wife had mentioned that a lot of activity happened in her husband's office, which was decorated with a lot of military antiques from around the world.

I told Jake we should go to the office and set up the session, he should be the one to sit and listen, and I would ask the questions. The "Frank's Box Session" is one of my favorite moments of investigating, yet it does drain the energy of the one listening and speaking for the session, so I tried to keep my eyes on Jake every time he sat down to do this so that I knew he was doing okay.

We all headed to the office, and I remember Jake having a little doubt that anything was going to happen. But as a good sport, he walked into the dark office and went to sit down at the desk. As soon as he sat in the chair at the desk, Jake was struck in the head by an object. "Whoa, something just got thrown at me and hit my head," Jake said, a little startled. We turned the lights on, and the cowboy hat that was a few feet behind him somehow was flung from the hat stand and at Jake.

Now having our attention, especially Jake's, he put together the Spirit Box and the headphones and turned it on, unable to hear anything from me, just what was coming through the box, and whatever came through clearly, Jake would just say out loud. I began asking who was here with us. "I am," Jake said, "I am watching." I thought maybe the spirit was wanting to speak, so I asked, "Where are you from?" A moment later, Jake said, "I am with him." Going through some more questions, it hit me that the spirit might be connected to the husband who lived there and that it had followed the husband, who was in the Army and had traveled the world. "Are you connected to the soldier in this house," I asked. Jake said, "Yes, I followed."

Through more questions, Jake and I were able to figure out the man's story. The spirit was that of a soldier who fought in a war and drowned in water trying to save his friends. He felt a connection to the Army soldier because the spirit himself missed his own family and had come with him to his house in Kansas to feel at home. After talking with the traveling soldier for a while, I asked, "Who is the boy that this family has seen?" Jake then said, "I have to go now; wait here." We sat there in darkness and silence when we heard footsteps coming our way to the office. Jake then said, "Here I am," as Jake broke from the session and said, "Jason, this voice is a child speaking, and he says he is behind you."

We spoke with the child for a while, and together Jake and I understood that the spirit of the soldier and the boy were the same person. To feel comfortable with the family and the kids, the older soldier spirit transitioned into a child form. As Jake finally took off the headphones, I went over all that we spoke about during the session because he did not understand all that was being said. Jake looked at me and asked, "Is it possible that we spoke with a spirit of a man and boy that were the same person, just so he could feel like part of the family here?" I looked at him and said, "He was a soldier overseas, saw the another traveling soldier, and just wanted to come home."

To this day, the soldier from far away is still at home with his new family. It's amazing what technology can do to help even those in spirit.

Jason Roberts has been interested in the paranormal, myths, lore, and the unknown since childhood. He is currently a team lead with Everyday-Legacy Paranormal and has been a tour guide/manager of Wichita Ghost Tours since 2009. In 2014 Jason took over ownership of Road Trip Paranormal during which he transformed the team into a public events group doing paranormal events all over Kansas. He is also co-owner of the Kansas Bigfoot Research Society as well as co-host of the Cryptic Heartland Podcast, which does live episodes on Facebook and YouTube. Roberts can be reached at roadtripparanormal.vpweb.com and everyday-legacy.com.

My Experiences with Death and the Afterlife
Daniel L. Galleher

Pets Are Never Gone

Our dear Katie (Boston Terrier) was such a special little girl. One of her trademark characteristics was lying down on her belly with her front legs sprawled forward and beating her paws on the floor like a drum. Towards the end of her life, she developed a heart condition that would cause her to have periodic seizures in her sleep, which, of course, scared her, and she would make a sound resembling that of a woman screaming. My wife and I would get up in the night and lay with her and hold her until it passed. Katie took her last steps in May of 2020. My wife had a portrait of Katie tattooed between her shoulder blades, and now in the evenings while my wife and I, along with our male Boston, sit to dinner or watch television, we can hear the thumping of her paws on the floor, a distant shuffling noise of a back-and-forth movement on the carpet as if she is on her back scratching it as Katie used to do so often. Once the noise subsides, then my wife will say, "Katie must be itching, because my tattoo is as well," as if she is letting her mama know she is still present and attending family time. Often, we will be awakened to what we both believe is Katie crying out from her room as if she is having another seizure. We'll go to the room only to find our male Boston standing in the middle of the room staring down at the floor.

My Father's Afterlife Experiences

In May 1986, my father died five separate times within a span of four hours following a car accident. While heading south on highway U.S. 177 in Kansas, the vehicle he was riding in left the roadway on an S-curve and went airborne. The vehicle flipped end over end four times before coming to a rest on the roof. My father was extracted from the sunroof of the vehicle during that time and was pinned under the car when it came to rest. Multiple bystanders responded to the accident and pulled the driver from the car but didn't realize that my father was pinned under the car, so they failed to attend to him right away. The sheriff's officer arrived and observed a bloodied shoe not belonging to the driver and began a search for my father. After a 15-minute search, the officer observed my father's torso exposed through the sunroof, so he and some bystanders lifted the vehicle from one side and stood it up.

My father lay lifeless and bleeding profusely from his head, right arm, and right leg. The paramedics classified him as "code blue" and began CPR. My father recalls staring down at his body while three paramedics ran lines and performed CPR. He also remembered that while one of the paramedics shocked his chest, he could feel the jolts of electricity running through his body but not be able to react while "watching" the process take place. At that moment, he felt a strong pull and a rush of pain all through his body and was now looking up into the eyes of a paramedic. He screamed out in pain, and moments he was loaded onto the life-watch helicopter to fly him to a trauma center 55 miles away.

During the flight, he coded two more times. He recalled looking into the helicopter for a moment as if he were flying alongside. Observing from the outside in, he felt drawn away and then everything became dark. He was now in what he could only describe as "nowhere but everywhere." It was darker than any dark he had witnessed. He could make out the voices from inside the cockpit but also familiar voices of his brothers who had previously passed away. They were calling to him, telling him to come home. But once more, the paramedics were able to bring him back. Now lying in the ER, more doctors and nurses ran lines, took X-rays, and once again, due to blood loss, he coded. As they performed CPR, he recalls floating back and looking down upon his body.

Hearing the voices coming from afar from his two brothers and his grandfather, he turned his back and tracked the voices, and then the darkness once again filled the void, although this time the voices who were so pronounced moments earlier were now silent. There was no light present to walk into and no voices to follow–just silence and darkness in every direction. Although he was touch and go for just a few moments more that day, he states that those few moments in the dark felt like forever. After a six–week stay in the hospital, my father was able to return home. Until his death in 2021, he never slept again without the television blaring throughout the dark night so he would not experience the darkness and silence that frightened him so much.

The year was 1976. My family had moved into a quaint two-bedroom 408–square–foot home–what is called a "shotgun" style home. From the time we moved in, the home felt heavy and uninviting. My mother, father, sister, and I would often hear what could only be described as a deep, gurgling, wet, raspy choking sound. On occasion, we would smell a strong stench of smoke as well as the odor of cheap pipe tobacco smoke throughout the home, but we attributed it to my parents, who smoked, though never in the home. One evening, my father drank a little too much, so he found himself sleeping the night away on the couch. A little after 2 AM, we were all awakened by a very loud gasping and gurgling sound coming from the living room, where my father was sleeping on the couch.

I ran into the room as my mother was trying to wake my father from sleep. But he was not asleep at all. His eyes were opened wider than I can every recall, fear was in his face, and his mouth was open, gasping for air, trying to get words out but none were vocalized. My mother grabbed his arms to try and sit him up and help him gain the ability to breathe, but she was not able to get him up. I then grabbed an arm and tried to help as well. We both noticed my father's stomach and chest were consistently sunken as if someone were sitting on top of him. As he tried to take a breath, you could see that his chest attempted to rise with no success. My mother screamed out, "Just stop! Just leave us alone, dammit!" As if something or someone could hear her request, my father took in a full chest of air and sat up.

We all looked up in awe as we saw a white, misty, and smoke-filled mass about five feet tall standing on top of the coffee table, just above a large 20–inch–by–12–inch–by–2–inch crystal ashtray. We heard a piercing cracking noise, and suddenly the ashtray burst into hundreds of little pieces as the smoke dissipated from above. Once again, silence filled the room.

the following day, my parents contacted the previous owners of the home to learn that in the home that was built in 1920, an elderly gentleman had fallen asleep smoking a pipe near the location of the couch, which had caught his chair and the carpet on fire. The gentleman woke up and began crawling to the front door but succumbed to the smoke and flames before exiting the house. With this news, my father found the need to renovate the living room area. Upon tearing out the sheetrock and flooring, he discovered several charred wall studs directly behind where the couch was situated; he replaced these as well. Although we still had activity until we moved from the home in 1985, we never experienced anything like that again.

After experiencing the paranormal at an early age, I have taken every opportunity to read on the subject, tour every location that I am within traveling distant of, and stay at every haunted location along those journeys. I met and joined my team doing just that, and in 2018 I joined road-tripparanormal.vpweb.com as a lead investigator/tech and researcher. I am also an investigator with our sister team, Everyday–Legacy Paranormal. My passion to learn more about the field has taken me across the United States as well as several other counties and to some of the most mysterious locations known in the paranormal world.

Pet Communication
T. MacGregor

In March 2019, our noble golden retriever, Noah, was diagnosed with cancer of the spleen. The vet wanted to operate immediately, but we wanted our vet to look at the X–rays and blood work, and we took Noah home. The next morning, he weaved into the family room and got on the couch with our other golden, Nigel, who was just two at the time. Noah put his head on Nigel's haunches and passed. It makes me choke up even now. I think he's around periodically. I had a reading with a wonderful animal communicator, Heather, who said that when he passed, "Buddy" was there. She didn't know if Buddy was a human or animal. Buddy was my dad–our daughter had given him the nickname. No way Heather could have known that. It's when I knew she was the real deal.

Heather said there had been another golden with him and my dad (Buddy) when he passed. She had no idea that we'd had a golden named Jessie before Noah entered our lives. It made sense that Jessie was with my dad because he was living with us at the time and adored her. My mother was in an Alzheimer's unit then, and Jessie used to visit the place with us in the evenings. None of the residents knew our names, but they knew Jessie's name and she loved on all of them.

One of the questions I asked Heather was whether Noah had been with us before. I always felt he had, in some form. She chuckled and said he'd been one of our cats and also had been a squirrel who hung around in our backyard. Noah loved to chase squirrels at the dog park. Would he be back? I wanted to know. She assured me he would but probably not as a dog. She also said that whenever we saw Nigel gazing off at nothing, he was seeing Noah, who would stick close to him since they'd been good buddies since we'd brought Nigel home at 10 weeks. The entire reading gave me such peace.

The Afterlife Chronicles: Exploring the Connection between Life, Death, and Beyond
Nicole Strickland

As I grew older, I made a point to research the paranormal realm during my middle and high school years. Prior to the Internet commencing, I relied heavily on books and articles written on the subject. However, it was an experience during my senior year of undergraduate college that catapulted my interest in investigating the paranormal field as an adult. In fact, you may hear many ghost researchers relay a life-changing encounter that propelled them into the field of the supernatural. For me, this particular occurrence involved the spirit of my maternal grandmother, Helen Lopinto. This singular, yet powerful, experience with the spirit of my grandmother sealed my quest in learning more about the unknown. Honestly, I don't know if I would be where I am today as a paranormal researcher and spirit advocate if it wasn't for this encounter. Perhaps her decision to appear before me in ethereal form was her way of letting me know the eventual path I was supposed to be on. Although some may argue that this experience was a bereavement hallucination caused from intense grief, I believe wholeheartedly that this was a pure spirit visitation.

"Hi sweetheart," my mom calmly said, as I picked up the receiver. As she echoed the words "I want you to know how much I love you ...," I instinctively knew that I was about to hear some tragic news. As I heard the remaining words, "... but I want you to know that Grandma passed away early this morning," sadness, anger, and shock permeated my body. After I finished talking with my mom, I sat in my bedroom as tears ran down my face–a cathartic release from my soul.

When I regained my composure, I made airline reservations to travel back home to San Diego to be with family and attend Helen's funeral services. The following day, our family had a private viewing for my grandmother. As she lay peacefully in her casket, I couldn't help but notice the three–part picture frame displaying the photos of her three grandchildren, a piece that for years sat on top of her bedroom vanity. But at that moment, it took on a different journey as it eternally comforted Helen's earthly remains in her beautifully adorned casket. Silence remained as our family convened; no words needed to be relayed as we all interconnected with each other's sadness and grief. As I touched her hand, I thanked her for many years of love and memories. I wished her well and told her to come back and visit in ethereal form.

After a few days in San Diego, I flew back to Tucson, Arizona, and continued with my studies. It took my entire mind, body, and spirit to glide back into the swing of things as grief and sorrow followed me around like my own shadow. As par for the course, I was plagued with fatigue and exhaustion for a few days; however, I started to notice a shift in my individual stages of grief. I was on my way to gradually accepting my grandmother's death–she was 96 years old when she passed on from this mortal plane, and she lived a happy, thorough life complete with lasting memories of those who adored her.

One night while I was studying, I distinctly heard my bedroom's doorknob rattle of its own volition. My logical senses kicked in, and I immediately examined the door to see if I could come up with any rational explanations for the event. But I couldn't. I chalked up this odd experience as some random event that I couldn't naturally justify. The following day,

I heard my apartment's front doorknob move in a motion as if someone was trying to open the door. With my spiny senses now at full force, I then asked myself, "Okay, what is going on here?" as these incidents had never before occurred. A few days and nights went by and I still came into contact with my doorknobs moving by themselves.

A few evenings later, as I was lying in bed studying for an exam, I felt the disembodied caress of a hand touch my face. The sensation felt eerily familiar as if it came from someone I deeply loved. These encounters culminated into something beautifully unexpected the following night as I again lay in my bed studying for my courses. Out of my left peripheral vision, I noticed someone standing in front of my closet doors. When my eyes scanned over to that exact location, I saw Helen as she appeared about ten years younger, adorned in her favorite blue and white house dress. With a glowing light behind her, she appeared rather peaceful with a slight smile across her face. My eyes stared at her for what seemed like an eternity. After her spirit form slowly disappeared, I was then engulfed in an extreme sense of stillness and tranquility. Perhaps I was tapping into how her spirit felt at that exact moment. Needless to say, Helen's ethereal being appeared before me for the next few nights, a profound encounter that many people go a lifetime without experiencing.

I immediately called my mom and told her that Helen was getting in touch with me from the spirit realm. After a lengthy discussion, both my mom and I agreed to openly talk with my grandmother and let her know that she was free to move on. In other words, she didn't need to carry any more worry about the family, as she was free from any earthly anxieties. It was then that my otherworldly occurrences with her ethereal form completely stopped.

Since my chance encounters with the spirit form of my beloved grandmother, I have been actively researching and investigating the unknown, with a chosen focus on ghosts, spirits, and hauntings. Retrospectively, I have often paused to look back at the very moment my eyes met Helen's ethereal energy, thanking her for paving the pathway for me as a paranormal researcher. It's as if she knew all along that I was destined to step foot on this trail.

Having empathic tendencies, I often sense Helen when she travels from the stars to pay her mortal loved ones a visit.

She stops by often, typically around holidays and/or special anniversaries. I do believe that my grandmother has evolved fully to spirit as opposed to remaining earthbound. Perhaps she needed a little reassurance from her loved ones that it was permissible to journey on to the divine.

> *Nicole Strickland is one of the leading afterlife/paranormal researchers on the West Coast. She is the founder/director of the San Diego Paranormal Research Society and serves as the California coordinator to the Ghost Research Society. Combining her love of history and writing, she's written several books, including her three bestsellers about the RMS* Queen Mary. *She's also a correspondent and writer for* Paranormal Underground *magazine. Nicole has presented on a variety of topics relating to the supernatural at well-known conferences and events. She is the executive producer/co-host of* Haunted Voices Radio *and host of the* Afterlife Chronicles, *which was selected by Feedspot as one of the top 25 podcasts on the afterlife in 2021. Nicole has been featured in numerous media outlets, including national and local television, film, radio, and print. Her website is http://www.authornicolestrickland.com.*

A Furry Friend from Beyond
Jason L. Roberts

Before I ever worked in the paranormal field, I worked ten years as a surgical technician for a veterinary hospital. I worked my way up from being a person who cleaned kennels, fed the animals with their meds, and walked them to being the clinic lead in charge of all surgeries and dental procedures. Many days working there would turn into staying overnight to watch the animals, or patients as we called them, to monitor their conditions. Now it was during these times that I spent the night there alone with the furry patients that I remember strange sounds and occurrences inside the clinic and hospital portions of the building. I just remember I needed to do my job and care for them the best I knew how, so I didn't pay much attention to the sounds and noises I would hear. A lot of these animals I got to know over my ten years being there.

Fast forward to a case in Council Grove, Kansas, where we were asked to investigate a very large bed and breakfast that had up to twenty rooms, all of which were proclaimed by the owners to be haunted. Our team went to this location to help assure the owners that they were in fact seeing spirits of both a little girl and an animal they claimed to hear. The owners claimed that the little girl walked all over the building, but it was the animal that they have seen their dog pawing at and interacting with.

We spent the night hoping for some voices or interaction from the little girl they claimed was there, but we ended up with nothing from her. As I started to think about wrapping up for the night, I got a radio call over the walkie talkie that I needed to head down to the main floor living room area. There, I met two of our investigators, and they explained that they keep seeing some strange movement over by the couch. The two teammates left me to take a break as I sat in a chair staring into the living room, focused on the couch. My teammates had also been seeing some movement there and wanted me to see it too. I sat there for a long time, not knowing what I would really see. Finally, I heard what sounded like a "meow" followed by some movement on top of the back of the couch.

I stared for a while, trying to understand what I was looking at. I had the lights off, but the residual light from outside was shining into the room giving us all a chance to move about. But as I sat there staring, I could see movement, but movement unlike anything I had seen up to now. The best way to explain what I was seeing in the darkness was what I remember from the *Predator* movie, where the alien was almost invisible, but you saw it move through a pixel-like state. I sat there watching this pixeled image with my own eyes, and I could make out the swishing of a tale that looked like a cat just calmly sitting there. Watching it for several minutes sitting on the back of the couch, I could see it jump and run off into the next room. This cat was there and seemed to be following its regular routine, regardless of us being there all night.

It now makes me think about all the nights I spent over at the vet hospital and what all I was hearing around me. I know now I was clearly not alone, as these furry friends were just keeping me company as I rested there. The meows, the bumps in the night, and the feeling of something jumping up on the bed were all these four-legged friends wanting to be near me, or so was my thought. Now each time I investigate, animals seem to be on my mind, which makes me feel safe and comfortable.

As for the little girl who supposedly haunts the bed and breakfast, after we spent time focusing on the spirit of the cat, we packed up and everyone headed out to the cars to load up. I was the last one in the building, taking one last look around on the second landing of the staircase. From the landing, I could see my team outside by the cars, when suddenly, I heard the voice and laughter of a little girl. I was alone, it was 4 AM, and all equipment was turned off and outside. I was the only one who heard her.... Go figure!

A Family Pet Never Truly Leaves

Working in the paranormal field and being interested in the unknown for so long, it never really crossed my mind about life after death for animals. It makes sense to me nowadays, and it is something I think about as I approach a family's home to help with a haunting. But in 2016, I had the awakening I needed in a home in Wilson, Kansas.

My team, Road Trip Paranormal, had been working a lot of paranormal events at the Midland Railroad Hotel, selling out the hotel for public events in which all guests investigate the hauntings of the hotel alongside us. During these events, we also got to investigate Grandma's Soda Shop around the corner from the hotel, giving us a lot more area to cover with our guests. During these events, we met the family of the Soda Shop and became friends with them, after which they asked if we could come to their house and investigate it. The Soda Shop's niece, Tiffany, told us all about their home, and to be honest, I was excited to go. So we set a date and came back to Wilson.

As the team set up the usual gear at their house, and we chatted with the family, I remembered I needed to go run an errand. As I was about to leave, Roth came over to me and said that the family was telling them about a spirit cat that ran around the house. It was their old black-and-white cat that passed away a couple years prior. Roth told me that the family would hear the cat cry out and that they would catch a glimpse of the cat running around inside and outside the house. Well, I just blew that off, because I have never encountered a spirit of an animal. So, I took off and ran my errand alone.

When I came back to the house, the whole team was excited and waiting for me to return, because they had been hearing the cry of a cat inside the house, yet they could not figure out where it was coming from. I rolled my eyes, something I feel bad about now, but I could not get myself to really believe that. We carried on and began investigating the house. I was more concerned about the spirit of the little boy the family had been seeing. I wandered off into an area of the house alone and was looking around when suddenly, I heard the cry of a cat!

This threw me off for a moment and then I heard it again and tried to follow it. The cry sounded like it was coming from the other side of the wall, so I ran around to the next room and saw nothing. I called out to it, as one does when you want a cat or any pet to come to you. I walked around the corner calling out to the cat, which I could still hear, and walked into Roth. He looked at me and smiled, "You heard it didn't you?" I looked away and growled quickly, "I did; shut up."

The rest of the night we could hear little cat feet running up and down the stairs–playing, or maybe just unsure of all of us being in his home. It got me thinking that maybe some of the haunting sounds people hear could really be the spirit of the animal that once lived there. We live in an amazing world and keep finding new answers to many things, which lead to more questions about everything. So, the question about the paranormal is not if there really is life after death for humans but rather if there is life after death for all of life on the planet. I took this moment to reexamine how I approach the realm of the paranormal, and it helped me understand what was in store for me in the near future with death and animals. Most important of all, though, is that your family pet never truly leaves your side forever.

Jason Roberts is a team lead with Everyday-Legacy Paranormal, a tour guide/manager of the Wichita Ghost Tours since 2009, owner of Road Trip Paranormal since 2014, and cohost of the Cryptic Heartland *Podcast. He can be reached at roadtripparanormal.vpweb.com and everyday-legacy.com.*

A Glimpse Beyond
Patrick Burke

Life after death … in our youth, it was something we rarely thought about as we were ever immortal. As we get older though, we tend to think about it. Is there something past this life we live? Is there a heaven? Is there a hell? What exactly can we expect once we shed this mortal body?

My journey in this field so far has been filled with both angelic and demonic interactions. As a sensitive (a person who hears, sees, and communicates with the spirit world), the event that started me on the path I currently take began the night my bed was lifted a few inches off the ground and slammed down on the floor. I was 12, and that started my exploration into the unknown. Now, at 64, I have seen and dealt with everything you would call paranormal. From experiences in battlefields, where traumatic death was instantaneous, to demon-infested houses, to crossing over soldiers, slaves, traumatized spirits, and fallen angels, I can emphatically say that there is life beyond our mortal bodies.

Here is a glimpse into this "shadow world"–how my team and I deal with the aggravated side of the spiritual world, or what I refer to as the arena of spiritual warfare. The struggle is real. Although many do not see it, it is darkness versus light, God versus Satan, good guys versus bad guys–call it what you will. I will share with you several events that have shown me that our soul and our energy move on once we leave this body. And I will discuss how some of the souls we have helped described to us what they saw as they crossed over into the light.

The very first time I crossed over a lost soul was during an investigation at a historic house in Fairfax, Virginia. It was one of the homes that became famous due to Confederate colonel John Mosby's raid during the American Civil War. When we did what is called the baseline walk-through, there were several areas that showed activity. The cellar is where I was most drawn. I took two ladies with me, both in training for their sensitive abilities. Immediately, a 10-year-old girl of color came through. Her name was Elizabeth, but her family called her Lizzy. As we interacted with her, we felt about a dozen more spirits start to gather around us. The temperature dropped to the point that we could see our breath, even though it was July, and the youngest of the team said she felt someone touching her shoulder. I asked Lizzy if she wanted to go to God's Grace. She told me she couldn't. Baffled by this, I asked her why. I told her God's love is all encompassing. She said she couldn't as she wasn't a full person. Being an avid student of history, and knowing she was a slave when she lived, I knew she was referring to the belief in those days that the black slave was counted as only three-fifths of a person. I told her again that in God's eyes, she was more than worthy to join the angels in heaven. I felt her energy shift; a gleam of hope surrounded me, and then it dashed away as she told me she couldn't leave her family behind. No worries, I said, all are welcome to enter God's Grace. I asked my spirit guides and the angelic presence I felt there to guide me in opening a portal, as this was my first time doing it. I formed the energy between my hands and instructed both women with me to direct their energy into the space between us. When I felt the energy formed, the angel told me to release it and I did, right between us, and all three of us saw a white pillar of light shoot up through the ceiling. Suddenly, over a dozen spirits, slaves, soldiers, and civilians from the 1860s stepped into the light. We could hear the jubilation as they crossed over. Lizzy was the last to go, and all three of us heard her say, "Thank you, it's so beautiful!"

From that moment on, no matter what investigation I am on, I strive to always close it out by helping any lost souls to cross over.

Sometimes when dealing with a person who had a traumatic death, the process of convincing him or her to cross over is more challenging. When it comes to traumatic death, it doesn't get more intense than on a battlefield. At the Gettysburg Battlefield, my team came across a Confederate soldier near the Bloody Angle, a place where hundreds of Union and Confederate men died in mere minutes. We had several electronic meters, an EMF meter, and a Trifield Natural meter in action. As we started to talk to a ghost soldier, our meters were going off the chart. We began to try and convince him to move on, that he was done here and needed to go to God's Grace. He said he couldn't, because he had killed men and, therefore, was not worthy. After five minutes of trying to convince him, I suggested to the medium that we try to call his family in. I opened a portal asking for spirit to allow any of his relations that he would recognize to help him cross over. Suddenly a young women stepped through and called out to him. The meters were going crazy. Suddenly, I heard him cry out very excitedly, and then abruptly the meters went silent. He had stepped through with the help of a loved one.

It's said that darkness cannot cross over to the light. Rubbish. For me, Yeshua (Jesus) is. His presence is all encompassing, and darkness has no power over him or those under his protection. With my faith firm, I have no fear of the darkness. At a historic theater in Pearisburg, Virginia, I ran into an old enemy called Legion. As we started the investigation, Legion came through the ghost box. It called me by name, saying I knew them. I had run into Legion while stationed in the military in Arizona in 1980. As the demons moved towards another member in our group, I wrapped them in Yeshua's light and gave them an ultimatum: Go to God's Grace or go to where they could do no harm. Interestingly, it was St. Michael who told me to give them a choice, so I did. Suddenly the ghost box said, "They went to the light," and the presence of Legion was not felt by us.

I share these stories with you so that you may know that there is life after this world. I never asked to see what the proverbial heaven or hell looked like because for me it was not important. What is important for me is knowing that we have free will–a choice to either work towards the betterment of ourselves and others or to walk down a darker path that leads to true enslavement to the Evil One and his minions. I choose the light.

> *Patrick Burke is a sensitive, spiritual warrior, and light work instructor.*

A Shocking First-Hand Experience
Larry Flaxman

Anyone who has ever heard me speak or who has read my books has likely heard me almost whimsically state that I consider myself to be about as psychic as a rock, which is a sentiment that I have repeated many times over the years. In my more than two decades as a paranormal theorist and researcher, I have had the incredible fortune of visiting and investigating hundreds of reportedly haunted locations. However, I have only experienced a few encounters in these areas that cannot be explained logically.

I will, however, discuss one of those exceptional occasions. This event was one that was just too complex and incomprehensible to dismiss out of hand.

Perched high in the Ozark Mountains, the spectacular Crescent Hotel in historic Eureka Springs, Arkansas, has had a tragic history that dates back to the Civil War. However, the most infamous and heartbreaking are those that occurred during the time that Norman Baker operated his cancer treatment center there.

Baker arrived at the spa and resort town of Eureka Springs in 1937 to discover a city that had fallen on hard times. He immediately fell in love with the Crescent Hotel and purchased it for $40,000. He practically stole it! The hotel had previously served as a retreat for the wealthy but had fallen into disrepair as a result of the Great Depression. Baker converted the hotel into a hospital, where he promised a surefire cure to hundreds of desperate and dying patients.

People suffering from cancer and a variety of other ailments rushed to the Baker Cancer Hospital, many of whom signed away their whole life savings in the process.

The therapies were the same no matter what ailment patients had: injections with one of his two formulae four times a day, every day except Sunday. The only problem was that Baker was not a medical professional, and he never claimed to have cured anyone of cancer. He was a liar, a forger, and a charlatan.

Baker's "cure" was a diabolic mix that contained carbolic acid, commonly known as phenol (which may cause organ failure), corn silk, ground-up watermelon seeds, clover, and water that he would inject into the bloodstream of his patients. Interestingly, around the same year, the Nazis began using this very method–carbolic acid injections– to euthanize detainees in their concentration camps.

Locals working at the Baker Cancer Hospital soon became skeptical of what was going on. One wing of the building was soundproofed and shut behind a door that was locked from the outside shortly after its opening. The "psychiatric wing" was designated for those patients who weren't improving.

Workers on-site also saw that patients were frequently proclaimed "cured" even though they were in a worse state than when they checked in. Later, it was discovered that these patients would only live for a few days after returning home.

Some didn't even make it to the station before passing out and dying on the train back.

Forty-four individuals died at the Baker Cancer Hospital throughout the course of its first two years of operation. Because these individuals were suffering from life-threatening conditions such as cancer, autopsies and inquiries into their deaths were not conducted.

In September 1939, Baker was arrested for mail fraud. According to postal inspectors, Baker was accused of defrauding his victims out of $4 million by using his newsletter. That's nearly $78 million in today's money.

After a three-week trial, he and two other "doctors" from his hospital were found guilty and sentenced to three years in jail at Leavenworth Correctional Institution. In addition, he was sentenced to pay a $4,000 fine. Since then, the hotel has earned the title of "America's Most Haunted," and it continues to draw tourists and guests from all around the globe–with good cause. The hotel is unquestionably haunted!

For the past 11 years, I've had the privilege of being called the hotel's resident paranormal investigator. A few years back, while attending one of the hotel's yearly paranormal events, known as the Eureka Springs Paranormal Weekends, I had an experience that I will remember for the rest of my life.

The morgue was my destination, and I was leading a small group of attendees there, which I had done hundreds of times before. I arrived in the basement morgue around 10 P.M. and immediately jumped into character. What character am I referring to, exactly? Well, I had just finished recording an episode of *Ghost Lab* for the Discovery Channel, and I was excited to try out a new method that I had witnessed being used.

In that particular episode, which was recorded on Alcatraz Island, I observed the stars of the show receive incredible spirit interaction by provoking and agitating them. Basically, the goal was to be as disrespectful and mean as possible. As someone who had never personally explored this method before, I jumped right into it and began attempting to communicate with the spirit of Norman Baker.

I was attempting to aggressively provoke Baker into reacting by addressing him in a variety of less-than-flattering words.

I was also digging into the morgue's floor drain to locate proof of claimed human autopsies that had taken place there.

While the visitors looked on in amazement as different pieces of equipment dispersed around the room began to light up, which signaled electromagnetic energy spikes, something else was taking place in the background.

Amid my verbal barrage, I suddenly felt an intense burning sensation on my lower back. It genuinely felt like someone had grabbed a hot poker and was running it down the center of my spine.

I had never felt such hot, searing pain in my life. Was this a heart attack or some other medical emergency?

I took a deep breath and reached around under my shirt, where I felt something strange. I lifted the back of my shirt and quietly asked one of the attendees to take a look.

I'll never forget the look on the gentleman's face when he shined his cell phone's flashlight on my back. It was pure, abject terror. He told me that there were deep, finger-like scratches running down my back starting at the bottom of my neck. I asked him to take a photo, and to my surprise, sure enough, there were two sets of red, extremely inflamed scratches present.

Oddly enough, when I awoke the next morning, those two large scratches had completely disappeared. I can think of only one possible explanation for how those fingernail scratches appeared–and the experience certainly taught me a valuable lesson. In addition, it is a principle that I have maintained to this day.

I still get a shiver every time I think about the events that transpired that evening. Prior to that occurrence (and thank-fully since!), I had never had any physical contact with a spirit in my more than 25 years of paranormal investigation.

Over the years, I suppose Norman Baker and I have devel-oped a certain amount of mutual regard for one another. Even though my personal sentiments towards him are strong, I continue to go out of my way to treat him with re-spect when investigating the hotel, and thankfully, no ad-ditional violent altercations have occurred.

Since then, I believe that I've been able to successfully communicate with Baker using a number of different spirit communications devices.

Symbols in Nature
K. Collins

When my grandmother died, we all saw them. Butterflies. Everywhere. She had *loved* butterflies and had tops and purses and even shower curtains with butterflies on them. All colors, sizes, and shapes. We could have passed it all off as coincidence, that there were just a lot of butterflies out that summer, but the truth is, we never saw any butterflies where we lived. Ever. So, after her death, seeing dozens of them everywhere was surely a sign that she was sending us from the other side.

About six months later, the butterfly sightings stopped. Since then, none of us see them anymore, which is very sad, because they did make us feel better and bring us comfort. But we talked about it and realized that she spoke to us for as long as she needed, and as long as we needed, and then she moved on. We had to move on, too.

Three years later, a close friend died of inoperable brain cancer. She loved rainbows. The day she was buried, there was an incredible double rainbow that was visible to everyone at the service. That evening, at an outdoor life celebration, there was another rainbow. Funny thing is it did not rain at all that day. Nobody could quite figure out the anomaly of rainbows that did not follow rain, although it was a little muggy out. Nobody really cared to question it, though, because it was a beautiful thing nonetheless and many of us said out loud that we knew who was behind them.

I have had many people die in my life that I never really got to know close enough to find out what they loved, so upon their deaths, there may have been symbols in nature, and I didn't even realize it. That makes me sad, that someone might have been waving or saying, "Hey, all is well" and I didn't notice. I try now to get to know people in my life more, to learn what they love and what brings them joy. I hope to see more signs in the future.

FURTHER READING

Abl–Tabatabai, Sean. "Scientists Say They Have Found Proof of the Human Soul." Newspunch.com, January 18, 2016, from https://newspunch.com/scientists-say-they-have-found-proof-of-the-human-soul/.

Alexander, Eben, *Proof of Heaven: A Neurosurgeon's Journey into the Afterlife.* New York: Simon & Schuster, 2012.

Almond, Philip C. "Friday Essay: What Do the 5 Great Religions Say about the Existence of the Soul?" *The Conversation*, April 15, 2021.

Bendix, Aria. "Researchers Who Study Near–Death Experiences Believe in an Afterlife." *Business Insider*, March 19, 2022.

Berthold, Emma. "The Animals That Can Live Forever." Curious, May 24, 2021, from https://www.science.org.au/curious/earth-environment/animals-can-live-forever.

Bhattacharjee, Sushruta. "Goodbye: Top 15 Weirdest Death Rituals around the World." IcyTales.com. August 28, 2020, from https://icytales.com/top-15-weirdest-death-rituals-around-the-world/.

Birchard, Robert. "What Can Science Tell Us about Death?" The New York Academy of Sciences, September 30, 2019, from https://www.nyas.org/news-articles/academy-news/is-there-life-after-death/.

Casey, John. *After Lives: A Guide to Heaven, Hell, and Purgatory.* New York: Oxford University Press, 2009.

Chalmers, David J. *The Conscious Mind: In Search of a Fundamental Theory.* New York: Oxford University Press, 1996.

Colman, Penny. *Corpses, Coffins, and Crypts: A History of Burial.* New York: Henry Holt, 1997.

Custer, Charlie. "The Age of Immortality Is Coming, and It's Going to Suck." Tech in Asia, March 15, 2016, from https://www.techinasia.com/disconnect-age-immortality-coming-suck#!

Desy, Phylameana Lila. "Tales Told by Children Remembering Their Past Lives." Learn Religions, January 10, 2019, from https://www.learnreligions.com/children-remember-past-lives-1731359

"Do Animals Have Souls?" *The Guardian*, January, 18, 2020.

Du Boulay, Shirley. *Cicely Saunders: The Founder of the Modern Hospice Movement.* London, England: SPCK Publishing, 2007.

Epstein, Adam. "Pope Francis Says All Pets Go to Heaven, but What Do Other Religions Say?" *Quartz*, December 12, 2014.

Ghost Hunting: The Science of Spirits. New York: Meredith Corporation, 2021.

Graziano, Michael. "Why You Should Believe in the Digital Afterlife." *Atlantic Monthly*, July 2016.

Harris, Trudy. "Evidence of Life after Death." *Guideposts*, March 16, 2015.

Isherwood, Damon. "Science at Last Explains Our Soul." ZME Science.com, June 27, 2016, from https://www.zmescience.com/science/science-explains-our-soul/.

Jensen, Lorenzo. "24 People Who Were Clinically Dead Describe What They Saw before They Were Revived." Thought Catalog, August 9, 2017, from https://thought-catalog.com/lorenzo-jensen-iii/2017/08/24-people-who-were-clinically-dead-describe-what-they-saw-before-they-were-revived/.

Jones, Marie D. *Celebrity Ghosts and Notorious Hauntings: Stories of Fame, Death, and Ghostly Immortality.* Detroit: Visible Ink Press, 2019.

———. *PSIence: How New Discoveries in Quantum Physics and New Science May Explain the Existence of Paranormal Phenomena.* Franklin Lakes, NJ: New Page Books, 2007.

Knapton, Sarah. "Humans Will Become God-Like Cyborgs within 200 Years." *The Telegraph,* May 25, 2015.

Kubler-Ross, Elizabeth. *On Death and Dying: What the Dying Have to Teach Doctors, Nurses, Clergy, and Their Own Families.* New York: Scribner, 1969.

Lewton, Richard. "Quantum Experiments Add Weight to a Fringe Theory of Consciousness." *New Scientist,* April 18, 2022.

Long, Jeffrey, with Paul Perry. *Evidence of the Afterlife: The Science of Near-Death Experiences.* New York: HarperOne, 2010.

Martin, Michael, and Keith Augustine. *The Myth of an Afterlife: The Case against Life after Death.* New York: Rowan & Littlefield, 2015.

McGraw, John J. *Brain and Belief: An Exploration of the Human Soul.* New York: Aegis Press, 2004.

McKie, Robin. "No Death and an Enhanced Life: Is the Future Transhumanism?" *The Guardian,* May 6, 2018.

Moran, Barbara. "Are We Hardwired to Believe We're Immortal?" Futurity, January 29, 2014, from https://www.futurity.org/hardwired-believe-immortal/.

Parnia, Sam. "What Can Science Tell Us about Death?" The New York Academy of Sciences, September 30, 2019, from https://www.nyas.org/news-articles/academy-news/is-there-life-after-death/.

Pester, Patrick. "Will Humans Ever Be Immortal?" LiveScience.com, September 29, 2021, from https://www.livescience.com/could-humans-be-immortal.

Seth, Anil. *Being You—A New Science of Consciousness.* New York: Dutton Books, 2021.

Shermer, Michael "Who Are You?" *Scientific American,* July 2017.

"Some American Indian Beliefs about an Afterlife." Native-AmericanNetRoots, June 22, 2015, from https://www.nativemericannetroots.net/diary/1936

Trosper, Jamie. "The Physics of Death (and What Happens to Your Energy When You Die)." *Futurism*, December 18, 2013.

Wagner, Stephen. "Visions at the Hour of Death: 13 People Describe Their Experiences with Deathbed Visions." LiveAbout.com, April 29, 2018, from https://www.liveab out.com/visions-at-the-hour-of-death-2594543.

Wallen, Jessica. "Why Is Society Obsessed with Immortality in Cinema?" Medium.com, May 2, 2018, from https://me dium.com/litpop/why-is-society-obsessed-with-immor tality-in-cinema-11449561c4a5.

Walls, Jerry L. *Heaven, Hell, and Purgatory: Rethinking the Things That Matter Most.* Ada, MI: Brazos Press, 2015.

Wyllie, Timothy. "The Enigma of Near-Death Experience: A Survivor's Reflections on the Afterlife." *New Dawn Magazine*, July/August 2015.

INDEX

Note: (ill.) indicates photos and illustrations

communication with the dead, 191
diet of the, 207
immortality in the, 219
resurrection in the, 227–28
use of in the afterlife, 24
use of in eulogies, 17
biocentrism, 56, 58–59
Birchard, Robert, 113
Blackmore, Susan, 146, 146 (ill.)
Blanke, Olaf, 138
blood
  and embalming, 13
  and immortality, 84
  as a lake in Hell, 89
  during NDEs, 101, 137
  and the soul, 62, 67
  at the time of death, 7–8
Blue Zones, 205–8
Bodhidharma, 230
bodhisattva Avalokitesh-vara, 75
Bodleian Library, 84
Bohm, David, 63, 65
Bombay, India, 36
bones
  of animals, 19
  cultural death tradi-tions, 33, 37, 43, 46
  decomposition of dead bodies, 8, 10, 186
  and immortality, 84, 210
  resurrection of the dead, 228
  turning of the, 41–42
  understanding death, 242
Book of Life [Christian], 88
Book of the Dead, Egyp-tian, 34 (ill.), 35, 72
Bor [biblical under-world], 228
Borjigin, Jimo, 101–2

Boston, Massachusetts, 147
Boston University, 119
Bow, Simmy, 86 (ill.)
Bradford, Thomas Lynn, 189
Brahman [Hindu divine reality], 54, 75
Braigu [Aboriginal Heaven], 77
brain
  of animals, 66, 111
  animate vs. inanimate, 109–12
  communication with the dead, 177–78, 182
  and consciousness, 97–116
  damage, 150
  death, 6, 137–38, 140, 144
  deathbed visions, 133–34
  ghosts in the afterlife, 158, 160–62, 169–70
  Heaven, Hell, and in between, 84
  holographic, 103–5
  illustration, 103 (ill.)
  and immortality, 84, 212, 214–15, 217, 222, 225, 233–35, 238
  life review, 100–102
  and the multiverse, 106–9
  near-death experi-ences, 135, 137, 144, 147–48, 150–52
  out-of-body experi-ences, 137–40
  prebirth experiences, 121
  and psychoactive drugs, 150
  of robots, 111
  and the science of death, 112–16
  and the soul, 49, 56, 58–59, 63–64, 66

spiritualism and medi-umship, 191, 201
understanding death, 1, 5–7, 242
Brandeis, Louis D., 69
Branford, Connecticut, 3
Brazil and Brazilians, 43–44
Breakthrough: An Amazing Experiment in Electronic Communication with the Dead (Raudive), 173
Bridge of the Separator (Chinvat Bridge), 72, 72 (ill.), 95
Brigham & Women's Hospital, 147
Bristol, England, 197
British. See England and the British
British Medical Journal [journal], 183
Brooks, Albert, 85
Brotherhood of the Cross and Star, 220
Broughton, Richard S., 169–70
Brown, Dan, 93
Brown, Rosemary Isabel, 200
Browne, Sylvia, 199, 202
Browning, Elizabeth Bar-rett, 198
Browning, Robert, 198
Brugger, Peter, 160
Brunelleschi's Dome, 89 (ill.)
Buddha [Siddhartha Gautama], 27, 80, 95, 126
Buddhism
  burial vs. cremation, 27
  cultural death tradi-tions, 36–37, 39–40, 44
  Heaven, Hell, and in between, 75, 80, 82–83, 95
  and immortality, 236
  and reincarnation, 126